Through Conflict
to Reconciliation

Through Conflict to Reconciliation

Edited by Augustine Meier and Martin Rovers

NOVALIS

© 2006 Novalis, Saint Paul University, Ottawa, Canada

Cover design: Audrey Wells
Cover image: © Jupiter Images
Layout: Pascale Turmel

Business Offices:

Novalis Publishing Inc.
10 Lower Spadina Avenue, Suite 400
Toronto, Ontario, Canada
M5V 2Z2

Novalis Publishing Inc.
4475 Frontenac Street
Montréal, Québec, Canada
H2H 2S2

Phone: 1-800-387-7164
Fax: 1-800-204-4140
E-mail: books@novalis.ca
www.novalis.ca

Library and Archives Canada Cataloguing in Publication Data

Through conflict to reconciliation / edited by Augustine Meier and
Martin Rovers.

(Saint Paul University research series)
Includes bibliographical references.
ISBN-13: 978-2-89507-797-8
ISBN-10: 2-89507-797-5

1. Conflict management. 2. Reconciliation. 3. Counseling. I. Meier,
Augustine, 1933- II. Rovers, Martin, 1949- III. Series.

BF636.6.T48 2006   158'.3   C2006-904570-4

Printed in Canada.

We acknowledge the financial support of the Government of Canada through
the Book Publishing Industry Development Program (BPIDP) for our publishing
activities.

5   4   3   2   1   10   09   08   07   06

Contents

Introduction

At the Heart of Conflict Resolution

Three years ago, Saint Paul University in Ottawa, Ontario, officially launched a graduate-level conflict resolution program. At the official ceremony, between two of the speeches, a Muslim man from a developing country who was experienced in conflict resolution leaned towards me (A. Meier) and stated that all conflicts begin in the heart (with oneself), then extend to the family, then to the extended family and then to the community and to nations. The implication of this statement is that a person who is in conflict with himself or herself will tend to re-enact this conflict in his or her relationships. Families who are conflicted will tend to re-enact their conflicts in relationship with other families; so too will conflicted communities and nations re-enact their conflicts with other communities and nations. Conversely, a person who is at peace within himself or herself will tend to create a home, workplace and community that is capable of collaboratively resolving its conflicts; so too a family, community or nation that is at peace with itself will help inspire other families, communities and nations to be at peace with themselves.

This peer-reviewed book, *Through Conflict to Reconciliation*, brings together scholars, researchers and professionals who are versed in conflict resolution. The book adopts a developmental, experiential, interpersonal and psychodynamic approach to the resolution of conflicts. Of importance to the resolution of conflicts is listening and responding to the needs, aspirations, desires and wishes of the conflicting parties. The mutual understanding and acceptance of each other's desires, needs, and so on leads to compromise and ultimately to the resolution of conflicts. This emphasis on desires, needs, etc., in the resolution of conflicts differs from problem-solving and solution focused approaches, which focus on changing the quality of behavioural and interpersonal interactions. Consequently, this book offers a different paradigm in the understanding and resolution of conflicts. The book limits itself to the understanding and the resolution of conflicts experienced by individuals within themselves and to conflicts between two or more persons. That is, it limits itself to the presentation of research, theory and practice regarding the resolution of interpersonal and intrapersonal conflicts.

Conflicts are part of the human condition; they are an aspect of human nature. To have conflicts is not the problem; acquiring the skills to resolve them is the real challenge. Every child is born into a society with a potential for conflicts. At birth, a child acquires two inheritances, a biological inheritance and a social/cultural inheritance. A newborn has no requirement to adhere to any of the social/cultural demands and expectations. The child lives primarily for the satisfaction of its own physical and physiological needs. In having these needs met by caring, loving, affirming and awestruck parents and family members, the child acquires a host of other needs and desires: to be loved, affirmed, appreciated, connected and recognized, as well as the need and desire for autonomy, exploration, independence, mastery and competence. This early love affair with others and with the world does not last for long. Beginning at a few months to a year into its life, the newly born infant is expected to accept and to adhere to reasonable demands such as sleeping and feeding schedules. As the child grows physically, socially and intellectually, more demands are placed on the child. The child is expected to dress and feed itself and to learn how to read, write and do arithmetic. The demands from the two sources – the physiological and social/cultural – signal the child's first experience with conflict. The child experiences being pulled by two demands. The child has the choice to comply with the social and cultural demands or to rely on its "wisdom" and act in accordance with its reasonable needs and preferences. The child who is affirmed for its reasonable choices learns the art of conflict resolution. The child who is unreasonably pressured to conform to social and cultural demands and is criticized, demeaned and humiliated for reasonable choices based on its own needs fails to learn how to resolve conflicts and remains in a conflicted state. Such a conflicted child lives his or her life not from an inner life-giving source, but from external demands and expectations.

When the demands for compliance to social and cultural expectations are exacting and the punishment for non-compliance is severe enough, the child develops feelings of sadness, depression, hate, anger and resentment and may act out these feelings in deviant and violent behaviours or may keep them inside and engage in passive behaviours, such as failing grades in school or abusive behaviours, such as self-injury. The child who experiences harsh and inconsistent parental responses for its behaviours is highly tormented, troubled and conflicted. For example, as a child, Leon (Whitey) Thompson (1992) was severely slapped by his father when Leon would lift items from a corner store and also when he gave a stick of gum to his best friend. Leon was criticized and demeaned regardless of what he did. He was not punished for what was culturally right or wrong; he was punished for being himself. Eventually he turned into an angry, hostile, conflicted and violent teenager and adult who became one of America's most hardened criminals, spending four years in Alcatraz.

Through the process of internalization, the child incorporates within his or her inner world (psyche) the conflicts that were experienced with others. The internalized conflicts begin to have a life of their own and continue within the child, and later in the adolescent and adult, in the same fashion as they originally took place in the external world with significant others. The child, adolescent and adult do not require that the person of the original conflict be present. The person carries on within himself or herself the same conversation that took place between him or her and the person who was the source of the conflict. The internalized conflicts take on the characteristics of a "working model" (Bowlby, 1988, p. 120) or an "internal representation" (Fairbairn, 1944/1954, p. 112) or a cognitive schema (Beck & Freeman, 1990) that influences how information is interpreted and impacts on the quality and nature of interpersonal relationships. An example of this type of conflict is the librarian who could not allow himself any pleasurable moments except when he took the dog for a walk, because it was expected that he play with the dog. The librarian was brought up in a home where the work ethic dominated and it was considered wasting time to engage in pleasurable pursuits. Achievement, success and accomplishments were affirmed. The librarian was conflicted between responding to his own needs and desires and responding to the socially and culturally transmitted values of achievement, success and accomplishment. The feeling of guilt prevented him from engaging in pleasure-related pursuits. Such a conflict has usually been referred to as an "intrapersonal conflict" or an "intrapsychic conflict" because the person "feels divided between two partial aspects of the self or tendencies ... which are experienced as in opposition" (Meier & Boivin, 2001, p. 99). The biblical figure Saint Paul echoed this conflict when he said that the things that he wanted to do, he did not do, and the things that he did not want to do, he did.

Complementary to such intrapersonal conflicts are interpersonal conflicts, which are discords or contentions between two persons. Often interpersonal conflicts are the re-enactment of intrapersonal conflicts. For example, Blayne, who is socially and culturally driven by the work ethic and does not accept the realization of his own desires and needs, will not accept that his colleagues take time to relax, play and have fun. Blayne is duty-bound, expects the same from his colleagues, and may not tolerate tardiness in the workplace. Blayne's own intrapersonal conflict leads to interpersonal conflict. Another situation that leads to interpersonal conflicts is a clash between opposing needs of two persons. For example, in a couple, Battina desires that she and her partner spend more time together, whereas her partner, Wolfgang, wants to have time for himself. The opposing needs lead to the interpersonal conflict.

Not all conflicts, however, are re-enactments of intrapersonal conflicts or of childhood interpersonal conflicts. Dumais (2001), in studying conflicts in the early church, states that some conflicts arise out of personal, cultural and societal differences (p. 25). Thus some conflicts are the product of the clash between environmental factors and circumstances, and the person's desires and needs. For example, a bright and gifted teenage boy, Siegfried, who had dreams of becoming an engineer, had to terminate his high school education and take on a low paying job to provide financial support for his single parent and for his four younger siblings. Since he left high school, Siegfried has been in constant conflict, because he does not like his work and he cannot afford to stop working to pursue the dream he left behind as a teenager. Siegfried is unhappy, angry and conflicted and suffers from a myriad of psychologically related physical ailments.

Conflicts can range in intensity from being mild to being severe. Reasonable requests – both internal and external – usually create mild and passing conflicts; unreasonable requests usually create intense and enduring conflicts. An example of a mild and passing intrapersonal conflict is the decision that a student has to make between going to a newly released movie and staying at home to complete a research paper due in two days. Typically, such conflicts are resolved by putting aside other activities so that the person can fulfill both the desires and the demands, or the person decides to go to the movie the following week. An example of an intense and enduring interpersonal conflict is that of a young woman who has not spoken to her older sister for 20 years because she feels that her parents favoured her older sister. This intense and enduring conflict can lead to social and health problems.

The source of conflicts varies in the degree to which they are apparent or visible. For some conflicts, the source is apparent, as when two persons claim the reward for having found and returned a lost pet. In other situations, the source of the conflict is "hidden" or, as Redekop (2002) says, the roots of the conflict are deep. The source is hidden from awareness and usually manifests itself in drawings, paintings, poetry, songs, dreams, re-enactments, and similar human actions. For example, Maxina, in her early 30s, was on a date for the second time with Michel. They were enamoured with each other. However, Michel's insistence that each pay his or her share of the bill troubled Maxina; she became conflicted about the relationship. The source of this conflict became apparent in a dream, where she dreamed that she and Michel were lifted off the ground in a parachute. Both were afraid but she took care of Michel. She became aware that Michel's insistence that each pay his or her part of the bill went against her deeper need for the other to rely on her, to be taken care of by her.

Conflicts routinely occur in every individual's life in at least three realms. First, as was mentioned earlier, conflicts occur within a person's intrapersonal realm and involve a person's competing desires, preferences, values and beliefs. Second, conflicts occur between people such as between Battina, who wanted to spend more time with her partner, and Wolfgang, who wanted to have more time alone. Third, conflicts occur between people and circumstances such as illness, financial difficulties and work disappointments (Heitler, 2000).

Not all persons are equally capable of resolving their conflicts. Some seek the help of a relative, a friend or a therapist, while others seek the help of a mediator or a conflict resolution specialist. During the past two to three decades, conflict resolution has become an increasingly important tool to settle disagreements within families, organizations, communities and countries. The significance of this approach is attested by the more than 47 million entries of this topic on websites. The task of a mediator is to talk to two people or groups involved in a conflict to try to help them to find a solution to their problems that is fair to both sides. Much of the published literature on the topic pertains to the resolution of conflicts in organizations, institutions, communities and countries. The broad goal of conflict resolution in these domains is to create communities and organizations that resolve conflicts in a culture of social justice and peace. It is believed that conflict resolution builds more rewarding relationships and stronger and more cohesive communities and organizations.

Some theorists question the use of the terms *conflict resolution* and *conflict management*. They suggest that these be replaced by the term *conflict transformation* (Lederach, 1995). According to these authors, *conflict resolution* carries an implication that conflict is bad and can be resolved permanently through mediation. *Conflict management*, on the other hand, suggests that conflicts are long-term processes, but the term incorrectly assumes that the opinion and feelings of people can be managed or directed. *Conflict transformation* recognizes the "dialectic nature" (Lederach, 1995, p. 17) of the conflict and works with it. It takes a deeper understanding of the conflict. In working through the conflict, the persons who are the source of the initial conflict are forever changed. For them, it can be a new learning experience.

The process of resolving both intrapersonal and interpersonal conflicts entails paying attention to the person's desires, needs and aspirations in addition to his or her feelings and cognitive processes. Meier and Boivin (2001) argue for a model that incorporates needs, feelings and cognitions in the understanding of human behaviour. According to this model, "needs are conceived to be prime directional motivators of behaviour, feelings are thought to be responses to either the satisfaction or the frustration of needs and thoughts pertain to the stylistic ways of construing reality, to solving problems, to managing reality, and to evaluating experiences" (Meier & Boivin, 2001, p. 96; see also Meier & Boivin, 1983, pp. 144–146). Needs, feelings and cognitive processes, therefore, form three interdependent systems. In their study on conflict resolution, Meier and Boivin (2001) observed that the process towards resolution begins with the persons expressing negative feelings and being judgmental. The second step of the process is the expression of positive affect and empathic responses. The process enters into the resolution stage with the expression and acceptance of mutual desires and needs. The expression of their mutual needs was an essential aspect of the resolution of their conflict. It was a transforming experience. This observation is supported by Fisher and Shapiro's (2005) experience mediating conflict resolutions. Among the needs that they identified are appreciation, affiliation and autonomy (p. 17). Redekop (2002) states that "deep rooted conflict occurs when the most significant human needs [e.g., for recognition, connectedness and security] satisfiers or a group are taken away or threatened" (p. 23). Conversely, deep-rooted conflicts are resolved when a person's significant human needs are responded to in a positive way. Mahler, Pine and Bergman (1975) state that two basic and enduring human needs are the need for connectedness and the need for separation or individuation. Every person attempts to seek a balance between these two needs. Kohut (1971) adds the needs for affirmation as a competent and capable person and affirmation for one's own person and goodness. The literature, therefore, makes it clear that an essential aspect of conflict resolution is for a person to be heard and to have his or her fundamental needs responded to and his or her dignity respected. The failure to respond to the fundamental needs of others inevitably leads to conflict, be it within oneself, between two persons, or in a family, community, organization, or country.

Often associated with the resolution of conflicts are forgiveness and exoneration (Rovers, 2001). This is particularly true when the source of the conflict is emotional hurt and sexual and physical abuse. In a general sense, forgiveness refers to pardoning someone for the harm caused and exoneration refers to absolving onself for one's own offences and destructive capacities (Meier, 2001, p. 91). A precursor to forgiveness and exoneration, however, is being empathic towards the other and towards self. In a study of two persons who were sexually and emotionally abused as children, Meier (2001) observed that the person who was able to forgive her perpetrator was able to empathize with him – that is, was able to see the good and bad in him – whereas the person who was not able to forgive her perpetrator was not able to be empathic towards him but only saw the bad in him.

It is apparent, then, that the resolution of conflicts is a complex process. Very little effort has been directed at the resolution of conflicts between individuals and within individuals themselves. It is well recognized that all major organizations, institutional and communal conflicts emerge from intrapersonal conflicts.

This book focuses on conflicts as experienced within oneself and between persons. It addresses the resolution of conflicts that emerge in the interactions of ordinary living. This theme permeates all of the chapters of this book. The book takes the position that by learning the skills to resolve conflicts within and between persons, one also learns the skills to resolve conflicts within larger groups – organizations, communities, and countries.

The book is meant for counsellors, chaplains and for all frontline professionals who work with individuals, couples and small groups in resolving conflicts. It is also meant for the individual who wants to learn the principles and process of conflict resolution to resolve his or her own conflicts. Some chapters of this book apply the principles and process of conflict resolution to diverse settings. Other chapters demonstrate how to integrate the process of conflict resolution within individual and couple counselling approaches. The distinguishing characteristic of each chapter is the application of the principles and processes of conflict resolution in establishing broader theoretical perspectives, resolving conflicts of actual cases, and in research. As was mentioned, this book is primarily meant for professionals and individuals who are interested in resolving interpersonal and personal conflicts. Nevertheless, the principles established in these chapters are also essential when resolving conflicts at the level of organizations, institutions, and communities.

This book is divided into four sections: theoretical aspects of conflict resolution, models of conflict resolution, conflict resolution applied to various settings, and research studies and ethics. The first part, *Theoretical Aspects of Conflict Resolution,* comprises four chapters that explore the role that faith, emotions, and nonviolent communication play in the resolution of conflicts or in their prevention. The last chapter in this section views collaborative justice in terms of conflict resolution. The second part, *Conflict Resolution in Diverse Settings*, comprises five chapters that present models of conflict resolution in various settings, including counselling with individuals and couples, and in working with brain injured persons and with transgender issues. Two chapters comprise the third part, *The Application of Conflict Resolution Models*, which presents the application of conflict resolution models to the resolution of intrapsychic conflict and to couple conflict. The fourth part, *Empirical Studies and Ethics*, which constitutes three chapters, reports an empirical study on the resolution of intrapsychic conflicts and on an interpersonal conflict. The section terminates with ethical considerations and procedures to resolve conflicts among professionals.

Part I: Theoretical Aspects of Conflict Resolution

Leslie Greenberg, in the first chapter, indicates the role that emotions play in couples' conflicts and which feelings need to be expressed to resolve the conflicts. He contends that communicating vulnerable feelings in non-demanding ways can help resolve conflict. In the first part of the chapter, Greenberg carefully distinguishes between primary, secondary, instrumental and maladaptive emotions and the role that these emotions play in the development and resolution of conflicts. He views all relationships within several parameters: the emotional need for connectedness and separatedness, need for identity and security, attachment needs for proximity, availability and receptiveness, and affiliation and dominance. In the last part of the chapter, the author applies these concepts and processes to the development and treatment of couple conflicts.

In his chapter, Richard Manley-Tannis argues for a practice of mediation that is faith based. The author conceives of faith not (only) necessarily in religious terms but also in human terms, suggesting that for mediation to take place one needs to have faith in the integrity of the other person and in the process.

Sherry Morley, in Chapter 3, makes a strong argument that crime is a form of conflict and that restorative justice is a form of conflict resolution. She describes the negative effects of criminalizing an offender's breach of the law. The dynamics and healing attributes of shame, guilt and remorse that lead to apology and forgiveness are essential components of restorative justice. Ms. Morley outlines the arguments for and against restorative justice. The chapter ends with a description of her experience with a healing circle.

Judi Morin, in Chapter 4, presents twelve habits for peaceful living – that is, habits to prevent the emergence of unnecessary conflict. These habits are based on knowing one's feelings and one's basic needs.

Part II: Conflict Resolution in Diverse Settings

Counsellors and therapists can at times experience a conflict between what they intend to achieve and what they actually achieve. In Chapter 5, Gilles Fortin and Judith Malette present a reflective practitioner model, whereby the counsellor or therapist can perform a self-evaluation of his or her interaction with the client. In this regard, the authors present theory underpinning this approach and then demonstrate how it can be applied in a training setting.

In Chapter 6, Marie-Line Morin proposes a pastoral counselling conflict resolution model for couples. To arrive at this model, the author analyzed current approaches to conflict resolution and to the integration of religions and spiritual dimensions in counselling. She then summarized commonalities among these models. Into these commonalities, she proposes the integration of a person's fundamental values. The resulting model, she suggests, provides a useful orientation for pastoral workers.

In the seventh chapter, Adèle Miles, Maria Cupples, Rose Robinson and Michelle Koyle, present a model used in a hospital emergency department to provide support and care to families and friends faced with the sudden death of a loved one. The model uses trained volunteers called Crisis Support Volunteers. The authors present the eligibility criteria and training required to become a volunteer with this support group. The chapter concludes with two case presentations that demonstrate how the volunteers helped the loved ones come to terms with the sudden death of a loved one.

Susan Tasker, in Chapter 8, argues for a new manner in responding to persons with brain injury. Rather than viewing brain injury as an outcome, one ought to view it as an event and as the beginning of a process. Within the context of this process the patient will need first to acknowledge the event and then to accept his or her new state. According to the author it is necessary to distinguish between acknowledgment and acceptance of the event and to emphasize the role of both processes.

In the first part of Chapter 9, Helma Seidl summarizes the historical, social and theoretical considerations of transgenderism. She notes that transgenderism existed prior to Christianity and that it has been received differently by the European cultures compared to the North and South American native cultures. The author then discusses the various classification systems for transgenderism and makes reference to standards for their care. Definitions are provided for gender incongruence, transgendered, transsexual, and cross-dresser. The last part of the chapter addresses clinical aspects and individual and group therapy for the transgendered. In the presentation of the chapter, Seidl always remains scholarly and sensitive to the feelings of others.

Part III: Application of Conflict Resolution Models

In Chapter 10, Susan Ford demonstrates how Virigina Satir's Human Growth Model can be integrated with Sandtray-Wordplay Therapy in the resolution of intrapsychic conflicts. The author briefly describes the Human Growth Model and the technique of Sandtray-Wordplay Therapy. A central technique in the integration of these two models is the Parts Party, as defined by Satir. The author applies the integrated technique to help a client make a decision regarding a significant person in his life.

Chapter 11, by Martin Rovers, tries to demonstrate how concepts from attachment theory and the use of the genogram can be integrated with Bowen's system theory of couple therapy. Concepts pertinent to this task are differentiation of self, family emotional and projection system, triangulation, multi-generational emotional unit and attachment styles. The author demonstrates how these concepts are useful to the therapist and to the couple in understanding and working through the relational problems. The author illustrates the therapeutic process by the use of excerpts from actual therapy sessions.

Part IV: Empirical Studies and Ethics

In Chapter 12, Seung Hee Kang, Thomas O'Connor and Suzanne Joyce present the results from a qualitative analysis of the transcribed interviews of a chaplain and nurse in resolving a conflict. Five themes emerged from the analysis: how the event was remembered, the turns of the conflict, qualities that facilitated conflict resolution, openness, and transformation of emotions.

Augustine Meier and Micheline Boivin, in Chapter 13, report their findings from a study using a conceptual model that integrates affects, cognitions and needs in the resolution of intrapersonal conflicts. The subjects comprised ten clients who resolved intrapersonal conflicts (Resolvers) and ten clients who failed to resolve such conflicts (Non-Resolvers). It was hypothesized that for the Resolvers alone, Need, and Positive Feeling statements predominate immediately prior to the resolution of the conflict, and Judgment, Thought and Negative Feeling statements decrease immediately prior to the resolution of a conflict. Five of the six hypotheses were supported. The findings were discussed with reference to object relations theory and to the necessity of simultaneously assessing many aspects of a client's inner experiences when studying the occurrence of significant in-therapy client events.

In the last chapter of the book, Peter Barnes offers a method of resolving ethical issues in organizations using a dialogue approach similar to that used in narrative therapy. The author cogently summarizes the negative effects of an adversarial approach to deal with ethical violations on the part of professionals. The author proposes the steps that might constitute the dialogue process in resolving ethical issues between a complainant and the respondent member.

This book presents the principles and processes of conflict resolution in diverse settings including theory, practice and research. It is hoped that the reader will find its contents challenging, informative and helpful.

Augustine Meier, PhD
Martin Rovers, PhD
Editors

References

Beck, A.T. & Freeman, A. (1990). *Cognitive therapy of personality disorders*. New York: Guilford Press.

Bowlby, J. (1988). *A secure base: Parent-child attachment and healthy human development*. New York: Basic Books.

Dumais, M. (2001). Des conflits, chemins de croissance? Un modèle biblique. *Pastoral Sciences, 20* (1), pp. 25–43.

Fairbairn, W.R.D. (1944/1954). Endopsychic structure considered in terms of object relationships. In W.R.D. Fairbairn, *An object-relations theory of the personality* (pp. 82–136). New York: Basic Books.

Fisher, R. & Shapiro, D. (2005). *Beyond reason: Using emotions as you negotiate*. New York: Viking.

Heitler, S. (2000). Conflict resolution therapy. In F. M. Dattilio & L.J. Bevilacqua (eds.), *Comparative treatments for relationship dysfunction* (pp. 247-272). New York: Springer.

Kohut, H. (1971). *The analysis of the self: A systematic approach to the psychoanalytic treatment of narcissistic personality disorders*. New York: International Universities Press.

Mahler, M.S., Pine, F., & Bergman, A. (1975). *The psychological birth of the human infant*. New York: Basic Books.

Meier, A. (2001). Adult survivors of incest and the capacity to forgive: An object relations perspective. In A. Meier & P. VanKatwyk (eds.), *The challenge of forgiveness* (pp. 87–124). Saint Paul University, Ottawa, Ontario: Novalis.

Meier, A. & Boivin, M. (1983). Towards a synthetic model of psychotherapy. *Pastoral Sciences, 2*, pp. 137–176.

Meier, A. & Boivin, M. (2001). Conflict resolution: The interplay of affects, cognitions and needs in the resolution of intrapersonal conflicts. *Pastoral Sciences, 20*(1), pp. 93–119.

Redekop, V.N. (2002). *From violence to blessing: How an understanding of deep-rooted conflict can open paths to reconciliation*. Saint Paul University, Ottawa, Ontario: Novalis.

Rovers, M. (2001). Forgiveness in post-affair couple therapy. In A. Meier & P. VanKatwyk, eds., *The challenge of forgiveness* (pp. 227–246). Saint Paul University, Ottawa, Ontario: Novalis.

Thompson, Leon (Whitey) (1992). *Last train to Alcatraz: The auto-biography of Leon (Whitey) Thompson.* California: Winter Book Publication-Fiddletown.

Part I

Theoretical Aspects
of Conflict Resolution

Introduction

"Let there be peace on earth, and let it begin with me" might well be the theme of Part I of this book. For this dream of peace in our world and in our lives to become a reality, the most important link in the process must be the individual – resolving intrapersonal conflict from the inside out. All those who work in the field of conflict resolution must begin the task with peace in their minds, hearts and spirits; the work at the heart of conflict resolution then stretches from the intrapersonal to couple and family, to communities, to the world. Each person's peacefulness is one less place for conflict to emerge. This inner sense of peace can have various expressions; peace of mind; peace of emotions; peace of faith; peace within oneself. Part I looks at various expressions of a commitment to peacefulness within the person. One person's commitment to and practice of peacefulness is a powerful force in our world. Leslie Greenberg carefully distinguishes the role that primary emotions play in the development and resolution of conflicts. He draws our attention to emotions as the basis of all social connectedness, and therefore potential conflict. Emotions are learned from birth and, as such, exercise much power in relationships. Richard Manley-Tannis argues for a practice of mediation that is faith based – that leads the reader to the heart of bringing peace to oneself, and therefore becoming one who resolves conflict intrapersonally. The author conceives of faith not necessarily in religious terms, but also in human terms, suggesting that for mediation to occur one needs to have faith in the integrity of the other person and in the process. Judi Morin presents twelve habits for peaceful living – habits to prevent the emergence of unnecessary conflict. Elements of honesty, empathy and being aware are central to living a life that promotes peace. These habits are based on knowing one's feelings and one's basic needs and therefore creating peace for oneself as a stepping stone to conflict resolution. Sherry Morley argues that crime is a form of conflict and that restorative justice is a form of conflict resolution. Justice is not seen as a sense of equality, but as a stage in the need for restoration and resolution of harm done. She outlines the arguments for and against restorative justice. The chapter ends with a description of her experience with a healing circle.

Mohandas Gandhi challenged us to be the change you want to see in the world. Part I of this book indeed goes to the heart of conflict resolution by drawing everyone's attention to the secure and mature self that can become the real peacemaker within oneself, within a couple relationship, within one's community, or within the world at large. Without such a sure footing, all conflict resolution would be doomed to confusing theories and inadequate techniques.

1

Emotions in Interpersonal Conflict Resolution

Leslie S. Greenberg

Introduction

In this chapter I will discuss the role that emotion plays in couples conflict and its resolution, and I will look at which feelings need to be expressed in resolving conflict and which are better dealt with in other ways. I will suggest that, in relationships in which reconciliation is the goal, communicating vulnerable feelings in non-demanding ways can help people resolve conflict. I will argue that automatically generated, amygdala and limbic system–based emergency emotions, at the core of the perception of threat, are a key generator of conflict, and I will present methods for working with emotions to resolve conflict.

Emotions

People's relationships with each other are a wellspring of emotional experience, and emotions are of great importance in the everyday life of relationships and in conflict. Emotions tell us the state of our intimate bonds, whether they are in good condition, if they have been disrupted or if they need maintenance. Emotions tell us when something is wrong; they tell us that our needs are not being met; they identify problems for us to solve, and rapidly communicate that there are problems.

Emotion forms the basis of social connectedness. They occur at the boundary between self and other and therefore are both intra-psychic experience and interactional events. Emotions connect inner and outer. They simultaneously organize both the self and the interaction. Emotions influence interactions in various ways. They change the interaction by changing the self. In anger, for example, the individual transforms by swelling up, thrusting forward, and is both physiologically and cognitively organized to attack or defend. The action tendency organizes the person to thrust forward or alternately to flee, thereby changing the person's relationship with the environment. The emotional organization plus the facial expression of anger in addition signals angry intent to the other. Emotion thus is our primary signalling system and influences interaction by non-verbal communication. Affective expression is a crucial form of communication that regulates self and other.

Members in a couple thus are highly connected to each other through the emotion system. People form emotional attachments through their emotion systems. Emotions are an important part of the glue that holds marital partners together and forms an emotional bond. This intimate bond is an important affect and self-esteem regulating bond providing both empathic mirroring and validation of the self. Our intimate relationships influence how we feel about ourselves. Partners read each other's emotional signals with great care and this reading dominates their interactions and connectedness. Emotional expression influences how others respond. Vulnerability, for example, disarms, and anger produces distance.

Types of Emotion

In our view conflict most often results from unexpressed hurt feelings and unmet needs related to security and identity. Thus it is important to help partners deal with their own and their partner's emotions and needs. However, not all emotions are the same, and simply helping partners get in touch with feelings or encouraging the expression of emotions will not resolve conflict. Rather, it is important to distinguish between different types of emotions, and decide which emotions need to be acknowledged and expressed, which need to be bypassed, contained or soothed, which need to be explored and which need to be transformed. Our approach to treatment is based on the idea that some emotions are adaptive and some emotions are maladaptive. We have found it helpful in understanding emotion to distinguish between different types of emotion: primary; secondary and instrumental (Greenberg, 2002). These are described below.

Primary emotions are the person's most fundamental, original reactions to a situation. They include sadness in relation to loss, anger in response to violation, fear in response to threat. These emotions are attachment- and identity-oriented and enhance self and intimate bonds. These are the emotions we want to help our clients access, symbolize and express. *Secondary emotions* are those responses that are secondary to other more primary internal processes and may be defences against these processes. Examples include feeling anger in response to feeling hurt, feeling afraid about feeling angry, or feeling guilty about a traumatic event by attributing responsibility to oneself for the event. They often are not responses to a situation but rather are people's responses to their own feelings or to prior thoughts based on prior emotions. Secondary emotions need to be explored, and the sequence of generators unravelled, to get at the more primary generators that were not expressed. The key here is that the awareness of adaptive primary emotions promotes attachment and identity. Thus accessing primary anger at unfairness promotes empowerment. Expressing secondary anger that obscures hurt and vulnerability does not promote listening and does not dissipate anger or provide relief. We have to get past the anger to explore the underlying hurt. *Instrumental emotions* are those feelings that are expressed in order to influence others. They are strategic and are conscious or unconscious efforts to get people to respond in desired ways, such as crying crocodile tears to get sympathy. These emotional expressions are problematic attempts to achieve an aim and partners need rather to learn to communicate their needs and wishes more directly without the fear of non-responsiveness that leads to instrumental expression. *Maladaptive emotions* are those old familiar bad feelings that occur repeatedly and do not change. They come most often from past trauma, or wounds or unfinished business with significant others. These are feelings such as a core sense of loneliness, abandonment, shame, worthlessness, explosive anger that destroys relationships, or recurrent feelings of anxious inadequacy that leads to clinging. These feelings do not change in response to changing circumstance or with expression; they do not provide adaptive directions and do not promote bonding or enhance identity. Rather, they leave people feeling stuck, often hopeless, helpless and in despair. These emotions lead to problems in relationships and are the emotions we want to help partners transform. Maladaptive responses are best transformed by contact with adaptive emotions (Greenberg, 2002).

When both partners enter maladaptive emotional states the escalating interactions intensify these states and lead them to say and do things which later often are seen as not representative or not real, or as having gone a bit "crazy." People will later say that what was felt and what was said in these states was untrue, it was really "not them." These "not me" states seem to have a mind of their own. These "not me" states are states of dysregulation that are self-reinforcing. Once in them, people may begin to yell at each other rather than speak to each other, or they may cut off and not listen. They think they have heard it all before. They probably have repeated these fights before and have resolved them or understood and forgiven each other many times. But it happens all over again. They can even see it coming, yet once they enter these unhealthy emotional states of threat, violation or humiliation, they are transformed into their other maladaptive selves. For example, in one of these dances of maladaptive states, a husband, sensing some abandonment, may experience this as a physical longing, and from deep within his body he may yearn for some form of reassurance from his partner, but he sees her as a cold, rejecting and impenetrable wall. Or the wife, on hearing a hint of anger or demand, automatically may feel a desperate need to protect herself from destruction. She fears becoming overwhelmed by her partner; she sees him as intrusively powerful, and closes up, becoming rigid, feeling icy and walling out any contact. These extreme states generally reflect that each partner has entered a maladaptive emotional state, often based on past wounds. These states also often are not partners' initial, primary responses to their partners. Rather, they result from both unhealthy internal affective /cognitive sequences and escalating interactional sequences.

Interaction

In working to resolve conflict in couples, it is important to look at interpersonal interaction as well as at emotion. Interaction reciprocally influences emotional states. Conflict involves escalating interactions that rigidify into negative interactional cycles. Ultimately it is an understanding of the emotion and interaction together that helps us resolve conflict.

There are two fundamental interpersonal dimensions on which interaction is best assessed: affiliation, (closeness-distance) and dominance (up-down). Reciprocal interactions along these dimensions lead to the emergence of destructive cycles in couples. Cycles on the affiliation dimension are ones such as pursue/distance, attack/defend, cling/push away and blame/withdraw. Cycles on the dominance dimension are dominate/submit, lead/follow, define/defer and over-function/under-function. In these cycles, the more one partner engages in one action, such as pursuing for closeness, the more the other engages in a reaction, such as distancing to get more space. The more the one partner distances the more the other partner pursues, and so we get a circular escalating interaction – and the struggle for connectedness and separateness begins. In one major type of cycle the pursuer pursues for emotional closeness, but does so by blaming and criticizing, and the withdrawer withdraws for emotional protection. In another major type of cycle the dominant person dominates, over-functions, makes all the decisions and then feels burdened. The partner, who feels more insecure, unsure or submissive, under-functions, doesn't do much, but then ends up feeling invisible, as though he or she doesn't exist in the relationship.

Destructive cycles such as these result from unexpressed primary emotions and needs. Cycles are maintained by the expression of secondary emotions such as blame and resentment that mask primary feelings, or by instrumental emotional responses, such as pouting as a means to get what one wants from the other person, or crying when one is angry. The cycles form around partners' most sensitive concerns, about what each one feels most vulnerable about, and needs most. One may want more closeness, be more anxious about connection and need more reassurance;

the other may be more inclined to feel inadequate, be over-concerned about being competent, need more compliments or may need space and be sensitive to intrusion. One partner may function more rapidly, be more decisive and more active, and become impatient if restrained. Partners' rhythms may be different: one may be quicker. while the other may be slower, need more rest and relaxation. One may be more bold, the other more fearful; one, more open, the other more closed. One partner may be more independent, the other more dependent. Two partners are never exactly the same. People sometimes do play different roles in different relationships, acting as a leader in one, follower in another, seeking out the other in one, and distancing in another. But in their primary relationship, people eventually become sensitive about just that issue that evokes their deepest anxieties and unmet needs. Partners' buttons usually don't get pushed by the same concern, or not to the same degree. One is concerned with closeness, the other with control. This leads to mismatched needs and to conflict.

Motivation

Relationships are a natural arena for the gratification of basic human needs for connectedness and separation. Needs for emotional connectedness (attachment) and for separateness (identity) are universal factors operating in couple systems. Conflict arises from the inability to resolve differences in desires for closeness and distance and for validation and control. These are struggles around needs for intimacy and identity, and the emotions expressed in conflict are related to frustration of these needs. Conflict thus emerges most fundamentally from unmet adult needs. Another way of saying this is that conflict comes from failures to resolve struggles for adult identity and security. Automatic, amygdala and limbic system–based emergency emotions are at the core of threats to identity and security and are key generators of conflict. Conflict thus results from emotional expression related to need, frustration and to the escalating negative interactions attempting to meet these needs which rigidify into negative interactional cycles.

Intimacy and Attachment

People have been primed by evolution to feel pleasant feelings when close to caretakers and unpleasant feelings when unwillingly separated from them. People basically feel joy when they are with loved ones and fear and anxiety when their bond is ruptured. Human beings are a species who need others to feel secure and happy. Healthy adult attachment and intimacy involves emotional availability and responsiveness, security and warmth. The need for other people only becomes unhealthy if a person cannot tolerate separation, and flies into a rage or becomes depressed at loss, separation or distance.

People are primed by evolution with both care-eliciting and caregiving capacities (Gilbert, 2000). Human infants, who are the most helpless at birth, need caring others to protect them, provide a safe base, feed and provide for them and over time help them to learn. Bowlby (1969, 1988) described this as part of an attachment system which essentially is an affect regulation system involving contact/comfort emotions such as pleasure at touch and at seeing the human face and positive affect from attunement.

The infant tracks at least three aspects of care crucial to survival: the proximity, availability and receptiveness of the caregiver (Gilbert, 2000). This same tendency to monitor proximity, availability and receptiveness is present in adults in close relationships. They become distressed when loved ones leave or are unavailable for any length of time. Touch and contact comfort regulate physiology, and protest, anxiety and withdrawal and depression result from loss. Adults' basic concerns in intimate relationships involve the same needs: a need for proximity (are you there when I need you?); a need for availability (can you give me the things I need such as affection, support, care?); and a need for responsive receptiveness to me (can you understand me and what is happening to me – do you understand what I need?). For the young child these are mostly automatic responses, but adults often (although not always) are able to articulate their felt needs and beliefs in regard to needs for care.

Care-eliciting tendencies without reciprocal, available and accessible care-providing tendencies to tap into would be useless.

Hence, caregiving tendencies that involve the motivation and behaviours to care, look after and provide resources for others to whom one is close are equally important for survival. Intimate caregiving also involves concerns with proximity, availability and receptiveness. The parent becomes alarmed if the child wanders too far. The parent is motivated to gather resources and make them available to the child (e.g., warmth, reassurance, food, opportunities for play), and the parent tries to intuit what the child needs and to match what is needed with the correct input. When the child is receptive, the role of successful-caring is achieved and is associated with positive affect. When the child is not receptive and there is mis-attunement, negative affect and behaviours in the caregiver may result.

As adults we have evolved potential abilities to be highly competent caregivers. We have developed capacities for empathy, sympathy and compassion. There may be all kinds of other reasons for wanting to care for others, self-serving reasons such as making one feel good, or to make others care for one. But the fact is that people are also motivated to be compassionate. People tend to help people in distress and to take care of them if they are suffering.

Identity and Self Esteem

In addition to attachment and intimacy needs, self-esteem and identity needs also are an important basis of relationships. If a person's sense of worth or self-esteem or social status is challenged, identity is threatened. When identity is threatened, issues of power and control, which are key concerns in couples, then become a source of conflict. Needs for control, however, become unhealthy if threats to identity lead to coercive dominance. Anger often is a response to challenge or frustration, and when it occurs in response to threats to identity and status, essentially it is an effort to protect a person's position in the eyes of self and other. Contempt emerges beyond anger as the most destructive form of attempting to maintain identity by establishing a superior position and looking down on another.

People are primed by evolution to compete and to be concerned about social rank and identity as well as to give and receive care.

Animals who are not acutely aware of their rank endanger themselves, miss opportunities for acquiring resources (food, mates and allies), and can be heavily put down by more powerful dominants for inappropriate resource seeking. Animals behave differently if they occupy high-rank rather than low-rank positions, and they change their behaviour when they change their rank. This is not learned, but is an innate, complex affective, cognitive, motivational, behavioural system just like attachment (Gilbert, 1998).

This tendency can lead to aggressive dominance, power and control. In both human and animal groups we do see aggressive dominants trying to control subordinates. We observe this in humans in bullying behaviour and in violence in couples and families. Nonetheless, humans compete for resources in a host of other ways that do not involve aggression, and it is not necessary to think of the needs for social rank and identity as only engendering hostility. For example, humans have evolved co-operation in small groups, adopted egalitarian life styles, and subordinates have formed alliances against dominants who were exploitive or aggressive. In doing so they were able to break free of the more typical primate group organization of linear hierarchies controlled by powerful and aggressive individuals, and developed different skills and social motivations for rank. Co-operation and group belonging have become more salient for survival and reproductive success (Gilbert, 1989). The way humans compete can be aggressive, but is more often an attempt to be attractive to others; people strive to have status, value and social place bestowed on them and benefit from recognition and validation of their identities (Gilbert, 1997, 2000). People compete to be seen as desirable friends, lovers, team players. In this context, for many people the central concerns are about avoiding low rank, being controlled by others, being at risk of exclusion or missing opportunities. To work to be seen as attractive to others one must stimulate positive affect in the mind of others not fear and/or fearful submission (as with aggression) (Gilbert, 1997, 2000, Gilbert & McGuire, 1998).

In social ranking, social comparison (Gilbert, Price & Allan, 1995), tracking other people's opinion and responding to potential threats or social recognition become major concerns (Gilbert, 2000). Non-verbal communication (which can be automatic) is an important aspect of social rank concerns and behaviours, as it is in attachment. For example, people in affectionate relationships (lovers, mothers and babies) stare into the eyes of each other, signalling desire and affection, wanting to look at and wanting to be looked at. However, in conflict situations, dominants stare, but subordinates don't. For the subordinate to engage in visual gaze would almost certainly increase arousal in both dominant and subordinate, increasing the chances of fighting. Imagine scolding a child who looks back defiantly at you, compared to scolding one who looks down and is inhibited. The child's signal of shame will have an impact on your anger. Patients who are in high states of shame commonly adopt submissive postures, have low eye gaze, and feel inhibited and unable to express themselves. This highly defensive, non-safe position is not a care-eliciting, caregiving, sexual or co-operative role. Rather, it is clearly a kind of submissive, defensive position and can click in even when a person consciously does not want it to. People have been primed by evolution with emotions such as embarrassment, shame and humiliation to adopt these roles. These emotions are particularly sensitive to how we *compare* ourselves with others, and arise when we feel socially threatened and our identities or feelings are being invalidated.

Vulnerable Emotions

The two main vulnerable emotions associated with threats to the needs for security and identity are fear and shame. These are the emotions that ultimately need to be accessed, expressed and responded to if conflict is to be resolved. Attachment involves needs for closeness and security. When these needs are threatened, the person experiences the fear of abandonment. The inability to express this feeling and need for others is a major problem and is driven by a fear of appearing weak and by shame about feeling inadequate. The primary vulnerable emotions involved in loss of security therefore are fear of being alone and shame at feeling rejected.

Identity involves needs for mastery and validation. When these needs are threatened, the person experiences the shame of feeling worthless. The inability to express this feeling and need is driven by the fear of being looked down on or by a fear of being controlled. The primary *vulnerable* emotions involved in invalidation of identity and threats to self-esteem thus are shame at diminishment or invalidation and fear from threat to one's standing, and control.

Conflict Resolution

The essence of conflict resolution lies in communicating, in non-demanding ways, feelings of the threat to basic need satisfaction, rather than by expressing protective or defensive feelings. The expression of authentic vulnerability tends to evoke compassion, while the expression of empowered anger sets a limit and evokes respect and attention.

Conflict resolution, in addition, involves the ability to recognize both self and other as subject and agent. The capacity to see the other as a subject, a person like oneself with feeling, needs and intentions, is required for empathy. And empathy is necessary for conflict resolution, forgiveness and acceptance. A couple's capacity to set up an empathic cycle rather than a vicious cycle is enhanced (a) by their ability to reveal their subjective experience one to the other so they provide material with which to be empathized; (b) the ability to see the other as being like oneself; and (c) the ability to experience compassion for the other, who, like oneself, is in pain. Empathizing with the other (even when the other is expressing opposing needs or views), accepting differences, and feeling compassion for the other, whom one recognizes as a subject like oneself, are all necessary components of healthy conflict resolution.

As we have seen, emotions both produce and maintain interactions, and interactions produce and maintain emotions. The interactional problems in conflict that need to be changed are the negative interactional cycles based on pursue/distance and dominance and submission. It is important to note that it is the display of emotion that is so important in effecting interaction. Seeing the face of each other evokes experience; we are impacted by the ways others face us. How we imagine the face of the other also is important in how we feel and what we do. The face, however, is an ambiguous text open to interpretation, and so how we react to others is also subject to our interpretation of the other. In therapy we want the person to express in such a way that there is no doubt about what is being felt so that it is not misinterpreted.

Problematic Emotions

It is instructive to look at predictors of divorce to see how central emotion is in marital conflict and to discern which emotions are most problematic. Gottman, Coan, Carrere, and Swanson (1998) found that rated facial expression of emotion was the best predictor of divorce. A wife's facial contempt or disgust, as well as a husband's fear and miserable smile and a wife's miserable smile, were the strongest predictors of divorce. Accompanying these facial expressions of contempt and fear, an elevated level of defensiveness (excused, denied responsibility) were found in both partners. Wives complain and criticize, while husbands stonewall and disagree more. The prototypic process leading to divorce appears to be one in which husbands become physiologically aroused in fear. The wife tries to re-engage, becomes physiologically aroused and blames. The wife then expresses criticism and contempt and disgust and eventually withdraws. There is then a lack of emotional engagement and they live parallel lives. Facial communications of affect seems to regulate this whole process.

The most troublesome emotions in couples' conflict are the expressed secondary emotions of anger, contempt and fear as well as the unexpressed primary emotions of fear and shame. Couples' conflict results then from negative interactional cycles supported by the expression of secondary emotional states. Thus we have cycles of attack and defence, supported predominantly by secondary anger and fear. The troublesome emotions fall into two classes. The first class involves the approach emotions involved in attack or blaming; the second involves the withdrawal emotions involved in walling off or avoiding. These emotional experiences and expressions, attempted solutions to a problem, become the problem.

The emotions expressed in blaming are anger, disgust and contempt. Anger in its adaptive form is empowering. It sets boundaries and is a territorially and hierarchically related emotion that is a response to challenge. In its non-adaptive, secondary form it leads to attack, promotes attempts to destroy and is focused on the other rather than on protection of the self. In these states people use "you" language. "You are bad, wrong, to blame, etc." Disgust comes from distaste in which we spit out that which is rotten, and contempt comes from dissmell, in which we lift our noses to move away from a bad smell. In their healthy form, these emotions help us get rid of and stay away from what is bad for us. In their unhealthy form, they become insult, indignation and denigration.

The withdrawal emotions in conflict are fear and shame. Fear in its healthy form helps us escape, and shame, in its adaptive form, involves shrinking away from the gaze of others to avoid being ostracized. It protects our belonging to the group. In its non-adaptive secondary forms, fear leads to avoidance, shame leads to hiding, and both lead to withdrawal from connection. These feelings arise when we feel socially threatened. If we are to help people resolve conflict, we need to help them deal with these emotions in themselves and in their partners.

Emotions and Interaction

Attachment, as we have seen, involves a quest for security via proximity to a caretaker. Fear and sadness are the emotions that occur in response to separation, followed by protest and anger. So threats to attachment-security produce fear and sadness, followed by anger and protest. This is a very important emotional dynamic in conflict. Caretaking involves love, warmth and compassion. This occurs in response to fear and sadness, but is not a natural response to anger and protest which rather beget defence, withdrawal or counterattack. Table 1 shows the primary and secondary feelings in both positions in both attachment and identity cycles. In the attachment cycle, the primary emotion in response to threats to security in the pursuer is fear, but the expressed secondary emotion is anger. In the withdrawer, the primary emotions are fear of inadequacy or anger, but the expressed secondary emotions are related to avoidance, and involve withdrawn depression, a cold wall or defensive rejection.

Through Conflict to Reconciliation

When the conflict is in the identity domain, the threat, however, is not to connection or security, but to identity and status. Here the dominant person's social status, sense of worth and self-esteem are challenged. As shown in Table 1, when people's dominant roles or view of self are threatened they respond with secondary or instrumental anger or contempt to protect their position in their own and in others' eyes. The primary emotions that are felt when there is a challenge to identity or dominance come from shame at diminishment or invalidation, as well as fear at loss of standing or control, in the eyes of others and oneself. In the submissive person we see secondary placating, caretaking or pleasing expressions, but the more primary feelings are fear and anger. Expression of underlying shame and fears would beget non-dominant and non- submissive and more empathic and compassionate responses.

Table 1. Emotions in Interactions

The Emotions in the One Partner

	Primary	Secondary
Attachment	Fear of abandonment	Anger
Pursuer	Sadness at loss	Contempt
Identity	Shame at loss of face	Contempt
Dominance	Fear at threat to position	Anger

40

Table 1 (cont'd)

The Emotions in the Other Partner

	Primary	Secondary
Attachment	Anxiety at abandonment	Defensive anger
Withdrawer	Shame at inadequacy	Absence of emotion/avoidance
	Anger at intrusion	Depression, Boredom
Identity	Shame/Fear	Caring
Submission	Anger at control	Placating

Dealing with Anger and Hurt: Two Major Elements in the Wall of Isolation

Without doubt, one of the most important ways couples get into difficulties is related to the inability to deal with their own and their partner's anger. Although, as we have said, anger in response to violation is a healthy feeling that needs to be expressed, anger is often a secondary response to the more primary feeling of hurt, or fear of feeling unloved or unsupported, or shame and powerlessness that cannot be tolerated. Many of the "harder" emotions partners express, such as anger, resentment and contempt, may often be aggressive attempts to protect themselves from their partner, or to protect themselves against their more painful "softer" emotions of sadness, hurt, fear and shame.

Anger is difficult to express without shaming or belittling the other or without attacking, demanding and controlling. It is very difficult to express hurt and anger without blame. Yet if partners don't express these emotions, they begin to build a wall. It is important to recognize that sadness generally underlies hurt, while hurt clearly often is at the base of anger. One of the difficulties is separating anger and sadness out from each other. The two often are fused into a hurt, angry ball of emotion expressed mostly as complaint, feelings of victimization and blame. Complaint arises from the difficulty of separating anger and sadness out from each other. Partners need to be able to express anger clearly and sadness cleanly, each emotion uncontaminated by the other. Anger needs be expressed without blame, and, if possible, with a show of good intention. A useful skill involves saying "I don't want to feel angry but I do feel angry at ...." This communicates a desire for harmony and can be reassuring to one's partner. People also have to learn to "own" their anger as their own. The tone must not convey contempt, or scowling, sneering hostility. Anger that wants to destroy will not work. Anger that asserts and informs partners of a boundary, or a boundary violation, although not always easy for the other to receive, is what's needed. "I'm angry you have not done what I asked. It makes me feel like I'm not important to you." It is partners' non-verbal communication and their attitude that counts. If they are contemptuous, their anger will be destructive. If they are respectful, it will not.

Anger in the form of unexpressed resentment and subsequent withdrawal or closing off is the poison of relationships. Closing off is often the attempted solution to resolving conflict by the withdrawer. It doesn't work. Contact works. Expression of hidden resentment is helpful. First it is helpful because it brings the withdrawer out of hiding. Second it is helpful, much to the withdrawer's surprise, because the pursuer finds the anger much easier to deal with than distance. It feels more contactful than stony, silence or cold distance. Contact is what the pursuer wants, and so expression of anger by a withdrawer can be contactful and enhance the intimate bond.

The problem is that anger often pushes partners away. Hurt and sadness, however, ask for comfort. When partners sense the other's anger, they will not be able to offer soothing comfort, because they are busily preparing a defense against the possible attack signaled by the anger. The hurt/angry partners meanwhile are waiting expectantly to have their hurt soothed, and they feel their partner's non-responsiveness as insult added to injury. In response to the insult of non-responsiveness, they now get really mad.

Another problem with anger is that it can escalate, or the interactions around it can escalate. Once partners become angry, unless they are met with an understanding response quite soon in the sequence, they will tend toward getting carried away. Sometimes there is almost a pleasure or joy in some people's expressions of anger. Once started, it is hard to stop. All emotions are a combination of letting go and restraint. An older client, who was hypersensitive to sound and who was losing some of his capacities to regulate different aspects of his functioning, began to get angry at his partner's use of a loud voice. He began by appropriately requesting termination of the provocation, but then couldn't stop his rapidly escalating irritation, which exploded into full-blown rage. Being able to regulate expression and not let it escalate is important.

Most problematic in couples is the runaway escalation of anger in both partners. One partner becomes angry, even in an acceptable way; the other partner responds with equal anger, feeling a boundary violation. Now we have two fighters poised in a ring, an attack-attack cycle. The general sequence is, as soon as one ups the anger, so does the other, and soon they are delivering blows below the belt. The spouse's character, mother and the kitchen sink, all become targets. These are usually painful and destructive fights. More often, however, only one partner prefers to fight. For this partner, the intense contact of anger feels better than the tense cold distance. The problem is the other partner is probably different and finds the fights too frightening or hurtful. Fights themselves are not the problem; it is the inability to resolve the fight that causes distance and eventual dissolution of the intimate bond. The worst case scenarios are when there is a very rapid escalation, when contempt is expressed and met with defiance, such as when a wife demands that the husband wash the dishes and he says, "Make me." These are signs of future divorce (Gottman, et al., 1998).

The solution to hurt and anger involves separating the sadness and anger so each come out in pure form. Anger should be an assertion of clear boundaries and sadness should be a call for comfort, unaccompanied by demand. Anger needs to be an expression of personal boundaries, firm, but in no way attacking. Hurt needs to be seen, not as an inevitable response to a damaging act, but truly as people's unique response based on who they really are and their own sense of loss. Rather than understanding the hurt as caused by the other, hurt must be understood as a function of one's own makeup. If, on the other hand, people see their partner as having intended to hurt or damage, then anger is the appropriate response.

What do therapists need to coach people to do with anger and hurt so that these emotions do not become bricks in a wall of alienation and isolation? How does a therapist help partners handle these feelings without turning them into the single most poisonous element of relationships – blame and the contempt it eventually develops into?

What Do Therapists Need to Do for Couples Who Are in Trouble?

In our research on how couples change in therapy, we found that the single most effective way of resolving couples' conflict, of moderate and milder forms, is to expose their vulnerable feelings to their partners, as well as their attachment and identity needs (Greenberg & Johnson, 1988; Greenberg, Ford, Alden & Johnson, 1993). Intimacy can be created by sharing feelings without complaining. Validation can be obtained by sharing feelings of inadequacy. Sharing vulnerable feelings can be the antidote to acrimonious relating. I am not suggesting this method may be used when violence is present or rage is too strong. However, partners in moderate conflict who revealed and expressed their previously unexpressed emotions of sadness at loss, fear at threat, humiliation at invalidation, and anger at offence, had a magical effect on each other. When partners actually saw each others' tears, heard their fear or anger, they snapped out of the trance of stating their position over and over again or defending it. Instead they became more alive, compassionate, softer, more interested and concerned. Couples can be coached quite quickly to realize that because emotions form the basis of relating, expressing genuine feelings has incredible powers to change interactions. Authentic vulnerability disarms and evokes compassion, while non-manipulative anger sets a limit and evokes respect and attention.

The key concept in resolving conflict thus is revealing the primary, or core, softer or vulnerable emotions underlying the hard secondary or defensive emotions. It is important to note that, although this metaphor of hard and soft is useful in evoking a picture of the process, sometimes anger, a "hard" emotion, can be a healthy primary adaptive attachment- and identity-related emotion. Not so, however, for contempt.

Many educators and therapists have talked about teaching the skills of good communication, such as making "I statements," being non-blaming, listening and so on. All are correct. All these skills will help people break the cycle that maintains the conflict. The issue, however, is more one of how people get organized to adopt these more conciliatory stances. By revealing their attachment- and identity-related emotions, partners evoke each other's compassion, caring, love and interest, and this organizes them to attend and listen.

How do therapists help people to feel the concern and caring that are so healing? And how do they help them elicit these from their partners? As indicated above, we have discovered something about how to help one partner facilitate these feelings in the other partner. By sharing vulnerable attachment- and identity-related feelings and needs, partners generally soften their stance towards each other (Greenberg, James & Conry, 1988; Greenberg, Ford, Alden & Johnson, 1993; Johnson & Greenberg, 1985). When people genuinely express their needs for closeness or identity in a non-blaming manner, their partner listens and relaxes. Then, once partners are feeling heard and seen, they are much more likely to be able to participate in a more conciliatory engagement and begin to access more loving feelings.

The best a therapist can do is to help partners to present their primary adaptive feelings and needs as honestly and openly as possible in such a way that each partner is most likely to hear and see the other. This does not mean that partners plead or become self-effacingly pleasing in order to win favour. Rather, with the therapist's support and validation of their primary experience, they become strong enough to risk revealing attachment and identity needs, and, if not responded to, to be able to tolerate the delay of gratification. The ability to tolerate non-responsiveness involves having the capacity to remember that the partner was available in the past and will again be available in the future. This faith in their partner's availability allows people to move away temporarily from their presently non-responsive partners and to do so graciously, even though they are not satisfied. If people are later able to turn back to their partner without resentment, but with humour, the ability to laugh at themselves, and the philosophical acceptance of the inevitability of conflict, this will help foster reconnection. Reconciliation is itself an art requiring the emotional intelligence of sensitivity and empathy to one's own and one's partner's state, and the skills of good timing.

In order to help people deal with maladaptive emotional responses that are evoked in a fight, coaches must help them learn to soothe themselves and each other. At certain times when partners are unable to soothe each other, they have to exercise the capacity for self-soothing. Some people may feel unable to self-soothe, because they lack the internal emotional structures or processes to relax and/or to calm or nurture themselves. They may not have received enough of this as children and may not have built an internal nurturing parent representation on which to draw. When relationships are momentarily disrupted, they feel desperate and have difficulty holding onto the sense of security generated by the lived history of the relationship. Then it is difficult for them to buffer even minor disruptions, and they are unable to project a vision of a secure future to the relationship. In turn, they experience tremendous threat or a sense of violation, as though the distance or slight rupture means the relationship is over. The development of the capacity to self-soothe is very important in helping resolve couples' conflict.

In a difficult fight with an intimate partner, at least one partner probably entered a state of anxious attachment or shameful inadequacy. That is probably why it escalated into a fight. One of the partners reacted from a vulnerability, a lost perspective, and they suddenly felt that unless this disruption was resolved and closeness was re-established immediately, their relationship, or they themselves, wouldn't survive. Partners who enter distressed states in conflict probably feel security or identity threats, and feel that unless they are heard immediately, they forever will be misunderstood or forever be invalidated by their partners. Neither partner necessarily believes this realistically, but an anxious part of each of them is acting this way in a do-or-die effort to protect something. Unfortunately, the attempted solutions of protecting by trying to point out, convince or blame usually become the problem. What is needed is to be able to calm oneself with images of past security and caring and the knowledge that bad moments in the past have again turned to good. Partners need to work with their own anxiety to soothe it by learning to breathe and by reassuring themselves that "this too shall pass," having already experienced this in the past. Therapists thus need to help their clients self-soothe at times when their partners are not able to be responsive.

Finally, another important piece of getting along is feeling and expressing appreciation of the other. People need to be able to express both the positive and negative feelings they have to their partner. Although it makes sense that people need to express more positives than negatives, people in relationship soon forget this golden rule (Gottman, 1999). Some couples get into trouble because the positives are so taken for granted that they end up expressing only the negatives. On the other hand, some couples feel they are not allowed to express the negatives and avoid them altogether. Neither of these strategies is constructive. Therapists need to coach people to express appreciation for each other and engage in giving behaviours that make each other feel cared for. A little bit of positive reinforcement goes a long way in helping people maintain good attachments.

Our goal then is to help people reveal the underlying and generally more vulnerable emotions of fear, shame, and in the case of withdrawers and submitters, the empowering emotion of anger, and to begin to engage in empathic responsiveness and appreciation of each other.

References

Bowlby, J. (1969). *Attachment and loss: Vol. 1. Attachment.* New York: Basic Books.

Bowlby, J. (1988). *A secure base: Parent-child attachment and healthy human development.* New York: Basic Books.

Gilbert, P. (1989). *Human nature and suffering.* Hove, England: Lawrence Erlbaum Associates.

Gilbert, P. (1997) The evolution of social attractiveness and its role in shame, humiliation, guilt and therapy. *British Journal of Medical Psychology 70,* 113–147.

Gilbert, P. (1998). What is shame? Some core issues and controversies. In P. Gilbert & B. Andrews (Eds.), *Shame: interpersonal behavior, psychopathology and culture* (pp. 3–36). New York: Oxford University Press.

Gilbert, P. (2000).Varieties of submissive behavior as forms of social defense: Their evolution and role in depression. In L. Sloman & P. Gilbert (Eds.) *Subordination and defeat: An evolutionary approach to mood disorders and their treatment* (pp. 3–45). Mahwah, N.J.: Lawrence Erlbaum.

Gilbert, P. (2003). Evolution, social roles, and the differences in shame and guilt. *Social Research, 70,* 1205–1230.

Gilbert, P. & Allan, S. (1998). The role of defeat and entrapment (arrested flight) in depression: An exploration of an evolutionary view. *Psychological Medicine, 28,* 585-598.

Gilbert, P & McGuire M. (1998). Shame, social roles and status: The psychobiological continuum from monkey to human. In P. Gilbert & B. Andrews (Eds), *Shame: Interpersonal behavior, psychopathology and culture* (pp. 99–125). New York: Oxford University Press.

Gilbert, P., Price, J.S. & Allan, S. (1995). Social comparison, social attractiveness and evolution: How might they be related? *New Ideas in Psychology, 13,* 149–165.

Gottman, J. M. (1999). The marriage clinic: A scientifically based marital therapy. New York: Norton.

Gottman, J. M., Coan, J., Carrere, S., & Swanson, C. (1998). Predicting marital happiness and stability from newlywed interactions. *Journal of Marriage and the Family, 60,* 5–22.

Greenberg, L. (2002). *Emotion-focused therapy: Coaching clients to work through feelings.* Washington, D.C.: American Psychological Association Press.

Greenberg, L., Ford, C., Alden, L., & Johnson, S. (1993). In-session change processes in emotionally focused therapy for couples. *Journal of Consulting and Clinical Psychology, 61,* 68–84.

Greenberg, L., James, P., & Conry, R. (1988). Perceived change processes in emotionally focused therapy. *Journal of Family Psychology, 2,* 1–12.

Greenberg, L. S., & Johnson, S. M. (1988). *Emotionally focused therapy for couples.* New York: Guilford Press.

Greenberg, L. & Mateu Marques, C. (1998). Emotions in couples systems. *Journal of Systemic Therapies, 17(2),* 93–107.

Johnson, S. & Greenberg, L. S. (1985). Differential effects of experiential and problem solving interventions in resolving marital conflict. *Journal of Consulting and Clinical Psychology, 53,* 175–184.

2

Faith Based Mediation: A Discussion

Richard Manley-Tannis

"Conflict is inevitable, violence is not."
Elizabeth Loescher (The Conflict Center: Denver, Colorado)

At the core of interest-based mediation lies the reality that the participants must, at some point, actively choose to open themselves to one another. The act of making oneself vulnerable, however, runs in contradiction to what we have learned culturally. For the process to succeed, a step of faith is required.

As with most vocations, those who operate within the field of mediation – and, more broadly yet those who practise within the various areas of Alternative Dispute Resolution (ADR) – are motivated in the craft by different catalysts. In general, ADR refers to those processes that are utilized instead of, or in addition to, the adjudicative process as best evidenced by the adjudicative process as it currently exists in most jurisdictions. A helpful tool that has been used to describe the various models of mediation can also aid the present discussion.

Transformative/ Relational	Evaluative/ Directive
Facilitative	Settlement/ Agreement

The model identifies the two basic approaches most often used: Facilitative and Evaluative/Directive. The subsequent quadrants – Transformative/Relational and Settlement/Agreement – are where, to borrow from a colleague, one lives in the process. The process can range from the purely practical – contract discussions – to the more intangible – parenting models and communication.

Facilitative mediation is an approach that is primarily concerned with consensus building among the disputants. A mediator in this mode will not make recommendations or directly influence the process. Within this model, a mediator is concerned with ensuring that the process itself is productive and allows those in conflict to come to a resolution on their own without outside influence.

Evaluative/Directive is a process that involves a mediator who is more hands on and who attempts to play the devil's advocate openly throughout the process. In such a setting, which is often associated with court-sanctioned mediation, there is often the assumption that the mediator is an expert in the field in which the dispute has arisen. In general, the mediator is not only responsible for the process, but s/he has a direct influence on the outcome itself.

Transformative mediation borrows much from the facilitative model, in that the hope is to offer the disputants a process by which they may find their resolution. Furthermore, a mediator is concerned with the enabling of her/his clients to maintain and hopefully enrich existing relationships. Finally, the parties involved often design the process itself and the mediator helps them in this task so that they may ultimately own the entire experience – process all the way to resolution.

Settlement/Agreement is often used when relationships are not necessarily of the utmost importance; however, the day-to-day realities must continue. This example of mediation is primarily concerned with balancing needs versus wants of the parties in order to arrive at a compromise with which all can live.

Often the practical will tend toward the Settlement/Agreement quadrant, regardless of the method utilized: Facilitative or Evaluative/Directive. It is, however, in the Transformative/Relational that a mediator finds herself when those in conflict will continue to be connected, even after the current conflict is resolved. For those who have found that previous attempts to resolve their dispute have failed – perhaps through court litigation or positional based negotiations, as only two examples – or that even with an adjudicative decision(s), they continue to sense something remains incomplete or unaddressed, mediation can be offered as more than just a means of resolution. When those in dispute arrive at a point where they are willing, even if reluctant, to uncover their interests, mediation can become a transformative tool.

Mediation offers an alternate paradigm to the win-lose adjudicative model that pervades our contemporary culture. While the media reinforces retributive justice and instant gratification of perceived wrong, mediation challenges those participating to look deeper, to take responsibility for their own resolution. By struggling with the process, by mucking around, not only is a more restorative model realized, but a new manner of communication, not only with one another, but with oneself, can be claimed.

Contemporary mediation within our Western context is perceived as something that is new or innovative. The birth of the current model, and the ADR field in general, can be pinpointed to the late 1970s and early 1980s. This was a time when the need for alternatives to the existing judicial mechanisms was increasing due to overload and the realization that the equity of the system was often over-shadowed by procedure and form. What has been lost, however, or has remained on the periphery of most discussions, is that mediation has an ancient divine origin. To discern this ancestry, therefore, as the Midrash story goes, the image of God as present in the mud with us offers a humbling, yet invigorating, reminder that our creative sense does not exist in isolation. Mediation has been and is a metaphor of the potential of our own transformative relationship with one another and in turn with God.

From a Christian context, Jesus acts as a bridge between humanity and God that leads toward restoration (for further biblical examples of Jesus as mediator, see Appendix A). Consider the following texts:

> All this is from God, **who reconciled us** (καταλλάξαντος ἡμᾶς) to himself through Christ and **has given us the ministry of reconciliation** (δόντος ἡμῖν τὴν διακονίαν τῆς καταλλαγῆς); that is, in Christ God was **reconciling the world** (κόσμον καταλλάσσων) to himself, not counting their trespasses against them and entrusting **the message of reconciliation** (τὸν λόγον τῆς καταλλαγῆς) to us. (2 Corinthians 5:18-19)

> For this reason he is the **mediator** (μεσίτης) of a new covenant, so that those who are called may receive the promised eternal inheritance, because a death has occurred that redeems them from the transgressions under the first covenant. (Hebrews 9:15)

The image of Jesus as mediator is very familiar, but in the context of the present discussion, we must dig deeper into the metaphor in order to fully appreciate its significance.

The tradition of justice that is offered by Jesus the Christ as mediator is more than a literary allusion. From the writers' perspective, the historical tradition that was referenced was revolutionary. When the early Christian audience, influenced by Greek culture, read these words, they understood them in context of a tradition that stretches as far back as the oral tradition of Homer's *Iliad* and *Odyssey*.

Greek arbitration was developed out of the community's need to resolve conflict. More importantly, Greek arbitration developed as a survival mechanism. The first indication of the use of mediation-arbitration in the Greek world comes from the Homeric description of the Shield of Achilles (*Iliad* 18.497-508):

But the people were gathered in the agora [communal gathering area]; there a quarrel had arisen, two men were arguing in regard to the blood-price of a man who had been killed; on the one hand one of the men, setting forth his case to the people, maintained that he paid everything, while the other man denied that he had received anything. By an arbitrator both men desired to take the decision. But the people were cheering for both of them, defending both sides. Straightway the heralds were restraining the people; the elders were sitting on polished stones in the sacred circle, holding in their hands the staves of the loud-voiced heralds; thereupon with these they started up, in succession they gave judgement. And in the middle lay two talents of gold, to be given to him who among them speaks the fairest judgement

λαοὶ δ᾽ εἰν ἀγορῇ ἔσαν ἀθρόοι· ἔνθα δὲ νεῖκος

ὠρώρει, δύο δ᾽ ἄνδρες ἐνείκον εἵνεκα ποινῆς

ἀνδρὸς ἀποκταμένου· ὁ μὲν εὔχετο πάντ᾽ ἀποδοῦναι

δήμῳ πιφαύσκων, ὁ δ᾽ ἀναίνετο μηδὲν ἑλέσθαι·

ἄμφω δ᾽ ἱέσθην ἐπὶ ἴστορι πεῖραρ ἑλέσθαι.

λαοὶ δ᾽ ἀμφοτέροισιν ἐπήπυον, ἀμφὶς ἀρωγοί.

κήρυκες δ᾽ ἄρα λαὸν ἐρήτυον · οἱ δὲ γέροντες

ἕιατ᾽ ἐπὶ ξεστοῖσι λίθοις ἱερῷ ἐνὶ κύκλῳ,

σκῆπτα δὲ κηρύκων ἐν χέρσ᾽ ἔχον ἠεροφώνων·

τοῖσιν ἔπειτ᾽ ἤισσον, ἀμοιβηδὶς δὲ δίκαζον.

κεῖτο δ᾽ ἄρ᾽ ἐν μέσσοισι δύω χρυσοῖο τάλαντα,

τῷ δόμεν, ὃς μετὰ τοῖσι δίκην ἰθύντατα εἴποι.

The Greek community, from the Homeric period forward, was constantly threatened by both internal and external violence. In order to address these dangers, the community as a whole created a method designed to resolve conflict. Greek arbitration was innovative, because the community's direct involvement legitimized the process. The community itself developed a model, likely through dialectic, which is akin to the modern process of mediation-arbitration (med-arb).

Med-arb is a combination of mediation and arbitration. "Med-arb is a process by which the parties attempt to resolve their differences through mediation, but agree in advance that if they fail to reach an agreement through mediation, the mediator will become an arbitrator and render a binding decision" (The Ohio Commission on Dispute Resolution and Conflict Management, 2002).

The ancient arbitrator's primary task was first to attempt to mediate the dispute, and, should reconciliation prove unattainable, he would then arbitrate. Public pressure was brought to bear in order to encourage the resolution of conflict. The oath was used in order to ensure the honesty of the disputants by involving the gods as witnesses to and protectors of the process. The expectation that disputants would resolve their conflict peacefully ensured, in turn, the continued stability of the community.

There are two items that must be gleaned from this discussion. The first is that the community — and not the state — had responded to very real dangers to develop the mechanism. And secondly, though the state would eventually formalize the process to a certain extent, most med-arbs remained in the purview of the private domain. In other words, these neutrals — mediators — continued to be utilized and relied upon to resolve very real and often potentially dangerous conflicts up until and including the contemporary period of the early Church. The mediator was an extra-judicial avenue that afforded people access to justice.

The New Testament references, therefore, can be seen to represent the historic reality of the influence of those who were expected to assist in an outcome of resolution. The revolutionary merging of the practical and the spiritual cannot be underestimated. This fusion is the task that now seems to confront the potential of Faith Based Mediation (FBM).

The remainder of this discussion will be used to consider some of the challenges and/or obstacles that exist should FBM develop into something other than mere deliberation. As with most initial discussions, this does not claim to be exhaustive. Rather, it is hoped that the process of reflection may prove in itself a catalyst to illuminate what, if anything, should follow.

The first question that arises, as indicated above, is whether or not anything formal should in fact be developed. Is it sufficient for those who feel a connection to the process to be able to discuss the matter in an open environment? The reason for this self-reflective scepticism also finds its precedent in the early formation of the ADR movement. Formalization has, and continues to be, something that the field has openly resisted. The reasons are varied, but the core of the objection is that formalization threatens the efficacy of the process. What this means is that the informal empowerment that mediation offers to those in need would be jeopardized if training and certification became institutionalized.

Trained incapacity is a term that is sometimes used when describing fields or jurisdictions that have become burdened with so many requirements that it now exists solely to self-perpetuate structure rather than content. This learned helplessness is a very real danger should formalization occur, even within an FBM model. There exists enough anecdotal evidence to suggest that an effective mediator is finally dependent upon personality and not upon formal training. Though some would argue that training is necessary, especially in some of the more institutional processes such as labour relations, often the transformative aspect of the process transcends education.

If formalizing the process were felt to be the logical evolution, where and how would that process begin? FBM would necessarily seem to require ecumenical and non-denominational encouragement. Who and where are those people and institutions that would be best capable to foster the ensuing and necessary dialogue?

One of the dangers and matters to keep in mind is that as mediation was a challenge to the limitations of the various aspects of the judiciary, FBM must be developed proactively and not reactively. Moreover, it would seem important not to adopt a parochial perspective that has previously hijacked valid innovations and failed to develop due to a misplaced sense of ownership. FBM should utilize an open-source concept that encourages participation, while hopefully avoiding proprietary dangers.

One of the challenges for FBM is the question of multi-faith representation. Though this outline has been used to demonstrate the foundations of an FBM structure from a Christian context, the fact is that most contemporary faiths share, in their own historic context, a desire to offer a peaceful and respectful resolution to conflict other than through the use of violence that is mirrored in the win-lose manner of the existing adjudicative model in many societies. FBM, therefore, should encourage dialogue among other faith groups to investigate a collaborative development of the process. The criteria of involvement in FBM, however, should also not be limited to religious affiliation. But, as our current state of international affairs demonstrates, neither should race be a limiting factor in developing an FBM model.

Who would practice FBM? Laity, clergy, specifically trained personnel? At the moment, it would seem unnecessary to limit those who might make use of potential curricula offered by or from an FBM structure. There could, however, be curriculum developed to address the specific needs and responsibilities of each relevant constituency.

Mediation, even for all of the positive potential it possesses, remains a reactive tool to conflict. The process, therefore, should not be seen or anticipated to be the end of an evolutionary structure, but rather a logical point in the ultimate aim. Mediation, at its transformative best, is a life skill that should be encouraged in all people, regardless of affiliation. The progression from reactive to proactive, therefore, must come to fruition in educating those who are not yet in conflict, so that hopefully, when they find themselves in such a place, they will be able to openly and honestly confront their dispute respectfully without the need for a third party neutral.

Regardless of where FBM may or may not end up, it is important to remain true to the potential that the merging of spirit and practicality offers. FBM offers an example of the struggle between organic and institutional learning. It also highlights the need in our present world to add responsibility, integrity and equity to a judicial process that is not only over-burdened, but that is also rationalizing where it currently is and how it has arrived there. Finally, such a discussion must be approached in the same manner that reluctant participants of a mediation must enter a facilitation: with healthy scepticism and possessing the knowledge that without taking a leap – without storytelling those things we would rather not divulge – there can be no honest resolution. (For further discussion in regard to FBM, please contact the author at rmmt@ perlucidus.net.)

Appendix A

Διακονία +Εὐγγελιον/Καταλλαγή
Definitions:

Διακονία: ministry, the ministry of the word, N.T. (Liddell and Scott, *An Intermediate Greek-English Lexicon*, 189).

Εὐαγγελιον: the Glad Tidings, the Gospel, N.T. (Liddell and Scott, *An Intermediate Greek-English Lexicon*, 322).

Καταλλαγή: II. a change from enmity to friendship, reconcile, Aeschylus (sense reinforced in N.T. see verb καταλλα᾽σσω) 2. reconciliation of sinners with God, N.T. (Liddell and Scott, *An Intermediate Greek-English Lexicon*, 410).

Romans 11:13-17

Now I am speaking to you Gentiles. Inasmuch then as I am an apostle to the Gentiles, **I glorify my ministry** (τὴν διακονίαν μου δοξάζω) in order to make my own people jealous, and thus save them. For if their rejection is the **reconciliation of the world** (καταλλαγὴ κόσμου), what will their acceptance be but life from the dead!

Romans 12: 3-7

For by the grace given to me I say to everyone among you not to think of yourself more highly than you ought to think, but to think with sober judgement, each according to the measure of faith that God has assigned. For as in one body we have many members, and not all the members have the same functions, so we, who are many, are one body in Christ, and individually we are members of one another. We have gifts that differ according to the grace given to us: prophecy, in proportion to faith; **ministry, in ministering** (διακονιάν ἐν τῇ διακονίᾳ); the teacher, in teaching; the exhorter, in exhortation; the giver, in generosity; the leader, in diligence; the compassionate, in cheerfulness.

1 Corinthians 12:5

and there are **varieties of ministries** (διαιρέσεις διακονιῶν); and yet there is the same Lord;

2 Corinthians 5:18-19

All this is from God, **who reconciled us** (καταλλάξαντος ἡμᾶς) to himself through Christ and **has given us the ministry of reconciliation** (δόντος ἡμῖν τὴν διακονίαν τῆς καταλλαγῆς); that is, in Christ God was **reconciling the world** (κόσμον καταλλάσσων) to himself, not counting their trespasses against them and entrusting **the message of reconciliation** (τὸν λόγον τῆς καταλλαγῆς) to us.

2 Corinthians 9:13

Through the proof that **this ministry** (τῆς διακονίας ταύτης) gives, they glorify God because you are submissive to **the good news** (τὸ εὐαγγέλιον) about Christ, as you publicly declare you are, and because you are generous in your contribution to them and to all;

1 Thessalonians 3:2

and we sent Timothy, our brother and **co-worker** (διάκονον) for God in proclaiming **the Gospel** (τῷ εὐαγγελίῳ) of Christ, to strengthen and encourage you for the sake of your faith.

2 Timothy 4:5

As for you, always be sober, endure suffering, do the work of an **evangelist** (εὐαγγελιστοῦ), carry out **your ministry** (τὴν διακονίαν σου) fully.

Philemon 1:13

I wanted to keep him with me, so that he might be of **service** (διακονῇ) to me in your place during my imprisonment from **the gospel** (τοῦ εὐαγγελίου);

1 Peter 1:12

It was revealed to them that **they were serving** (διηκόνουν) not themselves, but you, in regard to the things that have now been announced to you through those who brought you **good news** (εὐαγγελισαμένων) by the Holy Spirit sent from heaven – things into which angels look!

Μεσίτης

Definition: A mediator, umpire, arbitrator, Polybius, N.T. (Liddell and Scott, *An Intermediate Greek-English Lexicon*, 499).

Galatians 3:19-20

Why then the law? It was added because of transgressions, until the offspring would come to whom the promise had been made; and it was ordained through angels by a **mediator** (μεσίτου). Now a **mediator** (μεσιτὴ) involves more than one party; but God is one.

1 Timothy 2:5

For there is one God; there is also one **mediator** (μεσίτης) between God and humankind, Christ Jesus, himself human.

Hebrews 8:6

But Jesus has now obtained a more excellent ministry, and to that degree he is the **mediator** (μεσίτης) of a better covenant, which has been enacted through better promises.

Hebrews 9:15

For this reason he is the **mediator** (μεσίτης) of a new covenant, so that those who are called may receive the promised eternal inheritance, because a death has occurred that redeems them from the transgressions under the first covenant.

Hebrews 12:24

and to Jesus, the **mediator** (μεσίτη) of a new covenant, and to the sprinkled blood that speaks a better word than the blood of Abel.

References

Liddell and Scott. *An Intermediate Greek-English Lexicon.* 1889. Oxford: Clarendon Press, 1992.

Ohio Commission on Dispute Resolution and Conflict Management. "Introduction." 15 March 2002. <http://disputeresolution.ohio.gov/nf-pintro.htm> 25 May 2006.

3

Restorative Justice: Theory and Practice

Sherry Morley

Restorative justice is a humane method of dealing with crime and its theory is closely associated with that of conflict resolution.

The subject of crime and its emotional damage is complex. There really is no perfect solution to solving crime and providing healing for its subjects. Varied definitions and diverse interpretations of restorative justice exist, but with agreement regarding the nature of humanity, it is difficult to analyze this perspective because it raises issues around the inherent goodness of humanity, among others. Advocates of restorative justice argue that crime is a form of conflict and therefore can be resolved using conflict resolution. Yet this idea needs careful examination. Crime deals with a more severe level of conflict and emotional damage than a workplace conflict, for example. This is true in reference to compensation and trust, because compensation for harm is tangible in workforces, but in criminal conflict there is no direct form of compensation for fear, loss of confidence, physical injury or emotional trauma that might guarantee restoration (Cragg, 1992). The goal of restorative justice is to reach an outcome satisfactory to all parties involved including the victim, offender and the community. However, to work together to reach an agreement requires trust, and the more severely eroded the trust, the more severe the conflict is (Cragg, 1992). Criminal conflict falls into this category. These differences must be kept in mind when analyzing the potential for the theory of restorative justice to succeed in reality.

Restorative justice believes in using accountability, restoration and healing to attain "justice." This terminology raises another complication because the notion of justice is relative to the individual. Who are we to define justice for others? In general, the definition of justice in one community may be punishment, while in another it may be restitution. Who is to say which concept of justice should prevail? In restorative justice practices, what seems fair to the offender may not be to the victim.

Questioning the Notion of Justice

Perhaps the notion of justice should be dropped altogether from the restorative "justice" concept. The term is dangerous because it may lead to the interpretation of restoration as a matter of equality based on an eye-for-an-eye mentality. The "mathematical" concept of justice sees proportionality as the ultimate commendable feature of any system of law enforcement because it accords with a morality based on the need to "equalize" disturbed situations created by crime (Fatic, 1995). The emotional component of justice is based on vengeful feelings provoked by the offence and on the desire to "get even" with the offender (Fatic, 1995). Justice generally refers to getting even rather than restoration, and it requires equality: "Even with provisions for merciful treatment, compassion and forgiveness, the basis of justice is reciprocal victimization of the offender according to the victimization of his victim" (Fatic, 1995, p. 188).

Justice is always measured by a sentence, which means it is measured by a form of punishment to balance the scales of harm. Consequently, the term restorative justice should be changed so as to better inform public perception and to disconnect society from the focus of achieving "justice." To many, it is predicated on the notion of punishment. This attitude is largely driven by the media, who often encourage the demand for harsher sentences and urge the public to define justice by the amount of years an offender serves behind bars.

The key is to view punishment not as the purpose of justice, but as a key component of the resolution and restoration. Throwing an offender behind bars is a form of punishment and some may argue that it leads to restoration by deterring the offender from committing future crimes. However, incarceration does not necessarily prevent recidivism and is not a humane way of dealing with criminal conflict. With conflict resolution as the goal, punishment such as eliciting shame and taking responsibility is inflicted as part of the means to resolving conflict rather than achieving justice.

Proponents emphasizing the importance of symbolic reparation over material reparation should raise the question of whether undergoing punishment can count as symbolic reparation (Johnstone, 2002). The notion of punishment in this sense is not a method of "getting even," but is an integral part of the restorative process that in theory can lead to reparation of harm caused. Reparation is made by making or acting in a way that acknowledges responsibility for harm caused. Feelings of regret, shame and remorse can be seen as a form of punishment when offenders are encouraged to feel humiliation or shame (Cragg, 1992).

Viewing Crime as Conflict

Historically, crime was not distinct from conflict. It was dealt with as an issue of conflict between members of the community whereby rulers did not participate directly unless heresy was involved. However, the Western world developed the public system of judicial punishment for crimes of violence against property (Johnstone, 2002), and the system gradually transformed.

Conflict has been given a variety of definitions. Generally, it occurs when two parties have contrasting interests and when those separate interests interfere with each other in some way. Scholars suggest that conflict exists where "incompatible activities occur" (Picard, 2002, p. 3) or they define it as "an expressed struggle between at least two interdependent parties who perceive incompatible goals, scarce resources and interference from others in achieving their goals" (Picard, 2002, p. 3). This form of conflict might arise in the workplace or simply between friends arguing over who will buy the last pair of their favourite shoes at the department store. Conflicts over tangible resources are easily identified and therefore easier to resolve.

Conflicts dealing with deep emotion – esteem, recognition and respect – are more difficult to pinpoint and resolve (Picard, 2002). Perhaps this is part of the reason why the current justice system "appears" to work so well in many cases. The justice system defines criminal conflict simply as a tangible conflict between an individual and the legal rules defined by societal norms. Criminal conflict is defined by law and therefore allows for a concrete, straightforward and by-the-book resolution to be reached. A judge examines the facts of a given case, distinguishes or compares it to previous cases with similar circumstances and makes a judgment accordingly. Arguably, personal circumstances of the individual may be taken into consideration for sentencing. Yet, unfortunately, this formal method is an ineffective way of dealing with and resolving crime because it ignores the human and emotional consequences of criminal conflict. It ignores the root causes of crime and more often than not encourages more crime through the isolation and stigma associated with prison and with a person being labelled a criminal. This form of "justice" discourages offenders from taking responsibility and owning up to what they've done. As academics suggest, criminal conflict has either become people's property (lawyers) or is defined away by those in whose interests it is valuable to do so (McEvoy and Newburn, Eds., 2003).

Restorative justice humanizes crime by interpreting it as a conflict between people.

Conflict Resolution and Restorative Justice

The general goal of conflict resolution is to de-escalate conflict and reverse the spiral of destructive or negative interactions, while attempting to come to an agreement and find mutually satisfying outcomes (Cragg, 1992). Similarly, the goal of restorative justice is to hold offenders accountable for their actions and work towards reparation and restoration of harm caused. The victim and offender interact directly or indirectly, sharing emotions and viewpoints, communicating and co-operating to reach an agreement on reparation. It generally involves confronting offenders with the consequences of their unacceptable behaviour (i.e. when a victim shares how the crime impacted them), eliciting an understanding in the victim of what it was about the offender's lifestyle, company or habits that led them to offend, committing the offender to change their lifestyle, encouraging an apology, allowing victims a chance to express their feeling about what happened, and encouraging victims to take some steps towards forgiving offenders (Johnstone, 2002).

A key theoretical concept in restorative justice is harm. In accordance with the theory, crime is defined as harm to people and relationships. There are four dimensions to harm in the criminal context. Harm involves injuries that require healing – harm to victims, to individual relationships, to offenders and to the community.

According to Van Ness (1993), the restorative justice perspective is based on three ideas. Firstly, crime is primarily a conflict between individuals and only later is it law-breaking. Secondly, the aim of the criminal justice process is to reconcile parties while repairing hurt caused by the crime. Thirdly, the criminal justice process should encourage participation by the victim, the offender and the community rather than be dominated by the government to the exclusion of others (Strang, 2002). The restorative justice process involves people impacted by a conflict interacting for reparative purposes.

Many proponents of restorative justice have varied definitions of the concept. It is a broad term. Critics argue it is an idealistic and unachievable philosophy, saying the perspective has no foundation or developed methodology on how to achieve its goals – such as reparation. McEvoy and Newburn (2003) share their own reservations on restorative justice and peacemaking criminology:

> For some of us, criminal justice is a practitioner's field in which peacemaking seems quite alien. For others of us, peacemaking is something we do in our daily lives, something that seemed unrelated to our academic pursuits. A few of us are actively involved in attempts to humanize prisons. All of us were sceptical of the perspective of peacemaking criminology, not so much for what it represents, but for the apparent confusion surrounding the central tenets, the lack of clear strategies for implementation, and the inability or refusal of many adherents to address

the hard questions of how we, individually or collectively, ought to respond to specific instances of violence of all types. (p. 102)

Some argue restorative justice is easier said than done. Others argue it should only be used for first time, minor offences. Either way, one major positive component of restorative justice is that it identifies with humanity more so than the current criminal justice system. Restorative justice theory emphasizes an ongoing relationship with offenders, rather than focusing on the stigmatization offenders receive once they're labelled criminals – and the marginalization they and victims receive in the criminal justice process. It sees offenders as "one of us," not enemies from the outside, even though they may adopt conflicting attitudes and behaviours. By segregating and ostracizing offenders, offenders are further alienated by the community and further distanced from being reintegrated into society (Johnstone, 2002). Criminologists who examine the sociology of emotions in crime admit that popular responses to crimes of senseless violence are seldom predicated on a convincing portrayal of the reality of crime. They suggest criminologists need to insist that perpetrators of crime are moral subjects striving to give meaning to their actions before, during and after the crime (De Haan and Loader, 2002). By treating them as human beings whose feelings and experiences we consider and listen to through participation in conflict resolution, offenders may in theory be more willing to repent and take responsibility for their actions and therefore repair the damage they have caused to victims and the community.

This philosophy is centred on the notion that confrontation will draw out feelings of shame, guilt and remorse, paving the way for restoration:

In the very process of being confronted personally by their victims and hearing first hand of the actual harm caused by their behaviour... offenders will begin to grasp the true effects of their behaviour. The psychology they use to distance themselves from knowledge of these consequences will be penetrated. (De Haan and Loader, 2002, p. 13)

It is believed that when offenders come face to face with their victims, they will see the true impact of their behaviour. This awareness will be followed by feelings of shame, guilt and remorse for the harm they have caused, which in theory will lead to the desire for some form of reparation of harm done.

For victims, the restorative justice perspective encourages healing and restoration by allowing victims to participate in the process, confronting the person who has caused them harm. This process is meant to empower the victim, to restore emotional and material losses, reduce fear and receive answers to better understand why they were chosen as a victim (Strang, 2002). The victim would have more control over how the wrong against them is defined and over how it should be dealt with so that they can move on and better deal with the aftermath. Therefore, it is maintained that restorative justice helps to heal the wounds of crime suffered by the victim (Johnstone, 2002).

This theory has been criticized because of its broad perspective. Some restorative justice advocates may direct the process more towards the victim because it is the victim who has suffered harm at the hands of the offender. Marginalization of the offender could result if the focus is mainly on the victim, with fewer attempts made to satisfy both parties equally, as in conflict resolution. A practical example of this can be seen in the proposed use of a screening process sensitive to victims (Pressor, 1999). In this regard, the restorative justice model holds the potential for disadvantaging a claimed offender because the people screening offenders into restorative programs might engage in intended or unintended bias (Lemley, 2001). The same bias or marginalization could occur during the process of resolving the situation when coming to an agreement.

The community is a key component to the theory of restorative justice because it is the community's reception of the offender that can affect the outcome – and success or failure of the process. "Ordinary members of the community are needed to generate pressure for the settlement of a conflict" (Lemley, 2001, p. 14). Community members' involvement is necessary as a support system for the victim and offender. In his analysis of the key theoretical concepts of restorative justice theory, Lemely (2001) suggests that the community should be the prime responder to crime with specific responsibilities: community norm development and enforcement and problem solving targeted at underlying community or neighbourhood problems.

Restorative justice theory should require that supportive community structures be built to combat crime at its roots and to discourage individuals from committing offences. This means dealing with social issues such as poverty and neglect, for example. These realities are a causal factor of crime in our communities. This discussion once again emphasizes the importance of seeing criminality and justice from a human perspective. Because social structures and culture contribute to the prevalence of crime, we should look to resolving this conflict in a humane way. McEvoy and Newburn (2003) include a study on peacemaking criminology that suggests

> the destructive behaviours and debilitating social structures that often characterize our culture result from a variety of factors: constraining modes of knowing, ideological systems that maintain non-coercive conceptual machinery for maintaining an oppressive social order, social institutions that create and reinforce destructive and unjust social relations, and forms of interaction that perpetuate individual pain and suffering resulting from power inequities and inegalitarian social arrangements. (p. 119)

Restorative justice is built on the notion that we are in a struggle with the social forces suppressing human potential. Therefore, when a crime does occur, the goal of restorative justice is to encourage personal change as part of restoration. Once recognized, the goal is to change attitudes about and ways of social interaction. The theory invites personal transformation (McEvoy and Newburn, 2003).

This philosophy is crucial to understanding crime. Because crime is defined as harm to people and relationships, an offence must be understood in its moral, social, economic and political context (Lemley, 2001).

It seems likely that proponents who place equal emphasis on the offender and the victim in restorative justice are those who see crime as a form of conflict to be resolved so both parties' situations are improved.

Restorative justice will not occur if the victim and offender participate involuntarily. Making amends and reaching an agreement on the outcome cannot be achieved if one or both parties are not willing to co-operate or enter the process with the sincerest intentions of wanting to reach a resolution.

Shame, Guilt, Remorse and Forgiveness

Various theories exist on the appropriate use of emotions in the restorative justice process. Some proponents argue shaming encourages the offender to apologize and take responsibility for their behaviour while recognizing the victim and their emotions. Theoretically, this recognition empowers the victim, too. Shaming is the expression of the disapproval of an act rather than the offender. The goal is not to degrade or stigmatize the offender, which in turn could elicit a defensive reaction. If stigmatized, offenders may put up walls or employ defence mechanisms in order to maintain self-respect and dignity.

Some researchers argue shame is generated by conscience. The type of shame that leads to guilt and remorse is that formed by conscience, rather than defiance, denial and ingenuity:

> As victims recount their pain and sorrow, and family members and close friends communicate their estrangement from the offender, he or she becomes aware of the lost trust and feels ashamed. At the same time, the other participants respond with "empathic resonance": they share another's distress. (Stokkom, 2002, p. 343)

In theory, the restorative justice process elicits various emotions at different stages. The process is laid out clearly by Bas Van Stokkom (2002) in his article "Moral Emotions in Restorative Justice Conferences." Van Stokkom (2002) suggests the process begins with feelings of indignation and apprehension between parties. The offender may be fearful about taking responsibility openly for the crime and facing or owning up to what they've done. The victim may feel ashamed or vulnerable because of the crime committed against them. Revealing the shame felt by both parties is in theory a key component to the reparation process:

> The expression of shame offers an opportunity to put one-self in the other's place, particularly if suffering or sorrow becomes visible. The shame of victims is generally hidden behind anger and indignation, but as soon as they express sorrow, anxiety or pain, feelings of shame come above the surface. (Stokkom, 2002, p. 344)

It is also important to remember that appealing for shame directly from the offender by pointing out their wrongdoings or failure could hinder the restoration process because it might be interpreted as an attack on the offender's entire identity, one against which the offender will defend themselves (Stokkom, 2002).

The shame of the offender manifests itself in confrontation with the painful feelings of the victim and in an expression of regret or remorse. As Braithwaite (2001) proposes, "shame is a normal emotion that healthy humans must experience; it is as vital to motivating us to preserve social bonds essential to our flourishing as is fear to motivating us to flee danger" (p. 42). The "transformation of emotions that mask suffering into emotions that reveal suffering, and in particular the inducement of shame, seems to be the key to successful conferences" (Stokkom, 2002, p. 344). It is this process that makes understanding, reacceptance and reparation possible. Once one party has opened up and revealed their pain, the other lets down their defences because they no longer feel threatened. They may feel embarrassed or humiliated and better identify with their own emotions when they let down their guard.

Shameful emotions dissipate as the offender takes responsibility for his or her actions by apologizing and showing remorse. In theory, this in turn encourages the victim(s) to see the offender as a human being rather than defining the offender by their actions. At this point, Moore suggests that the victim is willing to forgive (Stokkom, 2002, pp. 341-342). Sharing feelings of shame, remorse and guilt in theory elicits respect from the victim, offender and the community. This lifts shame from the offender – "any shame the offender feels is a fundamental respect by others for the offender. This same respect needs to be shown to the victim" (Johnstone, 2002, p. 5).

Shame also impacts members of the community who are present to support the offender in the process. It prevents the offender from bearing his or her shame alone. Instead, the offender can share it in the comfort of others with whom they have a connection:

> The shame felt by friends and close relatives of the offender is, in part, a vicarious shame. It demonstrates their bonds with the offender. This explains the relative ease with which young offenders and their victims are pulled out of humiliation in the setting of a restorative conference. (Stokkom, 2002, p. 343)

In the final stages of the conference, participants feel relief. The victim is relieved to see that the offender and others share their humiliation at being demeaned by an offence. It shows them that they do not have to be ashamed of feeling ashamed, and the victim and offender achieve a level of empathy towards each other (Stokkom, 2002). In the eyes of the victim, the offender is now human. "They have adopted intuitively an egalitarian and non-competitive view of intrinsic human worth" (Stokkom, 2002, p. 342). The process becomes an exchange between parties: "Offenders observe the distress of victims and begin to grasp their point of view, whereas victims observe helpless offenders, thereby lightening the burden of their anger" (Stokkom, 2002, p. 343). Once guilt and remorse have been shared, the road is paved for the possibility of forgiveness.

Achieving symbolic reparation through this "emotional exchange" (Stokkom, 2002, p. 345) is much more important than material reparation. Paying money or offering community service work does not necessarily signify regret or remorse.

Some guilt theorists argue that shame is a self-directed, destructive emotion that leads to defensive behaviour, effectively blocking communication between parties. Yet remorse theorists argue that guilt is a self-focused emotion, a kind of "anxious self-pity" (Stokkom, 2002, p. 350). I suggest shame is a combination of these emotions essential to restorative justice theory and reparation because both induce human emotion and empathy from other parties. As a result, their defences are down and the floor is open for communication.

Shame is defined as an expression of disapproval and is a necessary emotion for the offender to experience in order to achieve reparation. Feeling shame shows that the offender in some way feels bad and acknowledges responsibility for the harm done. However, shame alone is not sufficient for reparation because it merely signifies that the offender accepts the harm they've caused. Depending on the individual, this feeling could be accompanied by guilt or remorse or perhaps defensiveness if the offender feels their core identity is being attacked.

Therefore, in dealing with shame, it is important that disapproval of the act is also expressed by the victim and members of the restorative justice process, rather than disapproval of the person as a whole. Stokkom (2002) emphasizes the need to distinguish between harmful and helpful types of shame in restorative conferencing: "focus questions upon the consequences of the offence and the emotions arising from those consequences. This helps to divert attention from the offender's person, thus limiting stigmatization" (p. 352). For this reason too, shaming, which means expressing disapproval, should be done by people the offender respects, as this may elicit more empathy and remorse in the offender (Stokkom, 2002).

In addition to shame, guilt is an essential emotion to restorative justice theory because it is categorized by many theorists as a moral emotion. "Guilt is a special case of empathy, involving feelings of concern coupled with a sense of personal responsibility for having caused distress... guilt feelings serve as evidence that offenders care about victims" (Stokkom, 2002, p. 348). The notion of caring is reassuring to victims. Yet some theorists argue that guilt is a more moral emotion than shame because shame is "self-focused" (Stokkom, 2002, p. 348) and likely to lead to re-evaluation of the self and one's core identity, with no focus on the offending behaviour and consequently the victim.

I propose that guilt has the potential of being almost as self-directed as shame, depending on the individual. If a person is so overcome by guilt (feels their behaviour hasn't lived up to the standards of others) depending on the extent or severity of harm caused, the evaluation of their behaviour may result in questioning of the self rather than the act alone. At this point, feelings of guilt could become more self-focused. This is especially more likely in restorative justice conferences where incidents are far reaching and offenders are confronted by relative strangers (the victim). The offender is no longer only surrounded by a support system to help them believe they can control bad things that happen to them. Instead, they are less in control and more likely to switch over to a negative self-evaluation, entering the uncontrollability of the shame domain (Stokkom, 2002, p. 349).

Nevertheless, feelings of shame or guilt or the combination of both are positive key theoretical concepts of the restorative justice perspective. These emotions demonstrate signs of distress and human emotion, which may in turn lead to empathy from others and a sort of understanding. As Stokkom (2002) argues, "without such signs, observers might believe the offender does not struggle with the consequences" (p. 349).

Remorse is also central to restorative justice theory. Remorse is an other-regarding emotion rather than a self-directed one and is defined as a feeling of "compunction or deep regret" (Stokkom, 2002, p. 350). By experiencing this emotion, the offender will be compelled to work at repairing harm done. Both guilt and remorse invoke similar responses, although theorists argue they are dissimilar. Guilt is characterized as a form of regret and remorse as deep regret – both have similar meanings and invoke a sense of wanting to undo the wrongdoing (Stokkom, 2002, p. 350). However, Stokkom (2002) alludes to one scholar's negative portrayal of guilt – that the person feeling remorse will see reparation as an end in itself, while guilt sees reparation as a means towards self-rehabilitation. I see both of these as positive components to restorative justice because the theory, similar to that of conflict resolution, is to satisfy both the victim and the offender. There-fore, self-rehabilitation elicited by feelings of guilt should not be seen as a negative aspect.

In the end, all of these concepts are essential to restorative justice theory. Shame, guilt and remorse have the potential to lead to empathy and reparation. These theoretical concepts are correlated and compatible, such as the notion of shame-guilt, which occurs when an offender realizes they have acted contrary to an ethical norm, has feelings of having done wrong, experiences concern that others have been hurt, and feels ashamed of oneself and one's act and anger at oneself (Stokkom, 2002, p. 351). The shame-guilt concept incorporates both self-directed feelings and other-regarded emotions. In theory, painful emotions experienced by the offender and revealed in restorative justice conferencing lead to compassion and understanding from other parties. These feelings pave the way for a resolution. This process may not lead to healing or forgiveness depending on the severity of harm, but the process can be a constructive way of dealing with criminal conflict. It is capable of accomplishing much more than the criminal justice system because it involves the healthy sharing of human emotions.

Guilt, shame and remorse are just a few of the emotions elicited in the restorative justice process. As well, emotion is just one of the key elements of the process. Restorative justice involves the parties meeting in person, with support systems for both victim and offender. Often there are one or more facilitators present to monitor and lead the process. All parties, including secondary victims and supporters for the offender, discuss what happened, how it affected them and how to address harm done. The emotional element contributes to understanding and leads to reparation and restoration. By sharing emotions and viewpoints, the parties come to understand each other, why the crime occurred, how severe the harm caused was and how to correct the harm done. In the end, the parties decide on an agreement that satisfies each.

Criticisms of Restorative Justice

Aside from its theoretical potential, there are many criticisms of the perspective that must be considered when analyzing the feasibility of the process.

First, in conflict resolution, as in restorative justice, a key element is maintaining equality and balance in the process between victim and offender to prevent marginalization and stigmatization of the offender. As emphasized earlier though, the harm caused by criminal conflict is often quite severe and is not a dispute with equal blame shared between both parties in the conflict. Therefore, it may be difficult to treat offenders equally and refrain from marginalizing or expressing disapproval with the offender themselves rather than their actions alone.

Furthermore, in placing an offender in a setting of strangers in order to elicit feelings of guilt from shame, the offender must have a support system present. However, not all communities or their members are willing to participate or support an offender. It is not a guarantee that the offender will have a support system they respect, who disapproves of the act and yet will stand by the offender. Also, being placed in a conference with strangers may elicit a defensive stance from the offender rather than an open one.

Moreover, with Western culture becoming increasingly individualistic, society facilitates avoidance. Opening up, sharing emotions and dependency are signs of weakness. As Stokkom (2002) himself suggests, "One must agree with critics that restorative justice conferences are the scene of an emotional collision highly unfamiliar to people nowadays" (p. 353). Restorative justice theory is emotionally demanding – especially with the moral pressure on an offender to expose themselves in front of strangers. The offender is asked to give up their defensive stance used to protect their dignity and pride, and to deliver themselves to the mercy of their victims (Stokkom, 2002, p. 353). This is not common practice and therefore could make it difficult for offenders and victims to achieve open communication, become vulnerable and reveal genuine feelings of shame.

Furthermore, there could be conflict in trying not to shame the offender directly so as not to elicit defensiveness while at the same time denouncing the harm and injustice caused to the victim, "to mobilize shame against wrongs" (Stokkom, 2002, p. 354). If indirect methods of producing guilt, remorse and apology do not work, the only option is for open, direct disapproval of the act – which could in turn block communication with the offender and produce destructive emotions.

It is also an assumption that the offender will feel shame, guilt and remorse for harm caused. Many individuals who participate in restorative justice are one-time offenders who, before they committed a crime, were not the type of person to do so again. They are individuals who genuinely feel ashamed by their actions and want to repair harm caused. However, some participants may be offenders who reject societal values and are able to distance themselves from the victim (usually a stranger) by denying that they themselves have caused any harm by committing the crime. Individuals react and deal with crime in different ways. For instance, offenders may absolve themselves of guilt and become defensive, seeing obedience to the law as disadvantageous. The restorative justice process may have no impact on these offenders, even though it may appear to.

Another assumption made by the theory of peacemaking criminology and restorative justice is that both reject the notion that human beings are innately violent and committed to self-interest. Determining whether humanity is inherently good is not an easy task. As both critics and advocates of peacemaking criminology even note, "human nature is an ambiguous concept that risks debates over whether behaviour and urges are socially constructed and contextual, or instead essentialist and hard-wired into us" (McEvoy and Newburn, 2003, p. 119). Critics also note that the restorative justice approach assumes a consensus on a spiritually correct and universal normative order; that all parties participate willingly and are not subject to norms subtly coercing obedience; and that status and other power inequalities will not intrude in the process (McEvoy and Newburn, 2003, p. 112). Seemingly balanced conversation may disguise potentially destructive realities within the process. Again, the restorative justice perspective requires individuals to act morally and to act on their responsibility to others. Consequently, many critics argue the theory is a utopian vision and a philosophy with no real substance as a model for processing offenders (McEvoy and Newburn, 2003, p. 114). Furthermore, the success of peacemaking and, likewise, restorative justice is dependent on the degree to which individuals can transform their interactions and themselves.

Even if the offender has feelings of guilt, and remorse and genuinely wants to make reparation, working together with the victim to come to an agreement involves trust; the more severe the conflict, the more severely eroded the trust. In his development of restorative justice theory, Wesley Cragg (1992) points out how Conrad Brunk (1988) describes escalating conflict:

> A well-known dynamic in conflict is that the less trust there is between the parties, the more difficult it becomes for them to communicate, the more they misperceive the nature of the conflict and the intentions of their opponent, and the more difficult it is for them to perceive a sincere, friendly gesture by the opponent as truly friendly. It is the classic "positive feedback mechanism where the conflict feeds on itself and expands." (p. 180)

Criminal conflict may be more difficult to de-escalate because of this eroded trust.

Cragg (1992) believed that principles of conflict resolution – such as undertaking to understand the opponents' position and to communicate one's own, as well as to be prepared to make unilateral gestures of co-operation – are more difficult to achieve when dealing with criminal conflict because of the high level and diversity of emotions felt by both the offender and the victim.

This is by no means an exhaustive list of cautions and criticisms of the restorative justice perspective. Rather, I am suggesting what just a few critics argue are some of the possible weaknesses of the theory in practice.

In the book that links criminology with conflict resolution and restorative justice, the problem with restorative justice theory is summed up in a paragraph:

the value of peacemaking lies in the degree to which individuals can transform themselves, their interactions and their social institutions away from a violent and hostile environment and toward one that is more conducive to fulfilling the "species being".... As a consequence, the criticisms that PMC is utopian, idealistic and ambitious remain valid. (McEvoy and Newburn, 2003, p. 130)

The restorative justice perspective, if successful, is an ideal way of dealing with crime not because of its potential to prevent recidivism and reduce crime rates and prison populations, but to heal and restore victims and offenders back to well being. However, the criticisms pointed out are realistic concerns that must be recognized by proponents of restorative justice.

Most restorative justice proponents do not advocate that this theory is the answer to crime prevention and the restoration of offenders. Yet even if full reparation is not achieved, the approach offers a kind of constructive method of teaching offenders and victims (those affected by crime) how to resolve conflict in a meaningful and humane way.

Critics of restorative justice proponents question the notion of punishment and often suggest one cannot practice both because they are opposing concepts. Some accuse restorative justice theorists of blurring the distinction between restorative justice and punishment when proponents suggest that restorative justice should operate in the shadow of punishment or that punishment should be an option if restorative justice does not work in a particular case. These accusations are unfair. Restorative justice is not a quick cure for crime or social injustices. Rather, it is a way of teaching and illustrating a new perspective for dealing with certain crimes. Individuals who break the law should not only take responsibility for violating societal standards, but also for the humane part of the committed action – for harm caused to the victim. Restorative justice cannot replace punishment because there are criminals who do not voluntarily want to repair harm done and do not want to take ownership for their offences. There will always be those who manage to distance themselves from their victims. Yet there are many people who commit a crime, who, once facing the victim, are inclined to own up to the harm they have caused and realize the impact of it. These are the people restorative justice is capable of helping.

Restorative Justice in Practice

I must admit that when I decided to observe a restorative justice circle, after much research on the subject and its criticisms, I was sceptical of the process and its ability to elicit emotions from both victims and offenders. As a human being, I have used defence mechanisms myself when I do not want to face or own up to responsibility for my actions or feel publicly ashamed.

My skepticisms were enhanced when the young offender involved in the youth justice circle I attended appeared to be going through the process with no real emotional involvement. There is validity in the suggestion that offenders can go through the motions without really feeling remorse or guilt. In this youth justice circle, though, the young offender did ultimately show signs of shame, guilt and remorse.

Two facilitators mediated the process. The circle included the primary offender, both of her parents, two primary victims and a secondary victim. The offender spoke first, explaining the string of events that led to her attempted break-in at a general store. At the time of the incident, the offender was living at a private therapeutic boarding school for girls with behavioural problems. The school was located in a small, close-knit community. The owners of the general store and inn were supporters of the school and offered up their rooms as a dormitory when the school first opened.

The offender said she felt she was forced to commit the crime because she didn't want to let the other girls down (girls who attended the school she was living in). The explanation for her actions and the regret the offender elicited at the beginning stages of the process appeared to centre on herself, with no regard for the victims. She said she questioned why she committed the act once she realized she was going to get caught by the police. The facilitators asked what her thoughts were before, during and after the crime, how she felt when the police came and how she and others were affected by her actions. The offender said she realized she shouldn't have committed the crime. She said she should have been strong and wanted to earn her parents' trust back. She said it did not feel good to not be trusted. She named the store owners as one of the parties affected by her actions, along with her family, the community and the police. Next, the secondary victim, who was the owner of the school, spoke. She said she was angry and interpreted the incident as a personal affront to the community, because as the school's owner, she had tried hard to convince the community that her girls were not bad kids. At this point the secondary victim made eye contact with the offender, and explained that she was embarrassed and felt partly responsible. The offender made little eye contact with the secondary victim and apologized for the embarrassment.

Following this discussion, the primary victims spoke about what they thought and felt as a consequence of the crime. The store owners said they felt violated and hurt, especially after they put up some of the girls in their inn to try to help them. Both owners began crying at this point as they shared their feelings. They also expressed feelings of being unsafe in their community now.

The parents of the offender spoke last. This was a noticeable turning point in the process, because the feelings shared by both parents elicited feelings of shame and remorse within the offender. The positive reaction of the offender to her parents supports in practice the theory that offenders are more likely to experience shame, guilt or remorse when they have a support system present or when their actions have affected not just strangers, but people whom they care about and whose standards they feel guilty for violating. In this case, it seems as though the young offender was able to maintain a defensive stance even though she had admitted what she did wrong – until she heard her parents explain how they felt and, more specifically, when her mother explained to the offender that the victim was not a complete stranger.

The father said that when he heard of his daughter's crime, his heart sank and he felt helpless. He said he felt a sense of loss because he had big hopes for her. He added that he had felt better about the incident over time, until coming to the justice circle to relive what had happened. The young offender's mother expressed her disapproval with her daughter's actions, and explained to those in the circle that the owners of the store had at one point served their family breakfast at the inn. At this point, the mother was in tears and the young offender began crying as well. Through tears, the young offender said she was so sorry for what she caused her parents and the owners of the general store and that she didn't mean any harm. The group worked out an agreement for the young offender to present her story about the incident to a group of young people in a similar situation. She also agreed to send a letter of apology to the owner of the school and already had sent a letter of apology to the owners of the inn and general store.

Clearly, the restorative justice process is not a quick fix. Confronting her victims and facing the consequences of her actions while owning up to them does not mean the young offender's behaviour and attitude have transformed permanently. Yet it does teach a better way of dealing with criminal conflict and injury caused to others. It also illustrates the human aspect of crime, the offender and the victims. Dealing with human emotion is crucial to healing. Keeping feelings pent up elicits resentment and bitterness and could prevent victims as well as the offender from moving on with their lives.

Ultimately, the restorative justice process did not solve the problems the young offender suffers from, in terms of her behavioural issues, but there is relief on the victims' and offender's behalf in their ability to put the incident behind them after having had shared their experience and emotions.

References

Braithwaite, J. (2000, July). Shame and criminal justice. *Canadian journal of criminology* 42(3).

Cragg, W. (1992). *The practice of punishment: Towards a theory of restorative justice*. London: Routledge.

Fatic, A. (1995) *Punishment and restorative crime handling*. Aldershot, UK: Avebury.

Haan, W. and Loader, I. (2002). On the emotions of crime, punishment and social control. *Theoretical criminology* 6(3).

Johnstone, G. (2002). *Restorative justice: Ideas, values, debates*. Oregon: William Publishing.

Lemley, E.C. (2001). Designing restorative justice policy: An analytical perspective. *Criminal justice policy review* 12(1).

McEvoy, K. and Newburn, T. (2003). *Criminology, conflict resolution and restorative justice*. New York: Palgrave MacMillan.

Picard, C.A. (2002). *Mediating interpersonal and small group conflict*. Ottawa: The Golden Dog Press.

Pressor, L. (1999). Restorative justice and offender screening. *Journal of criminal justice*, 27(4).

Stokkom, B.V. (2002). Moral emotions in restorative justice conferences: Managing shame, designing empathy. *Theoretical criminology* 6(3).

Strang, H. (2002). *Repair or revenge*. New York: Oxford University Press.

Strang, H. and Braithwaite, J. (2000). *Restorative justice: From philosophy to practice*. Aldershot, UK: Ashgate.

Weitekamp, E.G.M. and Kerner, H.J., Eds. (2002). *Restorative justice: Theoretical foundations*. Oregon: Willan Publishing.

4

Nonviolent Communication: Developing Habits for Peaceful Living

Judi Morin

It's your fault! You deserve to taste
some of the pain that I am experiencing

– or at the very least, you deserve to experience guilt.

I should!

You should have!

We're right!

You're wrong!

Does this sound all too familiar?

These statements come out of a paradigm in which many of us spend our lives. It is the paradigm of demands, blame and judgment in which we gobble up much of our limited energy in diagnosis and dishing out punishment or rewards. As a result we have little energy left to focus on naming and meeting our needs and the needs of others.

Marshall Rosenberg (2003) noticed this thinking style while he was growing up and became aware of the loss of energy it caused. At the same time, he noticed that some people responded in a different way to situations of conflict or "hard to hear messages."

They seemed to be able to hear and see the positive hope or longing of the other person beneath the destructive act, judgment or demand expressed to them. They also appeared to get their own needs met and at the same time were able to bring out the best in others. Marshall Rosenberg wanted to be able to communicate in this way and wanted this for others.

In carefully examining the communication of these people, Marshall discovered certain elements that characterized it. In conversation these people were able to:

1. Articulate what was true for them and listen for what might be true for the other. When making an *observation* they gave only what they saw, heard, touched, tasted, smelled, remembered sensed or imagined, clearly separating the *observation* from any *evaluation*.

2. Name what they were *feeling* without blame. "I am so anxious," instead of "You make me anxious," or "I 'feel' belittled."

3. Focus on the *need* that they hoped to meet.

4. Make a clear positive *request*.

   These elements he named *honesty*.

   He further noticed these people were able to:

1. Envision what the other was *observing* instead of reacting to an evaluation of what the other might be experiencing.

2. Guess what the other person might be *feeling* and check it out with the other.

3. Clarify with the other what he or she might be *needing*.

4. Imagine what the other is *requesting*.

   These four elements he named *empathy*.

Finally he became aware of the intention these people held. They appeared to seek ways to connect with the other. In doing so they facilitated the channelling of their energy towards working together and finding strategies to meet the needs of both sides.

So how do we change from judgmental thinking to the kind of communication that Marshall Rosenberg so valued?

Before we learn about this, I want to remind you that this is not simply a technique for resolving a particular conflict: *It is a way of being.* In this less stressful, peaceful way of being we facilitate interaction between both sides to meet their needs. To develop these skills requires developing several habits.

Habit 1 – Be Aware

Develop an awareness of our judgmental thoughts – and how we judge our judgmental thinking. Developing a habit of becoming aware of our thoughts is like panning for gold. When we find bits of gold, we do not throw them away: we refine them.

Here are several ways to develop this habit of awareness:

1. Practice awareness meditation. Sit quietly and just notice thoughts that are walking across your mind; without judging the thoughts, let them go. Return your focus back to your breath until you notice another thought.

2. In idle moments – at a stop light, in a lineup, as you walk or swim – notice the thoughts that come into your consciousness.

3. When you become aware of tightness in your body or a change in energy, stop and notice what you are thinking that has precipitated that change.

4. When you are aware of an uncomfortable emotion, notice the thoughts you are thinking. These are the cause of your feeling.

5. When you are aware of a peaceful or comfortable feeling, notice the thought that is causing it.

6. When you notice your thoughts, say them to yourself or out loud if you are alone.

Once we become aware of our thoughts we can begin the process of translation. Once we have found the gold, we can begin the process of refining. The following model developed by Marshall Rosenberg helps us in translating our thoughts.

Table 1. Basic Nonviolent Communication Model

	Honestly Expressing	Empathic Receiving
Observation	When I see, hear, remember, imagine ...	When you see, hear, remember, imagine ...
Feeling	I feel ... (one word)	do you feel ... (one word)
Need	because I need (hope, value, dream)	because you need (value, dream)
Request	Would you be willing to ... (positive, do-able)	and would you like me to ... (positive, concrete)

Habit 2 – Separate Evaluation from Observation

When something happens to us, or we remember or imagine something happening to us, we automatically leap to having a thought about it, evaluating the situation. What actually happens or what we observe does not produce feelings. Our thoughts or evaluations about what happens cause our feelings. So it is helpful to separate the observation from the evaluation.

Here are some practices to help develop this habit:

1. When you notice yourself evaluating, name what you are observing, e.g., "There is a lovely bouquet on my desk" (evaluation); "There are flowers in a vase on my desk: white flowers with yellow centres surrounded by red blossoms hanging from a stem." (observation)

2. When you find yourself with a feeling or energy shift, name what you are observing.

Habit 3 – Name What You Are Feeling

Children are sometimes taught the four basic feelings: glad, mad, sad, scared. Many of us have been taught that some feelings are not acceptable. Some of us have been taught that feelings don't count and so we try to ignore or bury them. I believe that feelings were given to us as a gift. When we experience an uncomfortable or painful feeling, we are being given a signal that we have a need that is not being met or even acknowledged. If our feeling is comfortable or joyful, we know we have a need that has been met and is wanting celebration.

If you are not accustomed to accepting your feelings or acknowledging them, you might want to start your practice by simply noticing when you experience the basic four: glad, mad, sad, scared. As you become familiar with noticing those four, you may want to develop your feeling vocabulary so that you can name your feelings more accurately.

Table 2. A List of Common Feelings

Feelings are about what is going on in me – not about what "they did"

FEELINGS WHEN NEEDS ARE NOT MET

<u>Gloomy</u> Blah Crestfallen Dejected Depressed Despairing Despondent Discouraged Downhearted Dreary Forlorn Hopeless Melancholic Miserable Mopey Mournful Pessimistic Resigned Somber Spiritless	<u>Sad</u> Agonizing Distressed Disenchanted Grief stricken Heartbroken Hurt Morose Full of pain Overwhelmed Sorrowful Unhappy Upset Woeful Wretched	<u>Anxious</u> Agitated Edgy Fidgety Frenzied Harried Hysterical Impatient Intense Irritable Overwhelmed Perturbed Rushy Stressed Uneasy Unnerved Unsteady Uptight	<u>Alarmed</u> Frantic In turmoil Incredulous Paralyzed Surprised Uneasy Upset	<u>Annoyed</u> Angry Cranky Cross Disgusted Enraged Exasperated Fed-up Frustrated Indignant Infuriated Irritated Miffed Ticked off Vengeful Vexed Vindictive
	<u>Afraid</u> Apprehensive Cautious Dreadful Fearful Frantic Guarded Hesitant In a cold sweat Insecure Jittery Leery Mistrusting Nervous On edge Panicky Startled Suspicious Terrible Terrified Wary Worried		Cautious <u>Hesitant</u> Reluctant Resistant Shy Skeptical Tentative Timid Unwilling	
<u>Argumentative</u> Disgusted Hateful <u>Hostile</u> Resentful Resistant		<u>Ashamed</u> Deflated Embarrassed Guilty Insecure Mortified Regretful	<u>Aloof</u> Apathetic Arrogant Callous Cold Contemptuous Critical Detached Disdainful Grouchy Indifferent Judgmental Nonchalant Passive Pitying Prickly Withdrawn	<u>Confused</u> Ambivalent Bewildered Curious Doubtful Hesitant Perplexed Troubled Uncertain Unclear Undecided
<u>Longing</u> Yearning Desirous Hungry		<u>Bored</u> Exhausted Fatigued Heavy Lethargic Listless Tense Tired Unconcerned Weary		<u>Envious</u> Jealous
<u>Amazed</u> Astounded Dazzled Surprised				<u>Disappointed</u> Discouraged Disheartened Dissatisfied

Table 2 (cont'd)

SOME FEELINGS WHEN NEEDS AND DESIRES ARE MET

Delighted	Calm	Absorbed	Amazed	Appreciative
Ecstatic	Cheerful	Alert	Appalled	Glad
Elated	Comfortable	Alive	Shocked	Grateful
Enchanted	Composed	Animated	Surprised	Gratified
Excited	Contented	Anticipating		Thankful
Exhilarated	Mellow	Ardent		
Exuberant	Peaceful	Confident	Carefree	Blissful
Gleeful	Quiet	Eager	Confident	Friendly
Jubilant	Relieved	Energetic	Expansive	Happy
Radiant	Satisfied	Engrossed	Free	Loving
	Serene	Enthusiastic	Gleeful	Joyful
Buoyant	Tender	Hopeful	Good-humored	Overjoyed
Effervescent	Tranquil	Interested	Relaxed	Radiant
Exhilarated	Vulnerable	Invigorated	Trusting	Splendid
Intense	Warm	Optimistic		
Keyed-up	Curious	Spellbound		Compassionate
Overwhelmed	Fascinated		Adventurous	
Upbeat	Inquisitive	Inspired	Confident	Proud
Wide-awake	Interested	Focused	Expectant	
Zestful	Intrigued	Open	Hopeful	Playful

Habit 4 – Name the Need to Which Your Feelings Point

Nonviolent Communication (NVC) encourages us to name our feelings and listen to what information they are giving us, usually pointing to a need. This habit is at the heart of NVC. Uncomfortable feelings point to a need, value, dream, hope that is, as it were, asking for attention.

The habit consists of listening to your feeling as it points to a need and to name the need that calls for attention. In my experience, as soon as I have named the need my feeling points to, the feeling diminishes.

Table 3. A List of Basic Needs of All People: Universal Needs

BASIC **NEEDS** OF ALL PEOPLE	PRIMARY NEED: HEART CONNECTION
AUTONOMY — Acknowledgment, Choice, Freedom, Individuality, Respect	CELEBRATION — Commemoration, Hope, Mourning, Remembering, Ritual
CLARITY AND UNDERSTANDING — Awareness, Experience, Insight, Knowledge, Wisdom, Wonder	CONTRIBUTION — Competence, Direction, Effectiveness, Purpose, Self-expression, Self-worth
CREATIVITY — Delight, Inspiration, Joy, Order, Play, Spontaneity, Vision	DIVINE CONNECTION — Life direction, Love, Peace, Serenity, Spirituality, Soul Nurturance
INTEGRITY — Authenticity, Meaning, Honour, Self-worth	INTERDEPENDENCE — Acceptance, Appreciation, Closeness, Commitment, Community, Compassion, Connection, Co-operation, Consideration, Contribution, Empathy, Equality, Harmony, Honesty, I count, Inclusion, Justice, Love, Reassurance, Respect, Support, To be heard, Trust, Understanding, Unity, Warmth
PHYSICAL NURTURANCE — Air, Ease, Exercise, Rest, Shelter, Space, Sexual Expression, Touch, Trust, Water	SURVIVAL — Emotional safety, Healing, Justice, Protection from serious threat, Reliability, Safety, Stability

Needs are general and make no reference to another person. I recognize something as a need when I can say that it is common to people in general; "needs are universal." For example, I need nurturing. Everyone needs nurturing. It is common to all people.

I may want you to nurture me in a particular way; this is not a need but a strategy for getting my need of nurturing met. There are many possible strategies for getting a need met. If I can name my own need and imagine what the other is needing, my focus becomes broader and my energy softens. Together we find strategies to meet the unmet need(s). I am responsible for getting my needs met.

Habit 5 – Use Anger as an Alarm Clock

Anger (or its relatives: vengeance, annoyance, rage, etc.) is a particularly useful feeling. Like an alarm clock, anger is there to wake us up. Anger reminds us that we are thinking judgmentally, and it invites us to look at our judgmental thought(s). That thought can connect to our unmet need. Often, when we become aware of what our unmet need is, anger changes to fear or sadness: fear that a need will be thwarted or sadness that a need has not been met. When the unmet needs are uncovered, we can then find strategies to meet the need(s). Here is a practice that I use:

I write the "story I am telling myself." This is what I am actually saying to myself about me and what I am saying about the other. Then, beside each statement, I write the unmet need that precipitated the statement:

Why do they always leave me out? .... Need: inclusion, belonging

Do they think I am just their servant? .... Need: equality

Or do they think I have no feelings? .... Need: to be heard

I am some sort of object that they can use as they like and then toss out when they have finished with it! .... Need: respect, to be valued

I am a human being. .... Need: to be heard

Don't they understand that? .... Need: to be heard, understood

Once I have named my needs, my focus changes from being angry at others to focusing on getting my needs met.

Habit 6 - Remind Yourself that Each of Us Is Responsible to Get Our Own Needs Met

Many people in this culture believe that other people are responsible for meeting our needs: wife, husband, boss, employee, parent, daughter or son. And if they don't meet our need, we take one of two stances: Power and Control, or Victim. In either stance, we spend much of our energy judging, blaming, denying responsibility or demanding. We see power and vulnerability as opposing forces. NVC offers another way: we can learn to live in power *and* vulnerability.

I find this exercise very helpful:

When you find yourself feeling powerless and choosing either the victim stance or the power and control stance, simply name your need and create one strategy to meet that need. (We will look at strategies or requests later on in the chapter)

Something else I find helpful is to say or sing this little ditty to myself, reminding me that I can choose to live in the power that is mine without diminishing anyone else's power.

Power and/or Vulnerability
Power and control
Is not really my goal
Insisting on having it my way.
Nor victim stance
Will my bliss enhance
Alone each takes safety and peace away.

But the two together
Can bring me great pleasure.
With both I don't bulldoze or cower.
When my power runs out
My vulnerability comes out
My named need gives me back focused power.

As my energy is freed
I can focus on need
And clearly, concretely request.
I keep focused in heart
I know it's an art.
It's the way I get each need met best.

Habit 7 – Clarify Your Intention and Change It to Help You Meet the Unmet Needs

Before you try to meet unmet needs or resolve a conflict, get clear on your intention. This demands honesty – at least honesty with your self. If, in any way, your intention is to punish or hurt or blame or diminish the other person, they will probably perceive it and resist. Your task at hand is to change your intention. You want to connect with them in such a way that you are working together to meet needs.

Here are some strategies to change your intention.

1. Be in the presence of Compassion (God, the Divine, the Compassionate One, Non-judgmental Energy). Experience Compassion hearing your intention and translating it empathically.

   – You: "I am pretty upset with George and I just want him to experience the same kind of pain that I am experiencing."

   – *Compassion*: "It sounds as if you are really hurting and you would like some understanding about how much you hurt. Is that it?"

   – *You*: "Yes. He just walks over me as if I am a doormat."

   – *Compassion*: "Are you wanting respect and equality in your relationship?"

   – *You*: "You bet I am and he just doesn't get it."

   – *Compassion*: "So you would really like him to see how much you would like to be in a relationship of equality and respect."

   – *You*: "That would be so nice."

Here you notice that your energy has changed. When your unmet needs are heard, named and acknowledged without judgment, you may notice your muscles relax and your energy changes. Usually at that time your intention might shift as well. When you experience being heard and acknowledged, you may be ready to hear the other.

2. In your imagination or in your journal, create a dialogue between Compassion and the one you had intended to diminish. Imagine what the other is saying to him/herself and imagine Compassion translating it into feelings and needs.

   – *George*: "Sometimes I get so mad at her. There she is giving me the silent treatment again and I can't stand it."

   – *Compassion*: "George, I am guessing that you are feeling pretty frustrated, that you want to be able to connect with Alice and you would love to know how. Is that true?"

   – *George*: "Yes, I do something she does not approve of and I am always having to guess what it is that she wants. I know what she doesn't want but I don't know what she does want and I haven't a clue how to find out."

   – *Compassion*: "So you really want some understanding and would love to have some help so you can know without guessing?"

   – *George*: "You've got it. How can I let her know that? I guess I have just now found out that this is what I want and have wanted all along."

As you watch George in your imagination, you notice that you have an insight that you had not experienced before. My guess is that your intention will have changed from wanting to hurt the other to wanting to really connect with the other.

Habit 8 – When a Need Has Not Been Met, Take Time to Grieve

There are times in our lives when we have not met one or more of our needs. Sometimes we keep ourselves in low energy by remembering (reliving the past and bringing it to the present) how awful the situation was. As a result, the joy in our present lives is diminished.

We can grieve by creating a ritual to let go of the past. I would suggest in that ritual to have an NVC conversation with the part of you that is sad.

- *Present Me*: "Would you be willing to tell me what it was like for you then?"

- *Past Me*: "I can't get anyone to help me – or even believe me. I feel alone and I am going into a shell where I do not trust anyone."

- *Present Me*: "Sounds like you are really needing someone to hear you and believe you so you can trust again."

- *Past Me*: "Yes, I can't seem to do it on my own."

- *Present Me*: "So you want some support? Would it help if I support you now?"

- *Past Me*: "It feels good to finally be heard without judgment or someone trying to fix me or asking me to snap out of it."

- *Present Me*: "Simply non-judgmental hearing."

- *Past Me*: "Yes, thank you. When you do that I seem to find some hope from inside me. I can trust me."

- *Present Me*: "Hope and trust of yourself. Wow!"

- *Past Me*: "Yes, and I am filling up with energy. Wow!"

- *Present Me*: "Would you like now for us to make a symbol of your loss?"

- *Past Me*: "Let's. And we can put it into the river and let the river carry it away."

Sometimes this can be a short process. At other times, it may take several conversations and rituals to be ready to let go. Once you have named and accepted whatever need had not been met, you might want to celebrate what you have gained from the experience. For instance, you may be more compassionate with some people or more capable in particular areas. Simply name the needs that are being met by this quality and the requests you make of yourself to further use this quality to contribute to life on this planet. Many people consider contribution our most important need after physical safety.

For further help in how to grieve, see Nancy Reeves' book *A Path Through Loss*.

Habit 9 – Learn to Make Requests to Meet Your Needs

Once we have named our unmet need(s), then we can create ways to meet that need. Requests are specific to a person, place and time. They are expressed in positive language. (I can't do a don't.) Ask for what you want, not what you don't want. It often helps the other disarm if we name the need(s) we are trying to meet, describe what we observed or what we are feeling, before making our request.

- "I need to understand. Would you be willing to tell me what you were thinking when you did that?"

- "I am feeling cold. Would you please close the door?"

- "I need assurance that you are okay. Would you be willing to phone me next time you know you will be more than half an hour late?"

Habit 10 – Remember to Hold Both Sides: Honesty and Empathy

When we are in the midst of a conflict, we can disarm ourselves and help the other disarm when we hold both their need and ours as precious. For instance, when someone brings the vehicle home later than they had said they would, and I had planned to use it, I might say, "I am guessing that you need flexibility and I need respect. Does that ring true to you?" This helps the other person realize that you are thinking of their needs as well as your own, and that you are prepared to hear their reality and not just express your own. Consider these examples:

- "When you said, 'You're so stupid,' I am wondering if your hope was to have me see this issue from your eyes. Is that it?... When I heard you say that, I felt pretty devastated, so I am wondering if, instead, you would be willing to tell me what you are needing."

- "When you close the curtains as you come in and I open them, I am guessing that you want privacy and I want light and openness. If this is so, let's find a way that we can meet both our needs."

Habit 11 – When You Find Yourself Judging Others or Judging Yourself for Judging, Laugh!

NVC is not about beating ourselves up. When I notice myself judging, I find that the most freeing response is simply to laugh and enjoy the show, knowing I have a choice. I can simply let go and then choose how I would rather communicate.

Conclusion

Nonviolent Communication is about people coming together, connecting with each other heart to heart, and finding ways to meet the needs of all. I have found it transformative in my life, and I hope that you, too, can develop these habits, so you can transform conflict into peaceful and creative situations, and use this energy to create a world of harmony.

References

British Columbia Network for Compassionate Communication: www.bcncc.org,

Center for Nonviolent Communication: www.cnvc.org_

Morin, Judi. *Learning guide*: Laminated sheets of the NVC Model including the list of feelings and needs are available at jmorin@ssabc.ca.

Reeves, N. (2001). *A path through loss*. Kelowna: Northstone.

Rosenberg, M. (2003). *Nonviolent communication*. Encinitas, CA: Puddle Dancer Press.

Part II

Conflict Resolution in Diverse Settings

Introduction

Where two or more people gather and interact there will be differences of opinion, conflict, disagreements, disputes and arguments. Conflict is an ever-present reality whenever people work and live together. It can manifest itself in differences of view, differences of opinion, differences of personality, and differences of interest. But conflict doesn't have to be destructive. It can be used constructively. A number of conflict theorists speak of *conflict transformation* rather than *conflict resolution* or *conflict management*. Practitioners and writers in this part of the book suggest that the destructive consequences of a conflict can be transformed so that self-images, relationships and social structures improve instead of being harmed by conflict. Highlighting people's differences in a constructive way can transform and therefore improve mutual understanding.

Part II presents stories and experiences from varied settings as conflict resolution is initiated, taught and practised. Each one of us can, at times, experience a conflict between what we intend to achieve and what we actually achieve. If peace is to begin with me, Part II outlines several ways where conflict resolution is being practised, especially by professionals working in the field. Gilles Fortin and Judith Malette present a reflective practitioner model whereby the counsellor or therapist can perform a self-evaluation of his or her interaction with the client. This self-reflection model helps counsellors to develop the art of becoming more congruent between what they say and what they do, and to become more competent resolvers of conflict wherever they work. Marie-Line Morin proposes a pastoral counselling conflict-resolution model for couples, proposing that a conflict-resolution model integrate a person's fundamental values.

Adèle Miles, Maria Cupples, Rose Robinson and Michelle Koyle present a model for how nurses, chaplains and crisis support volunteers provide support and care to the families and friends who survive the sudden death of a loved one in a hospital emergency department. Especially difficult in this setting is dealing with conflict in the face of deep personal crisis and, often, death. Susan Tasker argues for a new approach in responding to people with brain injuries. She suggests viewing brain injury as an event and as the beginning of a new process; the patient and family first need to acknowledge the event and then accept this new state.

Helma Seidl challenges trangendered people to bring resolution to potential intrapsychic and societal conflict that transgenderism and sexual orientation can create. She notes that transgenderism existed prior to Christianity and that the European cultures have received it differently from the North and South American native cultures. She addresses clinical aspects and individual and group therapy for the transgendered.

Part II straddles that part of conflict resolution that is both intrapersonal and interpersonal, but, in both expressions, is never far from the heart of the matter. Conflict resolution, in this part, is still very personal and existential, a heartfelt reality in people's lives. It carries the deep seams of emotional content outlined in Part I, and brings them into the real world of people and interpersonal relationships, a theme that will be picked up in Part III.

5

Using a Reflective Practitioner Model with Counsellors-in-Training to Promote Personal and Professional Congruency

Gilles Fortin and Judith Malette[1]

Counsellors at times find themselves in conflict between what they hoped to achieve and what actually took place in the counselling session. The reflective practitioner model provides an instrument whereby they can assess their interactions with their clients. This model comprises two complex stages – namely, efficiency and co-operation – that are described in detail. Concrete examples are given to illustrate how it can be applied in a counselling setting.

A number of authors suggest that a reflective practitioner model can be used as a tool to facilitate the reflective process within and upon an action. Chalifour (1999), for example, invites counsellors to reflect upon and within the relationship of counselling in order to use interventions tailored to the needs of the client, and to "determine his/her intention, to clarify his/her expectations (his/her motivation), to acknowledge his/her thoughts and feelings" (Chalifour, 1999, p. 235, translation by authors) towards the client. VanKatwyk (2003) proposes a supervision model, "the experiential learning cycle" (p. 128), which has four phases: being with, examining, evaluating and intervening. These phases are not necessarily sequential. With the "Helping Style Inventory," the counsellor can examine whether his orientation is directed

---

1   The authors are presented in alphabetical order.

more towards the intervention techniques than the person and whether he is more of a facilitator or a director. This model focuses on developing the counsellor-in-training's awareness of his way of interacting with a client in order to increase his feeling of competency. St-Arnaud (1995, 2003, 2004) proposes also a reflective model which emphasizes the questioning of premises, intentions and counselling strategies that can lead to the discovery of differences, contradictions and conflicts between one's declared model and one's actual practice. In problematic interactions, which are often a source of dissatisfaction and conflict, it is not unusual to observe differences between what the counsellor thinks he is doing and what he actually does. Based on this model, the counsellor must become aware of such conflict in order to act upon it. Ultimately, this awareness allows the counsellor to adjust his interventions more efficiently to the desired effect, and to obtain a higher level of personal and professional congruency and interpersonal skills. To our knowledge, St-Arnaud's model is the only one that includes a test of personal efficiency. We chose to focus on this model for this reason.

First, we will describe the reflective practitioner model and its origins. We will then explain the main theoretical underpinnings: efficiency and co-operation. On this last point, we will use as a resource the writings of St-Arnaud (1995, 2003, 2004). We will then describe in more concrete terms the analytical frameworks of efficiency and co-operation, which can be used at each of the stages of the process. Finally, we will give a concrete example to illustrate how to make the most of this model.

The Nature and Origin of the Reflective Practitioner Model

The reflective practitioner model comprises three stages. It denotes "knowledge drawn from the action and that can be used within the action, an interaction based on self-determination and a scientific thought process" (St-Arnaud, 1995, p. 182, translation by authors). In undertaking a process of reflective analysis, the reflective practitioner model aims to encourage the emergence of implicit knowledge found in the action. In the context of a professional intervention, self-determination plays a key role, since it views the client as having the capacity to make personal choices.

And finally, the changes that it tends to produce are based on scientific principles. This last stage emphasizes that if the reflective practitioner model focuses on greater counsellor efficiency, it is because it can be considered as a "second generation" of action-research (Dolbec, 2003, p. 512), as compared to "first generation" action-research, which aims first and foremost to change the environment in order to change the attitude of the participants. This second generation of action-research is based on Kolb's model of experiential learning (1984) which states that the counsellor can learn from his experience by observing, conceptualizing what he observed, and verifying his conceptualization against reality.

The concepts of action-science put forth by Argyris and Schön (1974) were taken up by St-Arnaud (1995, 2003, 2004), and served as a basis for the development of his reflective practitioner model. His main contribution has been the development of the personal efficiency test. This efficiency test comprises a systematic and coherent approach that can be of great use to the counsellor in reviewing problematic client interventions during counselling, thus allowing him to achieve the desired results (St-Arnaud, 2004). It is this model that we will describe in greater detail.

St-Arnaud's Reflective Practitioner Model

According to St-Arnaud (1995, 2003, 2004), the efficiency of professional practice is a function of the ability of the counsellor to manage the interaction. There is a strong correlation between the efficiency of a given practice and the degree of co-operation that is established between the partners (St-Arnaud, 1995, 2003, 2004). However, before looking at co-operation and the five rules that define it, we will focus first on the notion of efficiency, the first stage in the reflective practitioner model.

First Stage: Efficiency

Efficiency in a professional interaction can be evaluated from two perspectives: the first perspective, which is extrinsic, consists of verifying if the action follows the practice norms established for the discipline (St-Arnaud, 1995, 2003, 2004); the second perspective, which is intrinsic, involves evaluating the action from the point of view of the counsellor's internal norms. Thus, efficiency is measured relative to the effect that the counsellor wishes to produce (St-Arnaud, 1995, 2003, 2004). The reflective practitioner model is based on the latter perspective.

At the heart of the reflective practitioner model is the notion of intention. According to St-Arnaud (1995, 2003, 2004), all action is intentional. This means that, in a given interaction, the counsellor seeks to influence the client, and his behaviour is strategic, that is, he/she aims to produce the desired effect. Using as a basis the principle of intentionality, professional efficiency can be viewed as the counsellor attaining the desired effect, and as the absence of any undesired secondary effect within him (St-Arnaud, 1995, 2003). Efficiency therefore takes for granted the capacity to adapt to each situation.

Self-regulation

St-Arnaud (1995, p. 34) summarizes the objective of the reflective practitioner model in this way: "to give the actor criteria that will allow him/her to evaluate quickly, in the heat of the moment, the efficiency of his/her action and to adjust immediately if the desired effect is not achieved without any secondary undesired effect" (free translation). The counsellor, wishing to improve the efficiency of his interventions, has no other choice than to adapt, that is, to reflect first on the action and then reflect as well within the action if he wishes to attain the desired effect.

Formulating the intent

Self-regulation requires that the counsellor be able to determine his/her intention in a given situation, which is not an easy thing to do. There are four difficulties inherent in formulating the intention: 1) the complexity of the process; 2) the scattering of attention; 3) the non-quantifiable nature of the desired effect; 4) the difference between the declared theory and the actual theory used.

The complexity of the process

Intention comprises three distinct elements: the strategy, the desired effect and the motivation. The strategy is the means chosen to produce the desired effect. The desired effect is the observable effect on the client. The motivation harks back to the personal needs of the counsellor.

It is of utmost importance, for the counsellor wishing to become more conscious of his interventions and improve his efficiency, to make a clear distinction between each of these elements.

The scattering of attention

To determine here and now the desired effect implies an adjusted vision. The counsellor occasionally turns his attention to the long-term effect (presbyotic vision) or to his/her needs or strategy (myopic vision).

The non-quantifiable nature of the desired effect

Another difficulty related to formulating an intention is the non-quantifiable nature of the desired effect. The counsellor must strive to specify the desired effect from the point of view of an observable behaviour. This will allow him to determine if this effect has been produced or not.

The difference between the declared theory and the actual theory used

In the case of a problematic situation, we can observe a difference between the explanation that a counsellor gives for his behaviour and the actual theory used (St-Arnaud, 1995, 2003, 2004). St-Arnaud (1992) names this phenomenon "the law of Argyris and Schön."

Hidden intentions can sometimes lurk behind the formulation of intentions (St-Arnaud, 1995, 2003). A review of a dialogue can bring to light the coherence – or lack thereof – between a formulated intention and the resulting intention. To increase efficiency, one must first discover the hidden intention.

The challenge for the counsellor is to acknowledge that, behind the beliefs, the expressed theories justifying his intentions and his interventions, can sometimes lie intentions that are difficult to articulate for fear of confronting aspects of his personality that he may not find easy to accept. These intentions can be linked to needs related to competency (action domain) and consideration (affective domain) – this is an aspect that stands out the most from the students' dissertations – but also to well-being (health, enjoyment) and coherence (knowledge domain). These needs are all perfectly normal. They become problematic, however, when they dominate the interaction with the client, and particularly when the counsellor is not aware of them. In a situation of countertransference, the counsellor is unconsciously acting in relation to his own needs. He is thus interacting more with himself than with the client (the desired effect is to satisfy the need of the counsellor, which brings him to make different types of errors) (see below). Suffice it to say here that, in a counselling session, a counsellor often does not perceive the conflict between his declared theory and the actual theory used. It is even possible that the intervention seems coherent with his intention. It is only after reflecting upon this after the fact that the counsellor-in-training can see the conflict between his intention and his intervention.

Competency does not imply infallibility. A person is competent when he realizes the errors made and tries to correct them. Moreover, a lack of congruency between declared theory and actual theory is not exclusive to counsellors-in-training. Consider the studies by Weinrach (1990, 1991), demonstrating that Rogers, in his interview with Gloria filmed in 1964, interpreted much of what he heard. In the humanist approach, interpretation has a rather negative connotation because it is seen as leading the client away from his actual emotional experience and violating his autonomy by trying to impose an insight. Here are examples of interpretations made by Rogers: "I see. It really cuts a little deeper. If she really knew you, would she, could she accept you?"; "You sound as though your actions are outside of you. You want to approve of you but what you do somehow won't let you approve of yourself" (Weinrach, 1990, p. 287). Moreover, according to Weinrach (1990), Rogers used more the reflection of content (15%) than the reflection of feeling (8%). Could even the moments he chose to say "mm-hmm" not constitute a type of intervention (reinforcement)? Finally, in keeping with the humanistic approach, transference constitutes a means of evasion, a defence against the therapy and direct contact with the therapist. According to Weinrach (1990), Rogers appears to be the quintessential patriarchal figure to Gloria: loving, accepting – in short, a father that everyone would like to have had. Here is an example of transference:

> Gloria: "(...) all of a sudden while talking to you (...) I want you to approve of me and I respect you, but I miss that my father couldn't talk to me like you are. I mean I'd like to say, 'Gee, I'd like you for my father.' I don't even know why that came to me."

> Rogers: "You look to me like a pretty nice daughter. You really miss the fact that you couldn't open with your own dad." (Weinrach, 1990, p. 282)

The personal test of efficiency

The counsellor has at his disposal an innate self-regulatory mechanism (St-Arnaud, 1995, 2003, 2004) that informs him, via the emotions and feelings, regarding the efficiency of his actions. These subjective reactions are the barometer that allows him to judge whether the desired effect has been attained or not and, if needed, to adjust the strategy in order to produce the sought-after effect. The personal test of efficiency allows the counsellor to delve into his life experiences and become more aware of his intentions.

The three causes of inefficiency

St-Arnaud (1995, 2003, 2004) lists three possible causes of inefficiency: 1) technical error; 2) intention error; 3) factors beyond the control of the counsellor.

Inefficiency can be the result of an error in the means used (technical error). Without necessarily being wrong, the chosen means may not be the most adequate to produce the desired effect. The counsellor thus enters a level I self-regulation cycle, which consists of modifying the behaviour without changing the intention (St-Arnaud, 1995, 2003, 2004). Intention error involves persisting in wanting to produce an unrealistic desired effect. This error is evident in the escalation and in the "dialogue of the deaf" that is established between the client and the counsellor. To correct this error and finally adopt a more realistic view, the counsellor can enter into a level II self-regulatory cycle, which means that he must modify his initial intention. After repeated attempts to adjust his intention to the situation and after using a number of means, the counsellor may come to the realization that he cannot be efficient, no matter what he tries. St-Arnaud (1995, 2003, 2004) emphasizes that the nature of the mandate, for example, may force the counsellor to stick to the initial intention. The danger remains, as the same author points out (St-Arnaud, 1995, 2003), in attributing too quickly his lack of efficiency to factors that are beyond his control. "Knowing what we want and wanting what we can" (St-Arnaud, 1995, p. 63) – this phrase summarizes well the principle of self-regulation that we have just discussed.

Second Stage: Co-operation

The second stage of the reflective practitioner model is co-operation, a value commonly espoused by professionals working in the area of human relations (St-Arnaud, 1995, 2003). Co-operation comprises five elements: partnership, alternation, mutual agreement, non-interference and assuming responsibility.

*Partnership: seeking and defining a common interest
(St-Arnaud, 1995, p. 88)*

Partnership refers back to the nature of the structure that has been adopted during the interaction in order to attain the desired effect. There are three possible structures: pressure, service and co-operation.

In a pressure structure, the goal of the interaction is determined by the counsellor. By taking it upon himself to orient and direct the interaction, the counsellor shows little regard for the competencies of the client.

When the client alone determines the goal of the meeting and the counsellor becomes simply a performer, this is called a service structure since the competencies of the counsellor are used to attain the goal. In a way, the counsellor controls the interaction process while taking into consideration the requirements of the client, which differentiates this structure from the pressure structure. There is, therefore, a certain sharing of control during the actual interaction. It is acknowledged that the client has competencies, even if it is only when he/she articulates the goal of the consultation. Within this structure, the client remains passive and relatively submissive. Eventually, this type of structure can encourage dependence. When the counsellor and the client determine together the goal of the consultation and they work together to attain this goal, they create a structure of co-operation. The control of the process and of the goal to be achieved are bilateral. In acknowledging the competency of the client, the counsellor wields only minimal control over the client. Professionals favour this structure because it allows for the attainment of better results and it keeps the client active in the interaction.

The formula for ensuring partnership can be summarized as seeking and determining a common interest.

Alternation: "Changing frequently the channel of communication" (St-Arnaud, 1995, p. 109)

Alternation consists of using different channels of communication to better reach the client. St-Arnaud (1995, 2003) identifies four channels, which we will describe below: 1) reception; 2) facilitation; 3) support; 4) information.

The reception channel is the one whereby the counsellor listens to the client. If he is attentive to the client and listens carefully and is not distracted by his own experience, a climate of greater confidence in the relationship will result. According to St-Arnaud (2003), the counsellor can improve the quality of his listening if he decodes well the information that is communicated to him/her. The client communicates four types of information: facts, feelings, beliefs and intentions.

Using the facilitation channel, the counsellor can move the client to reveal himself, to open up. "Facilitation is an active extension of the reception strategy" (St-Arnaud, 1995, p. 101; translation by authors). It is a means to confirm with the client that he has understood correctly what the client was trying to say. Through his interventions (for example, reflecting, formulating, summarizing and asking open-ended questions), the counsellor can elicit a general verbalization, facts, responses, ideas or intentions (St-Arnaud, 1995, 2003). The questions and the reflecting flow from a facilitation strategy. The counsellor must be aware, however, that one question can often mask a suggestion and/or send a double message, which is no longer facilitation.

The counsellor calls upon the support function when he gives information on the process or when he/she structures the relationship. The support channel serves to prevent confusion in communication. It is useful for marking the passage from one stage of the process to another, to clarify the roles and responsibilities of the partners, to deal with the client's resistance. In being aware of what is happening between himself and the client, by maintaining this relationship, the counsellor increases the level of client co-operation, and, by the same token, his own efficiency by adopting interventions that are more relevant to both the client and the process. Opinions, observations, refocusing and confrontations – in short, all communication of information by the counsellor – are part of the information channel.

Alternation thus means to use the four channels of communication and to avoid favouring one over the others.

Mutual agreement: "Managing the process" (St-Arnaud, 1995, p. 127)

Mutual agreement presupposes the management of the communication process and the use of the support channel (St-Arnaud, 1995, 2003). The rule of mutual agreement includes coming to an understanding at the beginning of the meeting on a common goal. This is possible only if the competencies of each partner are taken into consideration.

Non-interference: "Sharing power" (St-Arnaud, 1995, p. 142)

Non-interference means respecting the power of the client. According to St-Arnaud (1995, 2003), there are three forms of power: 1) authoritative power; 2) expert power; 3) personal power. While the counsellor cannot help but influence his client, he can, however, choose the type of influence he exerts.

Authoritative power comes from natural authority or from an external mandate that gives the person the right to undertake actions in order to influence a given situation (St-Arnaud, 1995, 2003). Expert power is based on the sum of acquired knowledge, experience and recognized abilities whereby the person feels that he has the ability to intervene. Personal power flows from the person's charisma, his personality, and not from authority or expertise. It is this charisma that leads to action.

In order for there to be co-operation, the counsellor must recognize that the client has a certain level of competency when it comes to determining the goal of the intervention.

Assuming responsibility: "Respecting and getting respect"
(St-Arnaud, 1995, p. 167)

Assuming responsibility means recognizing the autonomy of the partners and the respective capacity to make choices. Each must assume his responsibilities. The counsellor must encourage the client to take on his responsibilities, that is, use his capacity to make his own choices. Respecting this role presupposes recognizing the strengths and competencies of each partner. As for autonomy, it is facilitated by respecting the partnership (seeking a common interest), non-interference (recognizing each other's competencies) and mutual agreement (a common path).

To summarize, professional efficiency can be evaluated from two perspectives: extrinsically, that is, as a function of external criteria, and intrinsically, that is, as a function of the actor himself relative to the desired effect. Self-regulation, a mechanism originating in evaluation, affords the opportunity to remain in constant touch with the action, to recognize errors, and to adjust the path relative to the desired effect.

To evaluate his efficiency, the counsellor must define his intention. As we have seen, this stage is not without its difficulties. The intention cycle is not only complex but it can be quite a challenge to sustain attention on the desired effect and to operationalize what the counsellor wants to attain in the here and now, not to mention the conflict between what he thinks he is doing and what he is actually doing.

After formulating his intention, the counsellor proceeds to evaluate the efficiency of his interventions. Inefficiency can be the result of various factors: a technical error (the means chosen are inadequate), an intention error (myopic or presbyotic vision) or factors beyond his control.

Ways to Analyze Efficiency and Co-operation

In the third part of this chapter, we will examine the different frameworks devised to analyze efficiency and co-operation. We will first make a few comments on the context in which these analyses are usually performed. To benefit the most from the reflective practitioner model, these analyses are usually done in a group, within the context of a supervised workshop. Each member of the group, a student at the Master's level in pastoral counselling, is invited to present his or her declared counselling model. This individual reflection is first done in writing, although the group facilitator may provide guidelines as a springboard to stimulate reflection. The main aim of this exercise is to identify the main theories that the counsellor claims to espouse. Each member then prepares a verbatim summary of an unsatisfactory counselling session that he has experienced, which is distributed to colleagues to study before the workshop. During the group session, the student shares personal reflections on what he or she perceives as the causes of his or her inefficiency, and the co-operation elements based on the stages of the St-Arnaud model. The student is then invited to deepen the analysis by considering the comments and questions of the other group members. Each participant has the opportunity to explain the action, to clarify the intention and to analyze the life experience. Proceeding in this manner allows participants to come to a better understanding of the different stages of efficiency and co-operation of the reflective practitioner model.

Analytical framework of efficiency

The evaluation of the efficiency of an intervention comprises several stages:

1. Identifying an unsatisfactory counselling situation and its at-tendant context.

2. Explaining why this situation is unsatisfactory.

3. Clarifying his/her intention. In order to define the strategies, the desired effect and the motivation, the counsellor is asked to complete the following sentence:

In this interaction, I wanted ...

... to do something, produce an action (strategy);

... the other person to do or say something (desired effect);

... to respond to my needs (motivation).

1) Analyzing the intervention sequence. The counsellor must write out the dialogue of an unsatisfactory situation and specify his or her personal experience throughout the interactions. The sequence of the interaction can be reconstructed from memory using the proposed framework (see Table 1). In the left-hand column is the counsellor's personal experience. In the next column, the use of different codes – green, yellow, red – gives an indication of the efficiency of the interaction. Green, symbol of a pleasant personal experience, indicates that the desired effect has been obtained; yellow, symbolizing a mixed personal experience, signals that the desired effect has not yet been attained but still might be; red denotes an unpleasant personal experience and, as such, produces the opposite of the desired effect. The counsellor/client dialogue is recorded in the following column. The next column, entitled "empathic decoding," aims to reconstruct the client's behaviour – the client can communicate four types of information: facts (f), feelings (a), rational [thoughts] (r) or intentions (i). The last four columns relate to the channels of communication: 1) non-verbal listening (R); 2) facilitation (F); 3) process management (Pr); 4) content information (Im).

Table 1. Analysis of an Interaction

Personal Experience	Code	Dialogue	Empathic Decoding (f r a i)	Channels of Communi- cation			
				R	F	Pr	Im
Personal experience and internal dialogue:		1 – Participant –					
Personal experience and internal dialogue:		2 – Participant –					
Personal experience and internal dialogue:		3 – Participant –					

Note. The table presented here is an adaptation from the work of St-Arnaud (1995).

Legend

Personal experience: What the counsellor experiences in terms of thoughts and feelings

Code: The level of satisfaction with the reactions of the client
· Green: pleasant personal experience
· Yellow: mixed personal experience
· Red: unpleasant personal experience

Dialogue: What the counsellor says or does: the numbered interventions

What the client did or said: indented interventions

Empathic decoding: (f: facts; r: rational; a: affective; i: intentions)

Channels: R: Reception strategy – non-verbal listening attitude
F: Facilitation strategy
Pr: Process management strategy
Im: Information management strategy

2) Analyzing the elements of the efficiency of the intervention. This stage allows for the updating of the causes of the inefficiency as well as the inadequate attitudes and behaviours of the counsellor. To define the cause of his inefficiency, the counsellor must question whether his expectations were realistic (intention error); whether the means used were relevant (strategy error); if factors beyond his control were present; and if the basic premises of his practice are valid.

The test of personal efficiency allows the counsellor to verify the divergence between the desired affect and the actual effect that is produced.

Analytical framework of elements of co-operation

According to St-Arnaud, five elements define co-operation: 1) partnership; 2) alternation; 3) mutual agreement; 4) non-interference; and 5) assuming responsibility. Each of these elements is discussed in detail below.

Partnership

Partnership refers to the structure of the relationship between the client and the counsellor. For St-Arnaud (2000, p. 69), the client's competency as recognized by the counsellor is "inversely proportional" to the amount of control he exerts. When the counsellor or the client defines the goal of the interaction, the relationship is one of pressure or service. Partnership requires joint definition of the goals. In his analysis, the counsellor must ask himself who defines the goals of the interaction, who wields the influence and who is influenced.

Alternation

Alternation presupposes the use of the various channels of communication. St-Arnaud (2003) proposes a formula to verify if there is indeed alternation. The percentage of alternation can be calculated by dividing the number of times the counsellor changes the channel by the number of coded interventions. St-Arnaud (2003) believes that a percentage of alternation of 50 or more encourages co-operation. St-Arnaud proposes the following formula to calculate alternation (2003, p. 158): Number of channel changes/number of coded interventions = % alternation. While St-Arnaud does not propose a formula to measure alternation in the response modes of the client, these must nonetheless be taken into consideration by the counsellor.

Mutual agreement

Mutual agreement requires that the counsellor adequately manage the interactions. For mutual agreement to occur, the counsellor must go beyond the content of the interaction and decode the process. One indication of mutual agreement is the appropriate use of communication channels. Certain questions can favour greater exploration of this phase of co-operation. The counsellor can, for example, question whether the initial situation has been articulated to his satisfaction and to that of the client.

Non-interference

Non-interference is related to the power that the counsellor wields and to the power that is attributed to the client. To verify this stage, the counsellor must examine his perception of power and the competencies he/she ascribes to himself and to the client. What form of power does he encourage? What power is he taking himself? What competencies does he acknowledge in the client? What are his areas of competency?

Assuming responsibility

Assuming responsibility reinforces co-operation because it calls upon the capacity to act autonomously and to make choices. The counsellor must become aware of his needs and find ways to meet them, so that they do not interfere with the process; in other words, they could compromise the completion of this stage of co-operation. To determine whether he has adhered to this phase, the counsellor can question whether he acknowledges his needs as well as those of the client, whether he encourages the client's autonomy or whether he refrains from sharing his personal opinions.

Sample analysis of an unsatisfactory situation

It would be difficult to understand the process of the reflective model without looking at a concrete example. The example presented below is taken from one of the dissertations that we have supervised (Cadieux, Crépeau, Guimond, Lafleur, Leblanc & Lepage, 2002), and deals specifically with the application of this model. In order not to make this paper overly long, we have restricted ourselves to the analysis of efficiency, setting aside the co-operation phase.

Context of the intervention

A female client consults a counsellor because of her difficulties in asserting her rightful place and in being authentic in her relationships. Married and the mother of two children, she says that she is dissatisfied with her relationship with her husband. The sample provided by the counsellor occurs at the end of a session that has lasted a little over an hour. The counsellor admits that she is satisfied with her interventions, because she has been working well with the client. However, the course of the session becomes somewhat complicated when the client tells her how good she feels after the therapy session. The counsellor's response starts the client off on another tangent, while what the counsellor really wanted to do was to end the session.

Counsellor's dissatisfaction or conflict

The counsellor is pleased to hear that the therapy is working well. In wanting to end the session, she chooses not to reflect her client's words, in order not to restart the interview process. Contrary to her intention, however, her response produces just the opposite effect. She feels that her interventions lead her away from her desired goal, that is, to end the session. In the course of the interaction with her client, she begins to doubt her professional competencies. She even fears that the client will stop therapy. The counsellor is visibly dissatisfied with the turn of events. She does not seem to be able to end the session in the way that she wanted and is surprised that she is not longer paying attention to what the client is saying.

Explanation of her intention

The desired effect that she has pursued with the client is as follows: that the client accepts the counsellor's decision to end the session and decides to get up and leave.

Her strategy consists of indicating to the client that the session is over. Since the client has done good work, the time seems right to end the session.

In wanting to adhere to a fixed goal, the counsellor wants to meet her own need to manage well the situation and thus to reinforce her own feelings of competency.

Description of the interaction

The interaction that follows is taken verbatim from the dissertation referenced previously.

Table 2. Example of a counsellor-client interaction

Personal Experience	Code	Dialogue/Facts	Decoding	R	F	Pr	Im
The moment is right to end the session. She is satisfied with the therapy. I am pleased. But I do not want this session to go on any longer.	Yellow	1. We will end the session and continue next week / Is that okay? - I did not feel well before coming here, / but just the fact of being here, of talking for an hour, I feel better already, I can breathe more easily.	a r		F	Pr	
Just a brief word to show I am interested in what she is saying, before concluding. It is true. But now is not the time to stop.	Yellow	2. That's what the therapy process is all about. It is a matter of talking about what you are going through, what you feel. Of course it is difficult but it can help. - But at some point, I'll have to fly on my own. I will not always be able to be in therapy.	i				Im
I will reassure her. She is excited about the idea of finishing therapy. Does she want it to end soon?	Red	3. You are making strides and you will make more of them. And then one day, you will certainly be ready to fly on your own. -Just to hear that makes me feel eager [to end therapy].	a				Im

Table 2 (cont'd)

Personal Experience	Code	Dialogue/Facts	Decoding	R	F	Pr	Im
I'm not sure I can help her to end therapy more quickly. How to explain this to her? It is beginning to get complicated.	Red	4. But it does not happen in a day. Your way of seeing things has been in place for a long time. - Just a short question before I leave. Is it by talking about and telling you what I lived through in my childhood, is that what will help me? There is something that I do not understand in all of that.	r				Im
Okay, I will try again. Is it clear enough for her to understand? Why does she say nothing?	Yellow	5. Of course, by talking things through, you discover certain difficulties that come from your childhood. You have experienced this before. But as well, by talking, it is a way of coming to grips with who you really are and how you see things. You will come to realize that there are things that can be changed. These changes will come about inside of you and your way of thinking will be modified. And your life will be better. -					Im

Table 2 (cont'd)

Personal Experience	Code	Dialogue/Facts	Decoding	R	F	Pr	Im
I hope she realizes that it will be a lot of work? I put too much emphasis on the time. It seems too long for her. What if she decides to stop therapy?	Red	6. Except that it will take some time. It does not all happen at once. - Can it take years? (said in a worried tone)	a				Im
I do not know what to say. Finally, I feel like I've come full circle. She says nothing. I hope I have not confused her too much and that she will come back.	Yel-low	7. I really could not say. We are always a work in progress. But at some point, you will most assuredly feel strong enough and you will say to yourself: I can continue on my own. - ...					Im
I am getting bogged down. What I am saying no longer relates to what I want to do. We have started up again.	Yel-low	8. You have some decisions to make about marriage. What you are going through is difficult. - I think about it every day, but it is not as bad. / What I do not like is the pretending.	f r		F		
I return to her reason for coming to therapy. She feels that I am with her.	Green	9. You would like to become more genuine, with time. You would also like to be true to yourself. - Yes, that is it. (tone of relief)	a		F		

Table 2 (cont'd)

Personal Experience	Code	Dialogue/Facts	Decoding	R	F	Pr	Im
At last, it is time to end the session.	Green	10. If you want, we can discuss this again next week. - Yes	r			Pr	

The analysis of the interaction leads the counsellor to realize that there is a difference between her declared theory and the actual theory used (see Table 3). Here are a few premises that the counsellor was able to identify: 1) the session must not end on an emotional note; 2) she does not have to listen to the client if she thinks the time is not right; 3) she must not take a stand and share her limitations; 4) the client's progress depends exclusively on the competencies of the counsellor. Such premises need to be reviewed in order to manage the interaction effectively.

Table 3. Summary of the counsellor's premises,
taken from the dissertation supervised by one of the authors

Premises from her declared theory	Premises from the actual theory used
I must accommodate the client with all of her attendant feelings.	A session must not end on an emotional note. I must do everything in my power to ensure that the client regains control of herself and that she leaves feeling peaceful.
I must listen to what the client wishes to broach.	I do not have to listen to the client if I do not think that the time is right.
An attitude of respect and authenticity forms the basis for a good therapeutic relationship.	I must not take a stand and share my limitations.
The client potentially has the competencies to resolve her own inner conflicts. My role is to work with her as she searches for her own solutions.	The client's progress depends exclusively on my competencies.

Conclusion

In summarizing his reflective analysis, the counsellor can thus discover the particularities of the model used and can thus be open to new means of increasing his efficiency and the level of co-operation with the client. With this process, he can more easily question his declared model, see its limitations in the case in point, and possibly validate the actual theory used. Becoming aware of the conflict between the actual model and the declared model can lead to a review both of his practice and of his premises, as well as to a greater personal and professional congruency and an increased interpersonal competency. We have observed this increased awareness with counsellors-in-training in the various workshops that we have led on the reflective practitioner model.

References

Argyris, C. & Schön, D.A. (1974). *Theory in practice: Increasing professional effectiveness.* San Francisco: Jossey-Bass.

Cadieux, J., Crépeau, F., Guimond, J., Lafleur, C., Leblanc, L., & Lepage, H. (2002). *La démarche praxéologique comme outil de développement professionnel en counseling.* Mémoire de maîtrise non publié, Université Saint-Paul, Ottawa, Ontario, Canada.

Chalifour, J. (1999). *L'intervention thérapeutique, volume 1 : Les fondements existentiels-humanistes de la relation d'aide.* Montréal : Gaetan Morin Éditeur.

Dolbec, A. (2003). La recherche-action. In B. Gauthier (Éd.), *Recherche sociale : De la problématique à la collecte des données* (pp. 505–540). Sainte-Foy, Québec : Presses de l'Université du Québec.

Kolb, D. A. (1984). *Experiential learning.* Englewood Cliffs, NJ: Prentice Hall.

Schön, D.A. (1994). *Le praticien réflexif : À la recherche du savoir caché dans l'agir professionnel* (traduit par J. Heynemand et D. Gagnon). Montréal : Les Éditions Logiques.

St-Arnaud, Y. (1992) *Connaître par l'action.* Montréal: Presses de l'Université de Montréal.

St-Arnaud, Y. (1995) *L'interaction professionnelle: Efficacité et coopération.* Montréal: Presses de l'Université de Montréal.

St-Arnaud, Y. (2003) *L'interaction professionnelle: Efficacité et coopération.* Montréal: Presses de l'Université de Montréal.

St-Arnaud, Y. (2004) L'atelier de praxéologie. Dans L. Mandeville (Éd.), *Apprendre autrement : Pourquoi et comment* (pp. 103–127). Sainte-Foy, Québec: Presses de l'Université du Québec.

VanKatwyk, P.L. (2003). Supervision in learning and teaching spiritual care. In P.L. VanKatwyk (Ed.), *Spiritual care and therapy: Integrative perspectives* (pp. 127–140). Waterloo: Wilfrid Laurier University Press.

Weinrach, S.G. (1990). Rogers and Gloria: The controversial film and the enduring relationship. *Psychotherapy, 27,* 282–290.

Weinrach, S.G. (1991). Rogers's encounter with Gloria: What did Rogers know and when? *Psychotherapy, 28* (3), 504–506.

6

Toward a Pastoral Counselling Conflict Resolution Model for Couples

Marie-Line Morin

Conflict resolution is a major component of therapeutic work with couples. One form of therapy, pastoral counselling, concerns itself specifically with religious and spiritual issues associated with conflict resolution. However, few researchers have dealt with such conflicts and their resolution from that perspective. To provide clinicians with sound therapeutic strategies, it is important to identify instruments or techniques that have already been proven effective in helping couples resolve conflicts and describe how they can be adapted to pastoral counselling. These can then provide a basis for devising empirical research designs in this area.

This chapter begins with a review of studies on conflict resolution in couples and on aspects of spirituality or religion related to the same issue. Most studies cover these subjects separately, investigating, on one hand, the effects of assessment tools, techniques or programs on conflict resolution and, on the other, religious variables associated with conflict resolution (spiritual variables were absent from the reviewed studies). This review presents a summary of practical techniques and strategies with indications regarding their degree of scientific reliability.

After defining the limitations of these studies, connections are made between the tools, techniques and programs presented and the religious variables pertinent to working with couples. Openings for pastoral counselling are thus identified. Finally, based on clarifications of specific dimensions of pastoral counselling, the author presents a conclusion in which she invites researchers to consider a model for conflict resolution in this field. This model includes the addition of religious variables to the instruments, techniques and programs reviewed, and ways of intervening based on partners' Fundamental Values (FV) associated with a third level of abstraction and change.

Studies reviewed

Among articles and books published between 1990 and 2003 in the field of psychology, fifty-two include variables such as "conflict resolution, couples, spirituality, religion and values." One study focuses on communication rules that need to be respected to resolve conflicts. Using mostly a psychologically based orientation, six present instruments, techniques and programs used in the context of conflict resolution with couples, and three deal with religious variables related to conflict resolution. A discussion of these ten studies reflects this order of presentation.

Communication rules

From a systemic perspective, it is understood that implicit rules regulate partners' ways of communicating and relating. Studies reviewed by Honeycutt, Woods and Fontenot (1993) reveal that rules are defined by Argyle, Henderson, Bond, Iizuka, and Contarello (1986) as "shared understandings of what behaviors should and should not be performed in various situations. Rules regulate situations and enable common goals to be attained and needs to be met." (Honeycutt, Woods, and Fontenot 1993, p. 286). Rules also "serve to co-ordinate behaviors and to define desired behaviors, [...] help enhance stability and predictability [and] provide cohesion by setting boundaries on relationships" (Argyle and Henderson, 1985, in Honeycutt et al. 1993, p. 287).

From the perspective of Argyle and Henderson (1985), violation of rules is associated with conflicts. When partners are in conflict, one may feel that the other has broken some rules and, when rules are violated, the relationship may deteriorate and be disrupted, and intimacy may be reduced. In such situations, conflict resolution requires that trust be rebuilt, thus implying that implicit rules be revised to prevent conflict patterns from resurfacing. Some rules may also need to be eliminated and others devised to ensure more effective communication (Honeycutt et al., 1993, p. 287).

Counsellors can benefit from knowing which rules are most likely to help resolve conflicts. Honeycutt et al. (1993, p. 286) identified three reasons for investigating rules in conflict resolution, based on studies of Yerby, Buerkel-Rothfuss, and Bochner (1990) and Burgess (1981): (a) to resolve conflicts and settle differences between family members, (b) to provide standards for negotiating conflict resolution, and (c) to inform marriage partners on the degree to which marital quality is associated with them (Honeycutt et al., 1993, p. 286). In a study with American couples (43 engaged and 56 married, first marriage), they identified four basic communication rules for dealing with conflicts: signaling positive understanding to one's partner, being rational, being concise and showing consideration for one's partner. These rules are associated with a number of underlying factors as in Table 1:

Table 1

Positive understanding	Rationality
Be able to say you're sorry	Don't get angry
Resolve problems so both are happy	Don't argue
	Don't raise your voice
Support and praise each other where it is due	Avoid combative issues
Listen to the other	
See the other's viewpoint	
Be honest and say what is on one's mind	

Table 1 (cont'd)

Conciseness	Consideration
Get to the point quickly	Don't talk too much
Be specific; don't generalize	Don't make the other feel guilty
Be consistent	Don't push your view as the only view
Keep to the main point	
Consideration	Don't mimic or be sarcastic
	Understand the other's faults and don't be judgmental.

These rules provide a basis for determining what to do and what to avoid in facilitating conflict resolution. Counsellors may use them to enlighten couples regarding what needs to be improved in their communication patterns. This will help couples rebuild confidence in their relationship and pave the way for effective conflict resolution.

Assessment tools

Before treatment begins, counsellors need to evaluate the nature of a conflict and its degree of severity. Lloyd (1990) developed a behavioural self-report measure of conflicts in everyday life, an area generally overlooked in global scales and detailed observations (Lloyd, 1990, p.265). With this self-report, clinicians can assess "how often a conflict arises [and how specific are the] disagreements that have occurred during an easily recalled period of time" (Lloyd, 1990, p. 266). The instrument evaluates four aspects of the conflict: *frequency, resolution, intensity* and *stability,* four variables having an impact on the maintenance of close relationships (Lloyd, 1990, p. 267).

Lloyd suggests that daily conflict be evaluated with two types of records: "an interaction record [for every interaction with the partner] and a disagreement record [for every argument] (Lloyd, 1990, p. 266). Results of her study with twenty-five couples show that greater ambivalence about a relationship is associated with increases in the intensity of conflicts, their frequency and the couples' inability to resolve them (for males). Also, stability of the conflict with partners and poor conflict resolution are significantly associated with discontinued relationships. These results support the reliability of a behavioural self-report technique for assessing conflicts in close relationships. Counsellors may therefore feel confident in using these instruments to gather information about the chances of maintaining a close relationship and the risks of an eventual breakup.

Hawley (1992) developed ENRICH, a 125-item self-report instrument used to assess conflict resolution along with twelve other dimensions of relationships: marital satisfaction, communication, [...] personality issues, financial management, sexual relationship, leisure activities, family/friend, equalitarian roles, religious orientation, children and parenting, marital cohesion, and marital adaptability (Hawley 1992, p. 95). Reliability and validity of this instrument were measured through psychometric evaluation by Fowers and Olson (1986).

Often used with individuals and in premarital counselling, this instrument is rarely used in marital and family counselling. Hawley warns counsellors not to rely solely on their observations and clinical experience to assess the nature and severity of a problem. He quotes Olson (1977), who notes that information provided by self-report instruments often does not corroborate therapist observations. Self-reporting is highly recommended to support clinical observations since it quickly sheds light on clients' perceptions of their relationship and progress in resolving conflicts (Hawley, 1992, p. 94).

Communication technique

Dealing with conflicts implies working with polarities. Therefore, conflict resolution supposes integrating the two opposing ends of polarities. Such integration is possible, from a gestaltist perspective, when those polarities are given the possibility to communicate and listen to each other. A dialogue between opposing parts is meant to result in transcending both sides of the conflict and reaching a *centering* point.

This conceptual stance may lead therapists to consider opposing sides as the expression of one partner's individual needs, beliefs or desires conflicting with those of the other partner. Mackay (2002) adopts a different point of view in research using Greenberg's (1979, 1983) Gestalt two-chair technique. The premise of this theory is "the more clients [individuals] come into contact with themselves (becoming aware of their beliefs, feelings, and actions and taking responsibility for them), the better they are able to make satisfying decisions" (Mackay, 2002, p. 221). For Mackay, therapy incorporating two-chair interventions should enable clients to become fully in touch with themselves, and thus facilitate decision making. The two-chair technique has two goals set forth by Passon (1975) and five underlying principles identified by Greenberg (1979, 1980). The two goals are (a) to assume responsibility for beliefs, feelings and actions and (b) to integrate aspects of the self into a unified whole (through awareness, splits are reintegrated) (Mackay, 2002 p. 222). The five principles are maintaining the contact boundary, taking responsibility (owning his/her experience), attending (becoming aware of his/her experience), heightening (increasing affective arousal) and expressing (acting out each side of the conflict) (Mackay, 2002 p. 223).

To verify the scientific basis of this theory, Mackay (2002) conducted an empirical study using the three-stage model (opposition, merging and integration stages – supported by Meier, A., and Boivin, M., 2001, who refer to opposition, empathic and collaboration phases) of the Gestalt two-chair technique. Using a Q-methodology, he expected factors of conflict resolution (CR) and Gestalt concept of contact with self (C) to interact before and after successful and unsuccessful therapy sessions (comprising six therapy sessions) using the two-chair technique for decision making. His subjects were eight participants ambivalent about staying married.

Results show that when therapy was successful, conflict resolution interacted with contact with self. When therapy was not successful, and when individuals experienced a great deal of interruption of contact, conflict resolution did not interact with contact with self. These results moderately support the use of the two-chair technique (and three-stage model) to facilitate pre-decision making. However, they do not explain why, in the process of decision making, conflict resolution and contact with self do not interact.

Although this research focuses on individuals' use of the two-chair technique to enhance contact with self and, thus, resolve conflict, clinicians may consider suggesting partners use the two-chair technique in dialogue with each other – the empty chair being used by each partner, in turn, as a neutral receptor of their conflicting needs, beliefs or desires. Such expression of couples' polarities may result in transcending opposing views of the conflict and reaching a *centering* point.

Therapeutic approaches

While the self-report instruments and the two-chair technique deal with individuals in relationships, systemic therapy and emotion-focused approaches address the escalating interaction cycles associated with conflicts and marital dissatisfaction. Goldman and Greenberg (1992) compared forty-two couples seeking help in resolving relationship problems. It involved two types of marital therapies – integrated systemic therapy (IST) and emotion-focused therapy (EFT) – and a control group.[1]

According to integrated systemic therapy, negative interactions are failed client attempts at problem resolution. Eliminating such undesirable behaviours interrupts the cycle of failure and sets the stage for effective conflict resolution. The primary aim in treatment is the "initiation of a reversal in the interaction" (Goldman and Greenberg, 1992, p. 962), involving reframing or positively connoting the symptoms or functioning of the system (or both). In emotion-focused therapy, interaction is understood as resulting from partners feeling a lack of entitlement to his or her unmet adult needs. The aim in treatment is to access primary feelings and unexpressed needs. Partner acceptance leads to interaction change. Interaction restructuring results from "facilitating the expression and acceptance of underlying feelings"

---

1   Couples were randomly assigned to one of the two treatments (10 free sessions – 4-month follow-up) or to a wait-list control group (tested after 10 weeks – no follow-up) – 14 couples in each group. Caucasians, average age, men 39.4, women 37.6, average length of partnership, 11.26 and no significant demographic differences (at .05 level).

(Goldman and Greenberg, 1992, p. 963). In Table 2, intervention steps used in both approaches are presented.

Table 2

Seven steps of systemic-interactional therapies	Nine steps of emotion-focused therapies
1. Define the issue presented	1. Define the issue as presented
2. Identify the negative interactional cycle	2. Identify the negative interactional cycle
3. Attempt restructuring	3. Facilitate the access & acceptance of underlying emotions
4. Reframe the problem using positive connotation followed by a prescription of the symptom	4. Redefine the problem cycle in terms of these emotions
5. Restrain, using "go slow" and dangers of improvement	5. Encourage the identification with previous experience
6. Consolidate the frame	6. Facilitate the acceptance of partners' positions
7. Prescribe a relapse	7. Encourage clients to state needs and wants
	8. Facilitate new solutions
	9. Help clients solidify new relationship positions

Both therapeutic approaches were found to be superior to the control and equally effective in alleviating marital distress, facilitating conflict resolution and goal attainment, and reducing target complaints at termination.[2] However, the IST couples showed greater maintenance of gains in marital satisfaction and goal attainment[3] when they were re-evaluated four months later.

---

2   MANOVA, Wilks's lambda procedure, $F(8), 72) = 5.80$, $p = .000$
3    $(F(4), 17) = 0.79$, $p = .547)$

Techniques and programs

When treating couples in which one partner is violent, conflict resolution involves multifaceted interventions. Tucker, Stith, Howell and McCollum (2000) illustrate the use of meta-dialogue (conversations between co-therapists in the presence of couples), based on Andersen's (1991) work, in a domestic-violence-focused couples treatment program. While co-therapists believe that clients have the resources needed to resolve their difficulties, Tucker et al. (2000) say they need to address problematic issues such as violence, disagreement, escalation, and stereotypical gender role assumptions. With the use of meta-dialogue, they become models for the couple, demonstrating non-coercive and non-abusive ways of managing differences (Tucker et al., 2000, p. 59). After having their clients describe their conflicts, they offer their own points of view on the situation, thus creating a basis for change in their perceptions of problems (Tucker et al., 2000, p. 59).

Meta-dialogue was shown to be useful in helping male perpetrators of violence against their female partners take responsibility for their actions and in assuring both partners greater physical and emotional safety (Tucker et al., 2000, p. 56). Table 3 presents nine activities of co-therapists in domestic-violence-focused couples treatment (meta-dialogue offered halfway through sessions).

Table 3

1. Ask solution-focused & reflective questions

2. Third role: observing team & stating observations of couple & musing aloud about possibilities (invite couples to step outside of constricted views & consider alternatives)

3. Adopt a respectful, not-knowing stance: encourages fluidity & possibilities, not foreclose reality from therapists' knowledge & decision making about what to do

4. Introduce difficult material (gently & indirectly while maintaining a neutral position)

5. Point out aspects of the clients' process: clients see new possibilities & alternatives to polarized positions, feel less scapegoated & emotional & open to alternative behaviour

6. Reduce escalation during conflictual interactions: shift focus from conflict to productive, reflective dialogue

7. Challenge stereotypical gender views: first step into gender-based roles to become clients' ally by identifying with clients' predicament & then suggest alternatives

8. Model how real people talk about problems: couples observing real people talking & seeking solutions

9. Compliment clients: indirectly introduce observations of strengths in therapy; do not tolerate denial

Conflict resolution often requires crisis intervention to deal with marital distress and destructive marital conflict. The Prevention and Relationship Enhancement Program (PREP) presented by Freedman, Low, Markman and Stanley (2000) is a prevention program for marital distress which applies principles underlying such intervention. Universal (targeting all couples, engaged or currently married) and empirically-supported.[4] PREP teaches conflict resolution and communication skills to help couples decrease relationship risk factors and increase protective factors (Markman, Stanley and Blumberg, 2001, in Freedman et al., p. 49). It empha-

4   Markman, Stanley, and Blumberg, 2001; Stanley, Markman, and Jenkins, 2002; Clement, Stanley, and Markman, 1997.

sizes the development and maintenance of intimacy, commitment and friendship, protecting couples from the negative ramifications of crisis events and decreasing the occurrences of crises (Clements, Stanley and Markman, 1997; Stanley, 1997; Stanley, Markman, St. Peters and Leber, 1995).

The revised and updated version of PREP makes couples aware of two keys to self regulation: (a) to refrain from making negative judgments of their partner's choices (especially present in women in unhappy marriages) and (b) to control physical reactions that accompany heated arguments (especially present in men) (Freedman et al., 2002, p. 50). PREP is also useful, in crisis intervention, to restore the individual's level of functioning by reducing external stress levels. As a short-term psychotherapeutic technique, it increases the level of adjustment and the ability to deal with internal conflicts rather than external stress. While encouraging the strengthening of social support networks of couples, PREP teaches couples to deal with sensitive issues and conflicts in a structured way. Research has also shown significant decrease of multiple indicators of marital distress and increase of marital satisfaction with its application.[5] These are only a few of PREP's many possibilities supported by research reviewed and presented in Freedman *et al.* (2002, p. 52-53).

PREP is generally administered in one of two ways: four to eight couples participate in three sessions (one full day on a weekend followed by two evenings during the week) or larger groups in an intensive weekend seminar. The eight major interventions used in the program are presented in Table 4.

---

5   Markman, Renick, Floyd, Stanley, and Clements, 1993.

Table 4

---

1. Teach the speaker-listener technique. The speaker has the floor, discusses an issue from his/her point of view. The listener listens without interrupting and then paraphrases the speaker's words. This continues until the speaker feels heard and understood.

2. Encourage weekly meetings to either talk about issues using the speaker-listener technique or focus on talking as friends.

3. Teach ground rules to keep conflicts from escalating.

4. Teach effective problem solving and the importance of discussing problems before proposing solutions.

5. Teach the use of XYZ statements: "When you do X in situation Y, I feel Z."

6. Analyze couples' negative interpretations of their partner's behaviours.

7. Focus on bolstering protective factors – tools are given to preserve and protect the friendship that brought them together (to ensure couples do not fall into a distressing interaction pattern). Encourage them to make time to talk and listen as friends, banning problem discussions for a while.

8. Encourage them to make sensuality a priority in their relationship as a way to increase their levels of intimacy.

Studies including religious variables

According to Butler, Stout and Gardner (2002), marriage and family studies tend to focus on "overt manifestations of religiosity [and] variables of religious affiliation and church attendance and its relation to individual physical and mental health [and] global correlations between religiosity and marital satisfaction, adjustment, and stability" (Butler et al., p. 20-21). Based on literature review they identified a need to focus on (a) comparative contributions of various spiritual conditions, practices, or both; and (b) processual mechanisms by which specific spiritual-religious practices, such as prayer, affect relationships (Butler et al., p. 21). They also found that religious practice such as prayer "received negligible empirical attention (Butler et al., p. 22) and suggest that more "relationship-oriented and interactionally focused studies of the effects of prayer are needed" (Butler et al., p. 22). Using a quantitative methodology and a qualitative design, they explore the effects of "prayer by religious spouses" (independent variable) on "ten themes"[6] (dependant variables) on a geographically and religiously diverse group of 230 Christian spouses.

Of the ten couple-reported effects of prayer, seven (statistically significant) were judged to have at least moderate clinical relevance:

(a) interactionally discernible "relationship" with a personified Deity together with an experience of mindfulness and accountability toward Deity, (b) reduced negativity, contempt, and hostility toward partner, with accompanying reduction in emotional reactivity (high contingency of negative exchanges), and an accompanying increase in one's relationship focus and partner empathy, and (c) increased self-change as opposed to partner-change orientation, together with heightened sense of couple responsibility to one another and to their relationship. (Butler et al., 2002, pp. 31–32)

Butler et al. (2002) conclude that the Person/Deity and Couple/Deity relationships are characterized by interactive communication and a sense that the Deity knows and cares about the

---

6   1. Phenomenological relationship with Deity (metaphysical relationship with personified deity), 2. Experience of emotional validation (feeling heard and understood), 3. Experience of mindfulness and accountability (remembering Deity throughout the day – thoughts and actions influenced by awareness of Deity), 4. De-escalation of negativity, contempt, and hostility (lessening of aversive feelings toward partner during time of conflict), 5. Reduction of emotional reactivity (decreased high contingency of negative exchanges) 6. Relationship and partner orientation and behaviour (increased focus on partner's feelings and relationship needs), 7. Unbiased/systemic perspective and partner empathy (bringing together the differing perspectives of each spouse through facilitating systemic/interactional perspectives and validating non-shared perceptions of experience), 8. Self-change focus as compared to partner-change focus (focusing on what one personally does to resolve conflict), 9. Couple responsibility for reconciliation and problem solving (self-reliant behaviour that encourages healing interaction and problem resolution within the dyadic relationship, 10. Incremental coaching (when spouses experience Divine intervention that is step by step and delineates what to do in the immediate time frame, versus resolving the entire problem).

individual, his partner and the marriage itself. As a result, the Deity is invited to become a third party, providing stability and support for the couple (Butler et al. p. 32).Conflict resolution is not independent of the way anger is perceived in the religious culture of couples. Marsh and Dallos (2001) verified the effects of the religious beliefs and practices on anger and conflict management in the marital relationship of ten Roman Catholic couples. Their interest emerged from attempts to resolve tensions between psychological and religious approaches to anger. Implicit messages received from personal therapy, clinical psychology, and counselling training convey that it is broadly beneficial to express feelings, including anger, and that it is potentially damaging to suppress such feelings. However, implicit messages received from both Christian and Buddhist teachings convey that "the expression of anger is likely to be harmful to others and indicates a lack of restraint" (Marsh and Dallos, 2001, p. 343). From these perspectives, both approaches are based on unstable foundations.

A single-group design was used within a qualitative paradigm. The study focused on 20 married participants (10 couples), practicing Roman Catholics for at least two years. A first, semi-structured interview with each partner generated transcripts that were analyzed using Grounded theory techniques and led to a second interview using Repertory Grids.

Of all the information generated, the most relevant refers to the effects on anger of religious practice and relationship to God. It was found that prayer, meditation, as well as attending Mass and going to confession, helped in a variety of ways. Among the effects listed are a reduction in the number of escalated conflicts, a general feeling of serenity and contentedness, a reduction in feelings of anger, an ability to open up to each other, to be less defensive, to listen better and to adopt the other person's point of view. These religious practices also helped couples come to terms with their emotions, adopt a meta-position regarding conflicts and emotions, and view the situation less personally. Family prayer was found to have "bonding effect by allowing the family to be together and to attend to each other's feelings and needs" (Marsh and Dallos, 2001, p. 348). Therefore, "creating a realignment of intentions for future behavior [prayer] helped participants introspect about their own responsibility in the conflict" (Marsh and Dallos, 2001, p. 348). Relationship with God is experienced as a source of peace and harmony. Anger can be accepted and contained by God, transformed rather than expressed or directed to the spouse.

Parallels can be made between a relationship with God and a relationship with a spouse: many spouses experienced a similar pattern of anger management/expression with God as with their spouse, while others found it complementary (God meets the needs not met by the spouse). Trusting in God's will helped many downplay their own needs and desires and led to a greater openness to the needs of the spouse and to a celebration of their mutual interdependence. "The experience of God's presence gave couples a sense that their relationship was blessed, unshakeable, or 'meant to be.' From this followed a sense of security and a feeling of optimism that God would deal with future conflicts in their relationship" (Marsh and Dallos, 2001, p. 349).

In the development of theory, Marsh and Dallos (2001) state that having identified different ways in which religious practices can influence individuals and their spouses, their study supports the notion of feedback between the couple and the religious system. They relate this to the concept of "space":

> Intrapersonally, religious practices expand "space" in a variety of ways: physiologically, through various slowing down and cooling off mechanisms; cognitively, by providing mental space for the believer to reflect on his or her own responsibility in a conflict, to consider the other person's point of view and to see the conflict from a broader perspective; affectively, by reducing the intensity of anger experienced, by facilitating impulse-control, and by putting physical space and time between the angry impulse and the desire to act. (Marsh and Dallos, 2001, p. 354)

Space is also expanded when tension can be defused by the integration of God as a triangulated figure. As partners learn to adjust to one another, they recognize that certain needs cannot be met by their spouse. To prevent tensions resulting from these unmet needs from destabilizing the homeostasis, needs are "detoured" (Minuchin, 1974) away from the partner to a "triangulated" (Bowen, 1978) entity. "Although this was sometimes the children, the study suggested that the triangulated figure may also be God who, in possible contrast to family members, cannot be hurt by any amount of anger, and whose love is unconditional (Marsh and Dallos, 2001, p. 354).

In a theoretical study, Propst (1997) presents a clinical view of conflict resolution against the background of Trinitarian theology. Her thesis is that her understanding of "the Trinity [...] enriches what we know about decision making and conflict resolution and provides ontological basis for therapy and a motivational tool in work with clients" (Propst, 1997, p. 58). According to her, in the light of Christian theology, there are three ways of dealing with conflict: (a) avoidance: not expressing an opposing opinion or leaving the presence of a person who is expressing such an opinion, (b) domination: suggesting something the other feels obliged to accept, and (c) confrontation: establishing one's position by openly disagreeing with the other person (Propst, 1997, p. 61).

Referring to the *Harvard negotiation project[7]: building relationships as you negotiate* and the way Christian theology deals with conflict, Propst suggests that since the individual fully exists only through the other, differences should be seen as "healthy and necessary; opportunities to deepen relationships" (Propst, 1997, p. 62).[8] She emphasizes the fact that, since God the Father, the Son, and the Holy Spirit are distinct persons as well as defined personal essences, according to the traditional Christian doctrine, "We can infer that for human beings to be created in the image of God (Genesis 1:26) is for them also to be at the same time distinct individuals" (Propst, 1997, p. 62–63). She makes a connection between a systems approach conception of the "whole [as] more than the sum of the parts [and] the trinitarian God [being] more than the three distinct persons of the Trinity" (Propst, 1997, p. 63) to support the idea that the relationship defines the spouses. She then infers a concept of persons from the image of the triune

---

7   Fisher and Ury, 1991; Ury, 1993.
8   She supports this idea by referring to Bonhoeffer, who parallels Martin Buber (1937) in *I and Thou* and by quoting Karl Barth (1960), for whom "the individual is fully an individual only after the I-thou-encounter. 'I am as I am in a relation.'"

God and uses this concept as the basis for recommendations on conflict resolution.

In fact, Propst recommends a process of conflict resolution in a trinitarian style where "individual differences are regarded as healthy and necessary for good relationships [and] persons grow (and thus change) as their relationships develop, but remain individuals" (Propst, 1997, p. 64). There are three principles to this approach: (a) state your own position clearly; (b) understand where the other is coming from; (c) be generous with one another. The first principle, *state your own position clearly*, implies that not doing so "does not tend to resolve conflict [or] leads to mutual satisfaction [and] may lead to various types of emotional pathology" (Propst, 1997, p. 65). The second principle, *understand where the other is coming from*, "dispose[s] clients to become more sensitive to, and respectful of, one another's opinions and feelings" (Propst, 1997, p. 67). The third principle, *be generous with one another*, is expressed in three types of behaviour: (a) frame issues positively and inclusively, (b) do not begin by disagreeing with the other, but rather empathize and summarize his or her position, and (c) compliment the other on his or her attempts at resolving the conflict (Propst, 1997, p. 70).

These studies provide a preliminary basis for developing a pastoral-counselling model. However, before devising such a model, it is necessary to identify the limitations of these findings. In the next section, we will relate the research on religious variables with those on psychology and identify possible connections between the two. We will then formulate certain conceptual suggestions for an effective pastoral-counselling model.

Limitations

Findings of the research on the impact of prayer on ten themes associated with couple experience of conflict (Butler et al., 2002) cannot be generalized beyond the Christian population (more than half of the sample – 230 individuals – were members of The Church of Jesus Christ of Latter-day Saints). Neither is the sample very diverse in terms of education, age, race or income. The research on the effects of religious practice and relationship to God on anger (Marsh and Dallos, 2001) did not include a focus on the impact of the partners' view of the relationship between God and religious practice. It is essential to consider how such representations influence the way couples handle anger and conflict management. The theoretical study by Propst (1997) is based on interesting principles. However, empirical research needs to be done to verify its application in the context of couples counselling.

As expected, the psychologically oriented instruments, techniques and programs do not address the spiritual or religious dimension. However, knowing that conflict may be the expression of deeper problems in the relational dynamic of partners, one would expect the studies presenting them to reach the third level of abstraction associated with family values, paradigms, and world view (Burr, 1991). The behavioural self-report technique presented by Lloyd (1990) and the Self-report Instrument: ENRICH, by Hawley (1992), leave little room for assessing information about values, paradigms and world views. With the two-chair technique (Mackay, 2002), contact with self may help identify values and other aspects of the system's third level of abstraction. However, the research does not explain why, in the process of decision making, conflict resolution and contact with self do not interact. This leaves room for interpretation based on variables other than contact with self. In that case, the technique may not always generate information needed by pastoral counsellors to work with spiritual or religious dimensions of therapy.

In their research on IST and EFT, Goldman and Greenberg (1992) present two therapeutic models that are effective in alleviating marital distress and facilitating conflict resolution. These models, however, aim at interaction reversal and access and expression of primary feelings and needs. Here again, values, paradigms and world views underlying couples' interaction patterns or feelings and needs are not addressed. Limitations found in the meta-dialogue (Tucker et al., 2000) and the PREP (Freedman et al., 2000) are similar to the ones identified in the research on IST and EFT; that is to say, there is no explicit indication on how to identify third level of abstraction issues. Nevertheless, as announced, certain connections can be established between religious variables and the therapeutic interventions and techniques of the aforementioned psychologically oriented studies.

Toward a model for conflict resolution in pastoral counselling

Points of connection

The information gathered in the studies (and their limitations) allows us to identify points of connection between, on one side, instruments, techniques and programs and, on the other, certain aspects of religious practice and relationship to God. These points provide a basis for determining how religious variables add an extra perspective to conflict resolution with couples. They are presented in Table 5 – authors' names (in the first column), the corresponding instrument, technique or program (in the second column), how parts of that instrument, technique or program can be complemented by a religious dimension (in the third column).

Table 5

Hawley, 1992	ENRICH Self-report	To the 13 dimensions measured by the instrument we can add *items measuring religious practice and the relationship to God* (Marsh and Dallos, 2001)
Mackay, 2002	two-chair technique	Use of this technique to dialogue with the inner God (Marsh and Dallos, 2001)
Goldman and Greenberg, 1992	IST and EFT	The aims of interaction reversal to interrupt the conflict cycle (IST) and access and express feelings and needs, and to have partners acceptance (EFT) can be complemented with *religious practices expanding "space" in a variety of ways, trusting in God's will to let go of needs and desires, and relating to God to feel care, support and stability in the relationship* (Marsh and Dallos, 2001)

Table 5 (cont'd)

Tucker et al., 2000	Meta-dialogue	Co-therapists taking a third-role (attitude 2), adopting a respectful stance (attitude 3), and maintaining a neutral position (attitude 4) can be applied to and enhanced in relationship to *God as a third party* (Butler et al., 2002), *source of peace and acceptance and helping to reach a meta-position* (Marsh and Dallos, 2001). To reduce escalation and shift focus from conflict to productive and reflective dialogue (attitude 6), *prayer, meditation or other religious practices* can be included (Marsh and Dallos, 2001). Finally, with modeling how real people talk about problems (attitude 8), it can be suggested that *God is also a model of interactive communication* (Butler et al., 2002).
Freedman et al., 2000	PREP	Teaching ground rules to prevent escalating (tool C) can be related to *religious practice that prevents escalating* (Marsh and Dallos, 2001). Encouraging weekly meetings (tool B) and making sensuality a priority in the relationship to increase levels of intimacy (tool H) can be complemented by *encouraging prayer or regular (daily or weekly) religious practice and relating to God as a source of inner-peace and mutual acceptance, a guide for anger management, a resource for help in letting go, etc.* (Marsh and Dallos, 2001).

This table provides suggestions for integrating religious practice and relationship-to-God issues with certain instruments or techniques, such as ENRICH self-report and the two-chair technique, and specific approaches or programs such as IST and EFT therapy, meta-dialogue and PREP. This implies, according to studies reviewed, that religious or God-related variables can facilitate conflict resolution. As for the behavioural self-report technique (Lloyd, 1990) and communication rules (Honeycutt et al., 1993), it seems unnecessary to add religious variables for them to be used effectively. The reference to Christian theology on the Trinity (Propst, 1997) is not included in the table because its theoretical orientation does not seem to offer practical openings to complement any of the clinically orientated instruments, techniques or programs studied.

Considering these parallels or complements, pastoral counsellors can anticipate ways of intervening with their spiritual or religious-minded clients. However, although these parallels constitute an important step in that direction, they do not go far enough to reach the level of values, which we strongly associate with pastoral counselling. In fact, the focus of the instruments, techniques and programs is on methods of communication and problem solving that tend to be limited in reaching the first or second levels of change. Adding religious variables does not necessarily provide a basis for dealing with underlying values in conflicts. To do so, one needs to consider what Burr (1991) calls the *third level of abstraction*. This level is associated with family values, paradigms, and world view.[9] It corresponds to the root of the systems' interactional organization from which conflict can originate. Identifying the systems' values, paradigms, and world view means reaching the deepest level of the systems, at the heart of many conflicts.

Reaching the third level of abstraction and third level of change

From the perspective of pastoral counselling, the third level of abstraction also includes values, beliefs and God representations that impact religious practice and relationship to God. This means that pastoral counsellors need to know how to identify and address issues that relate to: 1) values expressed in the quest for meaning and absolutes underlying a system's interactional organization, and 2) beliefs and representations associated with God and the community (religious or spiritual) that sustain a system's problematic interactional organization.

---

9   *First level*: specific, observable, concrete *patterns of behaviour* occurring in temporal, spatial, developmental, and ecosystemic contexts, also called *transformation processes* because they transform, change, exchange, and allocate such things as time, energy, space, creativity, distance and closeness, boredom, love, care, anger, etc. (this level corresponds to first-order change). *Intermediate level* refers to the structure of the system, the meta-communication and meta-rules level, metaphors' level, the social, political and legal decision making, the organizational change, the ability to change (this level corresponds to second-order change) (Burr, 1991, pp. 442–443).

The goal in identifying and addressing these issues is to help couples make the necessary transformations to move toward a non or less problematic interactional organization. Working on underlying values, beliefs and God representation means aiming for "third level changes." Such changes do not occur frequently because the risk of destroying the system is greater. However, for spiritual or religious couples, whose search for absolutes and ultimate realities is usually associated with a strong desire to reach the highest level of satisfaction and fulfillment, making "third level changes" is essential. Therefore, pastoral counsellors need to be skilled in helping couples identify values, beliefs, and representations at the heart of problematic interactional organizations. Changes at this level will follow naturally.

In a systems approach, values and beliefs (myths) are analyzed as ways of maintaining homeostasis. According to Jackson (1977), values can be used as a means of "demanding, imposing or justifying a certain type of behavior in a relationship" (Jackson, 1977, p. 39). For example, using a commonly accepted value of democracy in situations where the family norm prohibits all disagreement, whenever arguing takes place, one partner need only say "every one speaks in turn" and the "no-argument" rule will be respected. In that sense, values constitute a kind of homeostasis mechanism. This is why Jackson (1977) can claim that values, in systems' theory, are used as "interpersonal tactical means of sustaining or imposing a norm" (Jackson, 1977, p. 39). Identifying values shared by a system requires that individual values and advantages gained in a relationship through values be uncovered. Within such a framework, communication and fulfillment of values become acceptable substitutes for conflictive behaviour.

Although systemic therapy usually encourages working with all members of a system, reaching the third level of change re-quires identifying the specific influence of each individual within the system. Systems are built by individuals having idiosyncratic values.[10] Since partners bring their own identities and differences into a relationship, couples' systems have, at their root, similar

---

10   According to Jackson (1977) even though values may originate in a larger system (culture, ethnic group or social group), idiosyncratic values also exist outside the realm of system interactions.

or different values held by individuals constituting them. Thus, partner identities, preferences and differences underlie the interactional organization that maintains homeostasis.

Recognizing the place of values, beliefs and representations at the heart of a system also involves recognizing psychodynamic issues. In fact, research shows that early development and relationship-with-parent issues influence values, beliefs and representations of God and the community. Therefore, two basic questions need to be considered in our approach:

1. How do individual projective or defensive dynamics (personal fundamental conflict) influence the interactional organization of a system?

2. What are the individual's values, quest for meaning and absolutes, spiritual or religious beliefs and representations of God, and how do they influence the system's interactional organization?

Pastoral counsellors must identify the individual projective or defensive dynamics of each partner. This means recognizing projections of object or relation issues and defense mechanisms interfering in the relationship with the partner as "other" (not as a replica of a parent or significant caretaker). The systems' developmental and crisis stages (birth of a child, mid-life stage, empty nest, etc.) also need to be considered. However, no elaboration of this aspect is provided here; our focus is on the third level of abstraction.

Secondly, the individual's values, quest for meaning and absolutes, spiritual or religious beliefs and representations of God are usually associated with psychological dynamics. However, while the dynamics are a consequence of childhood primary experiences, they do reveal how a relationship is used to deal with past problem issues. Values, aspirations, beliefs and representations emerging from those issues reveal how personal yearnings for ultimate realities can constitute a basis for including God in problem solving.

Fundamental Values of Partners

When addressing issues at the third level of abstraction, we reach unconscious and shadow material generally associated with suffering. Counsellors need to tread softly here (for example, using meta-dialogue), and focusing on fundamental yearnings is a way of doing so. Previous research has shown that a client's values, aspirations, desires, etc., reveal his/her Fundamental Value. Thus, focusing on this Value means exploring the positive aspects of the repressed and unconscious painful material.

A Fundamental Value is defined as a dominant good that integrates all others, a core value that best expresses a person's psycho-spiritual identity (Morin, 2001). This concept finds a parallel in the concept of "hypergood" that Taylor (1989) defines as standing for a "higher-order good [ranked by individuals as] incomparably more important than others, [providing] the standpoint from which these must be weighed, judged, decided about [and giving] a sense of wholeness, of fullness of being as a person or self, that nothing else can" (Taylor, 1989, p. 63). Saint-Arnaud (1988), who developed this concept in pastoral counselling, borrows concepts of psychosynthesis (Assagioli, 1965) to say that the Fundamental Value is the expression par excellence of a Transpersonal Self which yearns for the ultimate good and selects one value among others as being most important. Thus, centering on the Transpersonal Self leads to the discovery of an individual's Fundamental Value (Saint-Arnaud, 1988; Morin, 2001, p. 14-34). Such recognition, in turn, sheds light on what individuals expect in their relationships with God and others.

Adding a theological aspect to the notion of Fundamental Value, Saint-Arnaud states that its complete fulfillment can only be found in a relationship with God; people and things can only provide partial fulfillment and act as reflections of what God has to offer. In that regard, he adds that the psycho-religious developmental process of individuals is to move away from expecting people and things to fulfill that Fundamental Value in an absolute way and move toward greater communion with God, the source of all good, who can offer such fulfillment. As a corollary to that, we can conclude that individuals in couple relationships should focus on God to find the *absolute* fulfillment of their Fundamental Value instead of trying to find it in their partner. This orientation is in line with the findings of Marsh and Dallos (2001) supporting the fact that relationship to God is understood as complementary to the relationship with the partner, where God fulfills needs that the spouse cannot meet. Their finding is illustrated by an extract from an interviewed subject, named Brenda: "No human being can be everything another human being wants [so] there has been a change where I would turn to my relationship with God and that would put me in a better relationship with Will" (Marsh and Dallos, 2001, p. 349). As partners progress in that direction, they learn to accept their partner's limitations in that regard, accept God's love for them, and become a reflection of that love for their partner.

Previous research has shown that individual Fundamental Values can be understood as constituting a homeostasis mechanism in the form of a paradigm at an unconscious level. Therefore, identifying the partners' Fundamental Value is essential to pastoral counselling with couples. Since it is the partners' ultimate good, it reveals important information on the way they developed their specific interactional organization. Relationship patterns can be understood as expressions of partner aspirations in attaining the fulfillment of their most fundamental or ultimate yearnings. From that perspective, each partner is thought to bring his or her Fundamental Value to the relationship, expecting the other to fulfill it. Doesn't the fact of falling in love include idealizing a man or a woman and thinking he or she is the ONLY PERSON who can satisfy one's desire for happiness?

From that point of view, we can say that relational patterns are developed with the hope of reaching such fulfillment. We can also infer that conflict occurs when partners, after years of co-habitation, realize their soul mate is unable to fulfill that yearning or does not correspond to their idealized image. By identifying Fundamental Values, pastoral counsellors will be able to help partners move away from unrealistic expectations of partners to communion with God and reflection of that communion on the other. Such an orientation implies the recognition that their partner can only offer partial fulfillment of their Fundamental Value and that, being a child of God, each one needs to refer to God for complete realization of themselves as individuals as well as in their relationship as couples. Having redirected their fundamental aspiration toward its ultimate source, partners can also be open to considering new ways of expressing their needs and yearnings, other than those experienced through the conflictive relational pattern.

In line with the identification of partners' Fundamental Values, religious values and beliefs can be identified and used as springboards for transformation. Among these are (a) values on which the couple was initially formed (What attracted them to each other and made them decide to get married or become a couple and what project did they intend to build together?) (b) values of fidelity (What keeps the partners together in spite of the conflict? Is it gratuitous love of the other for who he or she is?), (c) beliefs, such as "Truth will make you free" (John 8:32), that may help couples accept the truth about personal unconscious material or projection of parental figures on the partner and their impact on the relationship, (d) biblical exhortations such as "Why do you look at the speck of sawdust in your brother's eye, with never a thought for the great plank in your own?" (Matthew 6:7) and (e) beliefs about life after death based on the religious teaching on the resurrection. Recalling these may help stop the escalation of mutual blame, redirecting attention to one's own responsibility; it may also help partners face the suffering and mutual wounds associated with conflicts and set new goals for themselves in the relationship.

Many other references could be given to help move in the direction of interactional pattern transformation. Also, religious beliefs and God representations, presented earlier as being part of the third level of abstraction, can help identify Fundamental Values and be part of the recommended process of change. However, including these in our reflection is beyond the scope of this short chapter. That is why the last section focuses on the concept of Fundamental Value, assuming the presence of values, beliefs and God representation associated with it.

Conclusion

A pastoral counselling conflict resolution model for couples

The model we offer for conflict resolution in pastoral counselling includes two dimensions: (a) religious variables added to instruments, techniques and programs, and (b) orientations toward the third level of abstraction and change: reaching out to partners' Fundamental Values (FV). The first dimension was presented earlier in Table 5; the second is summarized in the following somewhat eclectic therapeutic process.

Our model for conflict resolution in pastoral counselling is based on the aims, steps, techniques and instruments presented above. It includes steps borrowed from the IST and EFT approaches, two-chair and meta-dialogue techniques, and attitudes and interventions derived from the domestic violence-focused couples treatment (where the meta-dialogue is presented) and the PREP. It also integrates the religious variables added in Table 5, and includes a variety of openings that provide access to the third level of abstraction and change (these openings are in bold) as well as interventions leading to the identification of the FV.

Our model has three main goals: (a) to alter negative interactions, (b) to help partners access and express primary feelings and needs, and (c) to facilitate interaction change. Altering negative interactions involves reframing or positively connoting the symptoms of the conflict or the functioning of the system (or both). Also, by reaching the root of the interaction structure through the identification of a partner's FV, couples can interrupt the conflict cycle and initiate the resolution of the problem. Similar results can be achieved by helping partners access and express primary feelings and needs, as well as values, beliefs and representations revealing the partner's FV and by facilitating interaction change through the acceptance of the partner's feelings, values, needs and limitations, including remembering that God loves and accepts the partner as much as oneself.

The steps of the model, borrowed from IST and EFT, are complemented with spiritual or religious variables and orientations. We understand that IST and EFT differ in their premises. However, knowing that, in practice, many therapists use both approaches at different times with different clients, it seems plausible to include both when our goal is to reach the third level of abstraction through the identification of partners' Fundamental Value. In that sense, going beyond the differences, our model includes 12 steps, presented in Table 6. Note that the numbers do not necessarily correspond to the IST and EFT steps and that some steps are combined for integration purposes. Complements are in bold; italics refer to items presented in Table 5:

Table 6

1. Define the issue presented

2. Identify the negative interactional cycle and **values, beliefs, God representations as revealing the FV that maintain that interactional cycle**

3. Facilitate access and acceptance of underlying emotions, **values, beliefs, God representations and FV** and encourage identification with them and trust in God's will to let go of needs and desires

4. Redefine the problem cycle in terms of these emotions, **values, beliefs, God representations and FV**

5. Facilitate the acceptance of partner positions and **relationship with God that contribute to experiencing the fullness of response to one's FV**

6. Encourage clients to state to partners **and to God, needs, values, etc., related to their FV**

7. Encourage clients *to practice religion and relate to God to feel care, support and stability* and **identify and encourage religious experiences that resonate with the fulfillment of their FV**

8. Reframe the problem using positive connotations **associated with partners' yearning for their FV**

9. Facilitate new solutions, attempt restructuring, or prescribe the symptom

10. Restrain, using "go slow" and dangers of improvement

11. Consolidate the frame and prescribe a relapse

12. Help clients solidify new relationship positions

Within the framework of this proposal, the integration process implies that, before facilitating access and acceptance of partners, pastoral counsellors consider identifying the values, beliefs and God representations as they reveal the FV. The same should be included in the facilitating of access and acceptance of underlying emotions, the reframing of the problem using positive connotation, and with the redefinition of the problem cycle and encouragement to identify with previous experiences. Our model also adds to the IST and EFT steps the encouragement to practice religion and relate to God to feel care, support and stability and to identify and facilitate having religious experiences that resonate with the fulfillment of their FV. Finally, among the positive connotations used to reframe the problem, we include associating the problem with partners' yearning for their FV.

Attitudes and intervention techniques

Our model respects principles and attitudes associated with meta-dialogue applied in the 12-session domestic violence-focused couples treatment. Connections made in Table 5 help identify areas where references to God are in line with some of these attitudes. Let us recall just a few: God as a third party and source of peace, acceptance, and help to reach a meta-position and God as a model of interactive communication. Helping partners relate to God in those perspectives means taking a stance in line with the attitudes suggested with the use of meta-dialogue.

Our model also uses intervention techniques from the PREP program complementing them with religious variables (Table 5) and elements that allow the identification and reorganization of interactional patterns based on partners' Fundamental Value (references leading to religious practice or experiencing God as fulfillment of the FV are in bold). In this model couples are

Table 7

A) taught speaker-listener techniques;

B) encouraged to hold weekly meetings to either talk about issues using the speaker-listener technique or focus on talking as friends and **to reserve time and space for regular religious practice (daily or weekly) and relationship to God as a source of peace and acceptance;**

C) taught ground rules to keep conflicts from escalating, **including religious practice (helps transform anger, letting go, etc.);**

D) taught effective problem solving, emphasizing problem discussion prior to moving on to the solution;

E) taught to use XYZ statements: "When you do X in situation Y, I feel Z" rather than accusations such as "You are such a slob";

F) **taught to pay attention to the FV emerging out of the expression of feelings, needs, wants, values, beliefs, God representations etc.;**

G) encouraged to analyze their negative interpretations regarding their partner's behaviours (ex: leaving the tube of toothpaste uncapped = lack of care);

H) invited to learn to focus on bolstering protective factors;

I) encouraged to make sensuality a priority in the relationship as a way to increase their levels of intimacy; and

J) **encouraged to make spirituality or religion a priority in the relationship as a way to increase experiencing God as a source of fulfillment of their FV.**

In this table, we consider that religious practice and relationship to God need to be encouraged as ways of fulfilling partners' FV, implying the identification of that value. That is why couples are encouraged to reserve time and space for such activities and to make spirituality or religion a priority in their relationship.

This model for conflict resolution in pastoral counselling, although grounded in reviewed research, needs to be put to the test of empirical experimentation. Recommendations for such research include using a diverse religious affiliation sample to verify if and how the identification of partners' FV correlates with the maintenance of the system's interactional pattern (other variables presented in the model need to be discriminated to avoid overlapping). Once the impact of these variables on the system is clearer, the pastoral counselling model can be used in structured counselling sessions, with a test group first and with a probabilistic sample later, to help couples resolve conflicts. A longitudinal study is recommended to verify if changes in the interactional patterns can be positively associated with conflict resolution when identifying partners' Fundamental Values.

References

Andersen, T. A. (1991). *The reflecting team: Dialogue and dialogues about the dialogues.* New York: Norton.

Argyle, M. & Henderson, M. (1985). The rules of relationships. In S. W. Duck & Perlman (Eds.), *Understanding personal relationships: An interdisciplinary approach*, pp. 63–84, London: Sage.

Argyle, M., Henderson, M., Bond, M., Iizuka, Y. & Contarello, A. (1986). Cross-cultural variations in relationship rules. *International Journal of Psychology, 21,* 287-315.

Assagioli, R. (1965). *Psychosynthesis: A manual of principles and techniques.* New York: The Viking Press.

Bowen, M. (1978). *Family therapy in clinical practice.* New York: Jason Aronson.

Burgess, R.L. (1981). Relationships in marriage and the family. In S. W. Duck & Gilmour (Eds.), *Personal relationship 1: Studying personal relationships.* London: Academic Press.

Burr, W. R. (1991). Rethinking levels of abstraction in family systems theories. *Family Process, 30,* 435–452.

Butler, M. H., Stout, J. A. & Gardner, B. C. (2002). Prayer as a conflict resolution ritual: Clinical implications of religious couples' report of relationship softening, healing perspective, and change responsibility. *The American Journal of Family Therapy, 30,* 19–37.

Clements, M., Stanley, S. & Markman, H. J. (1997). *Predicting Divorce.* University of Denver.

Freedman, C. M., Low, S. M., Markman, H. J. & Stanley, S. M. (2000). Equipping couples with the tools to cope with predictable and unpredictable crisis events: The PREP program. *International Journal of Emergency Mental Health, 4(1),* 49–56.

Fowers, B. J. & Olson, D. H. (1989). ENRICH marital inventory: A discriminant validity and cross-validation assessment. *Journal of Marital and Family Therapy, 15,* 65–79.

Goldman, A. & Greenberg, L. (1992). Comparison of integrated systemic and emotionally focused approach to couples therapy. *Journal of Consulting and Clinical Psychology, 60(6),* 962–969.

Greenberg, L. S. (1979). Resolving splits: Use of the two-chair technique. *Psychotherapy: Theory, Research and Practice, 16,* 316–324.

Greenberg, L. S. (1980). Training counselors in Gestalt methods. *Canadian Counseling, 3,* 174–180.

Greenberg, L. S. (1983). Toward a task analysis of conflict resolution in Gestalt two-chair dialogue on intrapsychic conflict in counseling. *Journal of Counseling Psychology, 28,* 288–294.

Hawley D. R. (1994). Couples in crisis: Using self report instruments in marriage counseling, *Pastoral Psychology, 43(2),* 93–103.

Honeycutt, J. M., Woods, B. L. & Fontenot, K. (1993). The endorsement of communication conflict rules as a function of engagement, marriage and marital ideology. *Journal of Social and Personal Relationships, 10,* 285-304.

Jackson, D. D. (1977). L'étude de la famille. In P. Watzlawick et J. Weakland, *Sur l'interaction, Palo Alto, 1965-1974, Une nouvelle approche thérapeutique.* Paris: Seuil.

Lloyd, S. A. (1990). A behavioural self-report technique for assessing conflict in close relationships. *Journal of Social and Personal Relationships. 7,* 265-272.

Mackay, B. (2002). Effects of Gestalt therapy two-chair dialogue on divorce decision making. *Gestalt Review, 6(3),* 220–235.

Markman, H. J., Renick, M., Floyd, F., Stanley, S. & Clements, M. (1993). Preventing marital distress through communication and conflict management training: A four and five year follow-up. *Journal of Consulting and Clinical Psychology, 61,* 70–77.

Markman, H. J., Stanley, S. & Blumberg, S. L. (2001). *Fighting for your marriage: New and revised.* San Francisco: Jossey Bass, Inc.

Marsh & Dallos, M, R. (2001). Roman Catholic couples: Wrath and religion. *Family Process 40(3),* 343–360.

Meier, A. & Boivin, M. (2001). Conflict resolution: The interplay of affects, cognitions and needs in the resolution of intrapersonal conflicts. *Pastoral Sciences, 20(1),* 93–119.

Minuchin, S. (1974). *Families and family therapy.* Cambridge: Harvard University Press.

Morin, M. L. (2003). Fundamental values and systems approach. In A. Meier (Ed.), *In Search of Healing,* Ottawa: Society for Pastoral Counseling Research.

Morin, M. L. (2001). *Pour une écoute en profondeur: la Valeur fondamentale.* Montréal: Médiaspaul.

Propst, L. R. (1997). Therapeutic conflict resolution and the Holy Trinity. In Robert C. Roberts & Mark R. Talbot (Eds.), *Limning the psyche: Explorations in Christian psychology,* Cambridge: Grand Rapids.

Stanley, S. (1997). What's important in premarital counseling? *Marriage and Family,* 1, 51–60.

Stanley, S., Markman, H. J., St. Peters, M. & Leber, D. (1995). Strengthening marriages and preventing divorce: New directions in prevention research. *Family Relations, 44,* 392–401.

Tucker, N. L., Stith, S. M., Howell, L. W., & McCollum, E. E. (2000). Meta-dialogues in domestic violence-focused couples treatment. *Journal of Systemic Therapies, 19(4),* 56–72.

Saint-Arnaud, Y. (1988). [Psychosynthesis]. Unpublished raw data from Master's thesis seminars, Saint Paul University, Ottawa.

Taylor, C. (1989). *Sources of the self: The making of the modern identity.* Cambridge: Harvard University Press.

Yerby, J., Buerkel-Rothfuss, N. & Bochner, A.P. (1990). *Understanding family communication.* Scottsdale, AZ: Gorsuch Scarisbrick.

7

Crisis Support Team: a New Dimension of Caring and Support

Adèle Miles, Maria Cupples, Rose Robinson and Michelle Koyle

The Moment When Everything Changes

Imagine a warm summer evening. You have just finished supper and are relaxing on your deck when the phone rings. When you answer, an unfamiliar voice says: "Hello, my name is Maria Cupples. I am a registered nurse at the St. Thomas Elgin General Hospital (STEGH) Emergency Department. Your mother has just been brought to our department by ambulance. She had collapsed in her apartment. She is in critical condition. Please come as soon as possible." When you arrive, Maria introduces herself and the Crisis Support volunteer with her, and then takes you to our quiet room. She tells you she will return with the Emergency physician to update you on your mother's condition.

The Birth of the Crisis Support Team

In 1998 STEGH called together a focus group to look at how families were supported when they experienced the sudden death of a family member in our Emergency Department. The group recommended creating a team of specially trained volunteers dedicated to the support of families in crisis. A committee of emergency nurses, physicians, ambulance paramedics, police, fire personnel and our Pastoral Care specialist then met to develop a position description and selection criteria (Table 1) for a Crisis

Support Volunteer (CSV). Many meetings and several interviews later, eight CSVs had been chosen.

Table 1. Selection Criteria

Educational criteria	Other qualifications
– training or experience in palliative care, or equivalent	– able to carry a pager and know how to use it
– training in bereavement support, or equivalent	– able to respond in twenty minutes
– training in end of life care, or equivalent	– no close bereavement in the past eighteen months
	– able to attend two hour, monthly educational sessions
	– able to take call for 108 hrs a week: from Friday 7 p.m. to Monday 7 a.m. inclusive, and then from 7 p.m. to 7 a.m., Monday to Thursday nights. In addition, to cover twenty-four hours a day on all statutory holidays
	– references and a police records check

In the fall of 1999, the CSVs began intensive training. Topics covered included active listening skills, crisis intervention techniques, an introduction to grief and bereavement support and a thorough orientation to the Emergency Department. Finally, in December 1999, they were ready to begin their on-call rotation. They received their first call on Christmas Eve 1999.

In its first five years of service, this group of enthusiastic, energetic, compassionate and empathetic volunteers has grown to twelve people. In addition to ongoing education at the monthly meetings, many individual volunteers have taken further courses to develop their skills in crisis intervention and bereavement support. As a result, the team has accepted new challenges. Originally, the CSVs only responded to sudden deaths of adults over 21 years of age, providing a ministry of presence from the time the family arrived until they were ready to leave the hospital. Today, they also respond to infant, young child and adolescent deaths, and support families of critically ill patients in the Emergency Department when the outcome is uncertain.

Dealing with Conflict in the Face of Crisis

A significant role of the Crisis Support Team is dealing with conflict or the potential for conflict in the face of crisis. The families they meet are usually in shock and disarray. Finding themselves in our Emergency Department was not in their plans for the day. Their emotional responses, as they begin to move past numbness, are often fairly extreme, from deep sadness to fear, high anxiety and anger. Families feel out of control and their normal coping mechanisms frequently fail them. Added to this are the strengths and struggles inherent in family dynamics. Families that struggle to function and work together in normal circumstances often break down in the face of the crisis they experience in the Emergency room. The result can be open hostility and the potential for violence. Substance abuse, either pre-existing or as a poor coping strategy, can further compromise family members' ability to function. Other factors that contribute to the potential for conflict are the sudden need for role redefinition, and the stress of decision-making around treatment or the withdrawal of treatment.

The Stories

The following cases illustrate some of our experiences, and highlight the interventions that help successfully defuse highly charged situations in our context.

Mary's Story

Rose Robinson has been a member of the Crisis Support Team since 1999. She is employed at STEGH in the Rehab Department. She tells the story of a call she received. Mary, a woman in her early fifties, was on her way to the hospital by ambulance. Her heart was not beating and she was barely breathing. Her prognosis was not good.

Rose arrived at the hospital and met with Mary's husband and only child (a daughter), who were waiting for information on her condition. After being briefed by the nursing staff, Rose went to check on Mary in the Resuscitation Room. She was not doing well. Respiratory staff were ventilating Mary manually. Rose then joined Mary's family, informing them of what was happening with Mary, and describing to them what they might see. Together, they entered the Resuscitation Room to be with Mary. In a very short time, the physician gave the family an update on Mary's deteriorating condition. Did they know what Mary's wishes were around resuscitation?

Conflict arose around substitute decision-making. Mary and her husband had a very close relationship. They were near retirement and looking forward to spending that time of their lives together. Struggling with his feelings, the husband could not answer. He did not want Mary to die. Their daughter, who was approximately seven months into her first pregnancy, was also distraught. She had happily anticipated the arrival of her baby and sharing this special event with her mother. This was supposed to be a happy time.

Parent–child roles were reversed when the daughter spoke to her father about what her mother's wishes had been. Mary had been a nurse for many years. She had spoken many times about what she wanted in the event she might not be able to speak for herself. She had clearly articulated to her husband and daughter the decisions she would like made on her behalf. The daughter shared that her mother had stated, "I don't want to be bedridden and not know what is going on. Just let me go." She repeated many times, "You know that's what Mom would want, Dad." Rose reflected back the daughter's statements and was able to affirm her in honouring her mother's wishes.

In the end, the decision was made by both family members that medical intervention be stopped. The CSV reassured the husband and daughter that Mary could still hear them and encouraged them to take all the time they needed to say goodbye. The husband and daughter stayed with Mary while she took her last breath. The daughter turned to her father, saying, "We let her go, Dad. We did the right thing." The family stayed until they were ready to leave. Hugs and thanks were given by the family as they left the hospital.

The type of interventions used by the CSV include (a) listening to the daughter, (b) reflecting feelings, etc., (c) affirming the daughter's honouring of the patient's wishes, (d) being present with the family at withdrawal of treatment, and (e) facilitating goodbyes and assuring the family that the patient can hear them.

Sam's Story

Michelle Koyle joined the Crisis Support Team at STEGH in November 2002. She is a full-time caseworker at Ontario Works. Michelle was called to Emergency to accompany Sam's family. Sam was a 46-year-old man, found collapsed with no vital signs in his home, by his best friend and his fiancée.

When Michelle arrived at the hospital, Sam had already died. His fiancée, best friend and sister were present in the Resuscitation Room. Sam's son, Brad, had been called, and was on his way to the hospital with his wife. Michelle was briefed by the Emergency staff and a second CSV upon her arrival. Michelle supported Sam's sister, Betty, and his best friend, John. The other CSV supported Sam's fiancée, and later his son, Brad, and Brad's wife. Everyone present was in shock over the sudden death. Though Sam had recently been diagnosed with a serious illness, it was not life threatening.

Sam's sister, Betty, anxiously awaited the arrival of her nephew, Brad. While waiting she spoke of the family discord. Sam and his son were mending a relationship. Betty felt that her nephew's wife was the source of the conflict between Sam and Brad, describing Brad's wife as a dominant person who had alienated the family. When Brad arrived, Betty struggled with his wife's presence. It quickly became clear that separating both parties was essential.

Betty remained in the quiet room. She was distraught, as she spoke of her parents' deaths from natural causes. She and Sam were the only family left. She disclosed that her younger sibling was killed instantly in a motor vehicle accident as a child. She was the first to arrive at the scene and carried her brother's limp body back to the family home. As she talked, Betty was reorganizing her life as the last living family member.

Michelle provided Betty with information about community resources including the 24-hour Crisis Line and local bereavement counselling organizations. Michelle also explored coping strategies. Eliciting past coping mechanisms is critical in empowering the bereaved to move forward through the first few days following a death. Betty's way of coping was to keep busy – she was returning home to paint her kitchen, living room and bedroom.

Sam's best friend, John, was very quiet and Michelle respected his silence. Later, John requested that Michelle accompany him outside while he had a cigarette. John expressed guilt for leaving Sam at home and not encouraging him to seek medical help, repeating, "If only I made him come to the hospital." John and Sam had grown up together and maintained a close friendship. John described Sam as his only "true friend." Michelle allowed John to express his feelings. She validated his feelings of guilt as a normal response in these circumstances.

Sam's fiancée was overwhelmed with Sam's sudden death, bewildered by the fact she had been planning a wedding, and suddenly she found herself planning a funeral instead.

Sam's son, Brad, was struggling with the unsettled relationship he had had with his father. The CSV reinforced the positive steps they both had taken to re-establish their relationship.

Further conflict arose over the choice of a funeral home. While the ultimate decision was to be taken by Sam's son, Brad, Brad's wife immediately stepped in and took over the decision-making role. The conflict between Betty and Brad's wife intensified. Both the CSVs present intervened by helping to set appropriate boundaries around decision making, and supporting Brad in taking on his rightful role as substitute decision maker. Again, the CSVs had to separate both parties. Experience has taught us that two or more CSVs are essential when there is family discord. Separating the family was crucial in this case to allow both parties to grieve the sudden death and to support each person appropriately.

After the family left the hospital, the two CSVs debriefed each other before writing their report and going home.

In working with Sam's family the type of interventions used by the CSV include (a) calling in a second CSV, (b) separating family members in conflict, (c) listening to stories, (d) recovering and reinforcing coping mechanisms, (e) helping focus on the positive steps towards reconciliation, and (f) helping establish appropriate boundaries.

Evaluating Outcomes

The Crisis Support Team has had a significant impact on caring for families in crisis in our Emergency Department. While we have not done a formal survey of families who have received support from the Crisis Team, we have received unsolicited feedback which has affirmed the importance of the team and the difference they make for families.

What's more, the Team has had a significant impact on the Emergency Department staff. We recently surveyed all department personnel, distributing 69 surveys and receiving 34 responses (a remarkable 49% response rate). A copy of the survey can be found in Appendix A at the end of this chapter.

The Crisis Support Team received very high marks on their contribution to the care of families in crisis in Emergency in the following areas:

- emotional support of families
- providing a communication link between family and ER staff
- continuity of care
- impact on family satisfaction
- impact on stress of the Emergency Team

What was interesting to us is that the lowest scores were in the areas of defusing potential conflict between families and the Emergency Team, and defusing potential conflict between family members. While most respondents still gave the team high marks, there were some who felt the team contributed no benefit to this area. However, these same respondents offered the following unsolicited comments which we found very telling: (a) no situation has ever arisen, (b) haven't seen any yet, (c) I've never seen a problem, and (d) not usually any conflict.

These comments indicate to us that the Crisis Support Team is highly effective in the work they do to de-escalate and resolve conflict. They do their work so well that conflict does not spill out into the department, impacting other patients and staff. In their presence and their interventions, the Crisis Support Team is highly effective in facilitating the resolution of crises and moving families forward to cope with their situation.

Success Factors for the Use of Crisis Support Volunteers

After five years, the CSVs have reached a point where they have become a true team working, learning, questioning and supporting each other. They have become a central part of the care we offer families in our Emergency Department at STEGH. Some of the reasons for our success from the perspective of the CSVs and from the team's co-facilitators are listed in Tables 2 and 3 respectively.

Table 2. Success factors from the team's perspective

- we feel we are accepted by and are a part of the Emergency Staff
- our availability and quick response time frees up the Emergency Staff
- providing continuity of care to families in need and providing someone for them to bond with and confide in
- we diffuse conflicts and provide information to families, Emergency Staff and sometimes police
- the pastoral care we receive from Adèle keeps our minds continually learning and our hearts open
- the connection we have fostered with the Emergency Staff is greatly due to the hard work of Maria who encourages the team. She is highly respected by her peers and is the core compassion of the team
- the team brings compassion, accountability, respect and simplicity to grieving families, enabling them to reach their tomorrow

Table 3. Success factors from the co-facilitators' perspective

- careful selection of the team members has given us highly motivated individuals
- attention to orientation and ongoing training
- acceptance and respect of Emergency Staff
- monthly meetings where volunteers debrief on each case they attend
- mentoring of new volunteers by experienced volunteers
- peer support
- excellent retention – still have 50 per cent of original members
- recognition by the Hospital for volunteer hours
- have received awards of recognition for their role in the Emergency Department
- good needs assessment before setting up team
- support from facilitators and peers
- attention to team building
- assuring adequate team numbers to prevent burn-out – increased team from 8 members to 12 members
- strong liaison / anchor person from Emergency

Conclusion

In its sixth year of operation, the Crisis Support Team continues to provide invaluable service to families in crisis in the Emergency Department at STEGH. Their skillful and timely interventions prevent escalation of conflict and strengthen coping mechanisms in the people they accompany. As a result of the Crisis Team's work, STEGH Emergency Staff experience less stress and greater satisfaction in the care they provide to families and patients in the event of sudden death or critical illness. The Crisis Support Team model has proved to be an innovative and effective strategy in a community hospital context for providing support to families in crisis.

Acknowledgments

In addition to the authors listed, Crisis Support Volunteers Colleen Burns, Lynn Deneire, Joanne Dowswell, Katie Dowswell, Marilyn Hunter, Carolyn Mayo, June Newman and Vicki Ryckman all participated in the design and content development of this chapter. Their contribution and their support are greatly appreciated.

Appendix A – Survey of Emergency Department Staff

St. Thomas Elgin General Hospital
Survey of the Emergency Team on the Use of
Crisis Support Volunteers
April 2004

1. Are you aware of the role of the Crisis Support Volunteer in the Emergency Department?

   YES   NO

2. Do you know how to contact the Crisis Support Volunteer?

   YES   NO

3. Have you ever called in a Crisis Support Volunteer to provide support for a family in the event of a sudden death or for a critically ill patient in the Emergency Department?

   YES   NO

4. Please indicate your experience of the contribution made by the Crisis Support Volunteer to **the care of families in crisis** in Emergency by placing a checkmark on one of the lines between each pair of terms:

Helpful	___ ___ ___ ___ ___ ___ ___	Harmful
Compassionate	___ ___ ___ ___ ___ ___ ___	Insensitive
Pleasant	___ ___ ___ ___ ___ ___ ___	Annoying
Effective	___ ___ ___ ___ ___ ___ ___	Incompetent
Knowledgeable	___ ___ ___ ___ ___ ___ ___	Unskilled
Supportive	___ ___ ___ ___ ___ ___ ___	Inconsiderate

5. Please indicate your experience of the contribution made by the Crisis Support Volunteer to **the work of the Emergency Department Team** in caring for families in crisis by placing a checkmark on one of the lines between each pair of terms:

Helpful   ____ ____ ____ ____ ____ ____ ____   Harmful

Compassionate   ____ ____ ____ ____ ____ ____ ____   Insensitive

Pleasant   ____ ____ ____ ____ ____ ____ ____   Annoying

Effective   ____ ____ ____ ____ ____ ____ ____   Incompetent

Knowledgeable   ____ ____ ____ ____ ____ ____ ____   Unskilled

Supportive   ____ ____ ____ ____ ____ ____ ____   Inconsiderate

6. Please evaluate the role of the Crisis Support Volunteer in the following areas by circling the appropriate response:

   a) Emotional support of families

   Very Beneficial   Beneficial   No Benefit   Negative   Very Negative

   b) Communication link between family and Emergency Team

   Very Beneficial   Beneficial   No Benefit   Negative   Very Negative

   c) Continuity of care

   Very Beneficial   Beneficial   No Benefit   Negative   Very Negative

   d) Defusing potential conflict between family and Emergency Team

   Very Beneficial   Beneficial   No Benefit   Negative   Very Negative

   e) Defusing potential conflict between family members

   Very Beneficial   Beneficial   No Benefit   Negative   Very Negative

f) Impact on family satisfaction

Very Beneficial   Beneficial   No Benefit   Negative   Very Negative

g) Impact on stress of Emergency Team

Very Beneficial   Beneficial   No Benefit   Negative   Very Negative

7. How important to you is the work of the Crisis Support Volunteer in the Emergency Department? (circle one number)

Important   1   2   3   4   5   Not Important

8. What do you believe are the key success factors for the use of Crisis Support Volunteers in the Emergency Department?

9. What suggestions do you have for improving the work of the Crisis Support Team in the Emergency Department?

Thank you for taking the time to give us your feedback.

- *The Crisis Support Team*

8

Acknowledgment and Acceptance: Two Different Constructs in the Psychological Recovery Process after Brain Injury

Susan L. Tasker

While recognizing the variability across brain injury in terms of etiology and outcome, this chapter generalizes across all brain injury. More specifically, the focus of this chapter is on the *emotional and psychosocial adjustment* of people with brain injury as well as their families, and is addressed to all levels of audience: the person with brain injury, family members, clinicians, and to other professionals involved in the reassembly of lives ruptured through brain injury. There are four goals for this chapter. The first is to show the short-sightedness and growth-retarding or growth-defeating nature of the uncritical and premature acceptance of a life-changing event such as brain injury. The second goal is to frame brain injury as an *event* and not as an *outcome*. Third, in reaction to the first goal and building on the second, is to emphasize the critical role of conflict in psychological recovery from trauma. Alternatively stated, the third goal is to propose and impose, if you will, a moratorium on "acceptance" in the resolution (or grief?) process. To this end, the constructs of *acknowledgment* and *acceptance* will be distinguished. Fourth, a process-model of psychological recovery will be delineated that includes these notions of acknowledgment and acceptance and draws on Erikson's developmental theory of identity formation (1959, pp. 110–112) and Bowen's theory of differentiation of self within the context of the family system (1978, pp. 467–547). On balance, the purpose of this chapter is to suggest how the process of resolving intra- and interpersonal conflict consequent to brain injury mediates acknowledgment as the crucial and requisite antecedent of acceptance of brain injury as a major life event.

In the acute care setting, and to a large degree contingent upon the expertise and treatment decisions of the attending medical corpus, the body and the brain are treated and restored to the best state possible within the neuroanatomical and neurophysiological range of the insult's organic impact. However, it is in the "chronic living" of brain injury that the collateral costs of brain injury are experienced by survivors and their families and selectively visited by research and applied interests and service bodies. Although the physical and cognitive collateral costs to the survivor and his or her functioning are researched, described, documented, treated and discussed as front of mind concerns, psychosocial costs receive scant attention at best, and emotional costs are typically ignored and cast as symptoms of either the reluctance or failure to "accept."

But recent findings documented by the Canadian Ontario Neurotrauma Foundation (see Bassett-Spiers, 2003) cogently expose this imbalance. In consultation with consumers to define a research agenda with the express purpose of qualitatively and directly contributing to the day-to-day lives of persons with brain injury, eleven issues were identified as important for research and understanding. Of these, seven (i.e., 63.6%) concerned *emotional* and *psychosocial adjustment* issues: (a) the challenge of behaviour, (b) stress and depression, (c) health and aging, (d) maintaining family life, (e) self-acceptance, (f) social expectation and stigma, and (g) the challenge of relationships, isolation and integration. Interestingly, these findings corroborate the findings by a study conducted by myself (Tasker, 2003). Here, the study comprised the collection of narrative data over a seven-week period from five adult survivors of brain injury. Brain injuries ranged from moderate (GCS = 9–12) to severe (GCS < 8) as categorized according to the Glasgow Coma Scale, and the participants' mean age was

41.4 years (range, 28–53 years). Importantly, the mean time from date of injury to study participation was 7.2 years (range, 3.1–9.11 years), meaning that all five participants were considered to have passed the acute and initial stages of recovery from their brain injuries and were thus well into what I conceptualize as the "chronic living" of brain injury. A systematic analysis of content was conducted and the findings described the same psychology of the brain injury survivor as reflected by those of the seven emotional and psychosocial issues identified by consumers of brain injury as important for research and understanding as recently reported by the Ontario Neurotrauma Foundation.

If we frame brain injury as an *event* rather than as an *outcome*, and recovery as a *process* that begins with and from the time – or *event* – of the brain injury, then we begin to appreciate the temporal nature of brain injury. Using the metaphor of life as a performance, brain injury does not enter life's stage as a foreclosed outcome and brain injury does not exit lives through premature, rushed or passive "acceptance." My thesis is this: While the *event* of brain injury necessitates the acute-phase casting of *the brain injury* as stage-front soloist, the *process* of recovery merits no soloist performances and no imperative to "accept." Rather, the rage, resentment, confusion, frustration, fear and despair consequent to the lived-conflict between "life-before-brain-injury" and "life-after-brain-injury" need to be entertained, played out and tolerated. The unexplored and uncritically accepted state of life as "life-after-brain-injury" is a life-denying outcome and may well be the result of two things: (a) the confusing of *event* with *outcome,* and (b) the rushing and pushing of those whose lives have been altered by brain injury into an unexamined "accepting" and "getting on with life."

Rather, in order for both the person with the injury and his/her family to begin to reconsider life again – to look at life with clarity and perspective – two major landmarks need to be reached in the *process* linking the *event* of brain injury through conflict to the *realized outcome* of brain injury. While the *place of acceptance* is the place of departure for the resuming of life, seeking[1] must be allowed to precede "arrival" at the *place of acceptance*. All too often "acceptance" is hurried, pushed, or proffered as key to psychological recovery to the cost of emotional and psychosocial adjustment and well-being. What is forgotten, neglected, overridden or simply not considered, is the penultimate place of arrival in this process-model of psychological recovery: *the place of acknowledgment.*

Figure 1. A process-model of psychological recovery from brain injury.

The *event* of brain injury

Discharge from Acute-Care Setting	Major Landmark 1 **THE PLACE OF ACKNOWLEDGMENT**	Major Landmark 2 **THE PLACE OF ACCEPTANCE and *realized outcome***

Minor Landmark 1 **THE PLACE OF DEPENDENCE**	Minor Landmark 2 **THE PLACE OF CODEPENDENCE**	Minor Landmark 3 **THE PLACE OF INDEPENDENCE**

Pothole 1 **Alienation, Isolation, or Cut-off**	Pothole 2 **Alienation, Isolation, or Cut-off**	Pothole 3 **Enmeshment**

---

1   I am indebted to my colleague Rev. David McInnis for his suggesting that my questioning of uncritical acceptance is analogous to the notion of belief-without-first-seeking (in conversation, December 2003).

For expedience and accessibility across audience, the *process* of recovery will be broken down and described in terms of "landmarks" and "potholes." The process of recovery is facilitated and bridged by communication and, adopting a functional communication perspective, communication here includes behaviour. That is, behaviour is viewed as a form of functional communication or, in clinical terms, as a "red flag." To the degree then that behaviour is always purposeful and often communicative, it is important that behaviour is not shut down without first questioning the psychology driving the behaviour.[2]

The *event* of brain injury is experienced as a time of shock, disbelief, uncertainty and overwhelming numbness typically followed by the reign of confusion and questions. Following discharge from an acute-care setting, similar yet differently sourced states of shock, disbelief, bewilderment, numbness, confusion, uncertainty and questioning ensue. It is from this point of discharge from an acute-care setting that the psychological process of psychosocial and emotional adjustment to life with a brain injury really begins. The process-model articulated here describes the progression towards acceptance through conflict and acknowledgment. (Note: Acknowledgment and acceptance are characterized as the two "major landmarks" in this process-model of psychological recovery from brain injury.) Perhaps more indirect and subtle, however, are the "minor landmarks" visited along the way. Specifically, the minor landmarks of Dependence and Codependence are found between the outset (i.e., time of discharge) and The Place of Acknowledgment, and Codependence (again) and Independence between The Place of Acknowledgment and The Place of Acceptance. And, at any point and at any place along the way, survivors and their families can get stuck or stay at, and sometimes even return to, a previous place of being (or way of coping) in the process of psychosocial and emotional recovery from brain injury.

Let us now track the process – and difficult work – of reconsidering life with a brain injury beginning with discharge from an acute care setting. For the person with the injury and the family, questions will now proliferate, dominate and preoccupy at-

---

2   My thanks to Dr. Joel Hundert and Dr. Nicole Walton-Allen for introducing me to and for making me think about the communicative function of purposeful behaviour.

tention. Why? Where to now? Where will this end? How do we move forward? How do I move forward? What do we do with him (or her)? What am I going to do? What are we in for? What am I in for? How do we look at life again? How do I look at my life again? What about the future? Will I work again? How do we pick up and continue with our lives again? How do I continue in my life again? Will we ever get over this? Will I ever know myself as myself again?

The Place of Dependence is the first minor landmark typically and inevitably reached by persons with brain injury and their families. The Place of Dependence is typically a place and time of denial, disavowal, overload and/or repression of brain injury and its possible implications in terms of an altered life. It is also a place and time of hope against hope, hopefulness, hopelessness, or a wild ride of both capricious hope and hopelessness. The first pothole (see Figure 1, Pothole 1) emerges from the sense of hopelessness. When families or individual family members perceive their situation or the implications for the future as intolerable or unbearable, the experience of hopelessness may be associated with alienation and "cut-off" (Bowen, 1978, p. 535) from the survivor through distance taking, or, in the case of marriages, marital break-up through separation or divorce. Similarly, when survivors perceive their life situation as intolerable, unbearable or hopeless, they too are inclined toward isolation and cut-off from family, friends and life. Isolation and cut-off by the survivor is expressed through affective (mood) states of withdrawal and depression or in suicidal thoughts and actions.

The successful negotiation of dependency will move the survivor and family to the second minor landmark, The Place of Codependence, and a time of high reactivity. Most generally, a lot of "behaviour" as a result of anger, fear, depression and frustration is evidenced, and two potholes (see Figure 1, Pothole 2 and Pothole 3) are associated with this place of codependence. When this period of codependence in psychological recovery is not traversed because the attendant and variable challenges of behaviour and emotional conflict are shut down, shut up, minimized, disregarded, ignored or avoided, recovery is at risk for regression to alienation, isolation or cut-off, and with respect to the survivor, suicidal thoughts and actions (see Figure 1, Pothole 2). Pothole 3 is enmeshment or "emotional fusion" (Bowen, 1978, p. 494). In terms of the family, enmeshment is displayed through attitudes and actions of fixing, taking charge, taking over, telling, instructing, doing, "shoulding" and blaming; blaming the doctors, other people or perhaps even the person with the brain injury. Brain injury is seen as the persecutor and the person with the brain injury is typically spoken of in terms of the label, "Brain Injured." At the same time, however, and importantly, codependence for the family can be experienced as a time of hope against hope and hopefulness. For the person with the brain injury, states of high reactivity, anger, aggression, depression and withdrawal accompany the felt-loss of identity and autonomy, and the self is reduced to or thought of in terms of the label, "Brain Injured." Like the family, the enmeshed survivor casts brain injury in the role of persecutor and sees him or herself as both a biological and psychological victim of brain injury. Confused and vulnerable, the enmeshed survivor will uncritically assimilate hope/hopelessness from the opinions and beliefs of family members and involved medical professionals.

But, if communication is kept open and objective, and the challenges of behaviour and emotional conflict described above are tolerated, endured, understood and processed, the major landmark of acknowledgment can be reached. Acknowledgment means only this: the recognition or owning the truth of brain injury as an *event* but not as an *outcome*. The person with the brain injury recognizes brain injury as a *part* of his person and being ("I have a brain injury"), and the family member recognizes and unpacks brain injury as a *part of* the person who has the injury ("My child/sister/daughter/ husband has a brain injury"). In both cases, the person with a brain injury is *more than,* rather than *reduced to,* his or her brain injury. Acknowledgment ushers in a period of reality testing in the service of coming to know and understand *realized outcome.* Honest or genuine acceptance of brain injury as a new component of life-now is conditional upon knowing and understanding. But this is where the confusion of acceptance and acknowledgment as two mutually exclusive constructs is most evident. Most notably, we confuse acceptance and acknowledgment through our misuse and misunderstanding of the term *acceptance*. We bypass *acknowledgment* by hurrying and/or pushing *acceptance* as the "right thing," as something we "should do," or "have to do" so that we can "be strong" or "put up a good front" or so that we can "let go" and "get on with life." The question may be asked whether the purpose of the push or urgency to accept is really to smooth over the unbearable agony of brain injury and what it may or may not mean for the survivor and his or her family and their respective lives. However, accepting brain injury as an *outcome* at this early juncture in the recovery process as opposed to *merely* recognizing the truth of brain injury as an irretrievable, undeniable, historical *event* denies psychological independence to the person with the brain injury as well as to the family. Instead, three potential potholes exist: (a) a return to The Place of Codependence and Enmeshment, (b) a return to The Place of Codependence and Cut-off, and (c) getting stuck in The Place of Acknowledgment in the guise of Acceptance. What we think is "letting go" and "getting on" is really "putting away" and burying; but buried things permeate our well-being, become bothersome, and result in a sense of emptiness and reduced existence (Tasker, 2003) and/or find expression in behaviour. What then contributes to psychological independence? How is the trajectory from The Place of Acknowledgment toward the Place of Acceptance initiated and negotiated? The suggestion is this: through the explicit sanctioning of a moratorium or "time out" (Crain, 2004, p. 288) in acceptance. In more concrete terms, the suggestion is to facilitate and tolerate separation, struggle and reality testing.

The Place of Independence is the Arena for Separation, Struggle and Reality Testing

Families need to pick up some of the pieces of their lives – to resume work and social and physical interests and activities. The person with the brain injury needs to be given the implicit or explicit permission to ask and to wonder and to test (obviously within the bounds of reasonable regard for personal safety) the question: "Can I do what I could do?" Reality testing allows, introduces and will be associated with (more) failure, and yet some surprises, understanding, awareness, revelation, strain, stress, pain, despair and behaviour, too. Through reality testing, limitations, compensations and alternatives are identified. Permanent deficits and remaining difficulties are, for the first time, patent. Taken together, these experiences result in growth, change and surrender, the appreciation of *however*, the coming to know what is, and the understanding of *"yet-ness."* And together, these components, in my thinking, constitute the construct of *authentic acceptance* of brain injury as an event first and a realized outcome second.

Underlying the evolution of authentic acceptance then, is the enduring and tolerating of agonizing conflict. In arriving at The Place of (authentic) Acceptance we are free to leave and to move on with a sense of resolution. The Place of Acceptance is a time of knowing, a time of softening; a time of opening, and a time of remembering; it is a time of looking beyond and toward, and is our seed of transformation.

Conclusion

The focus of this chapter was on the resolution of intra- and interpersonal conflict consequent to brain injury. More expressly, this chapter was written with four goals in mind.

The first was to introduce the reader to the short-sightedness and growth-limiting nature of the premature imposition – indeed, acceptance – of acceptance before acknowledgment of and struggle with conflict. That is, the acceptance of brain injury prior to conscious struggle and, if you will, "conflict-completion." The second goal was to frame brain injury as an *event* and not as an *outcome,* and to distinguish between the constructs of acknowledgment and acceptance. The third goal was to react to the first goal and to build on the second by describing the critical role of conflict in psychological recovery from trauma and to call for a moratorium in the push for *acceptance* so that the momentum and fruitful functioning of necessary and life-defining conflict can run its course. Fourth, a process-model of psychological recovery was delineated that included these notions of acknowledgment and acceptance, and that draws loosely on Erikson's developmental theory of identity formation and Bowen's theory of "working toward individuation" (Bowen, 1978, p. 539) or differentiation of self within the context of the family system.

It has been my experience that conflict and struggle are associated with the acknowledgment of brain injury. Yet, conflict and struggle, endured and witnessed, enable authentic acceptance, the reconsidering of life and the eventuation of serenity.

Acknowledgment

To Headway, South Africa, and her people: thank you for giving me the opportunity to present this work in rough form to your Organization in September 2004. More so, thank you for enriching my thinking and for allowing me the joy of contributing to the deep experience of life.

References

Bassett-Spiers, K. (2003). Ontario Neurotrauma Foundation: Strategic update. *Ontario Brain Injury Review*, December 2003, 12–13.

Bowen, M. (1978). *Family therapy in clinical practice.* New York: Jason Aronson, Inc.

Crain, W. (2004). *Theories of development: Concepts and applications* (Fifth Edition). New Jersey: Pearson Prentice Hall.

Erikson, E. H. (1959). Identity and the life cycle. *Psychological Issues, 1*(1), 101–164.

Tasker, S. L. (2003). Acquired brain injury: Meaning-making out of lived trauma. *Illness, Crisis & Loss, 11(4),* 337–349.

9

Transgenderism: Part of a Greater Gender Continuum or Pathology?

Helma Seidl

Given that most people never question their gender, the above question leads to internal as well as external conflict. Generally, gender is a straightforward concept, imposed by biological differences and socially learned behaviours. However, for a small percentage of the population, gender causes uncertainty and dissonance. An individual's discomfort is increased through the socially dominant discourse of a mutually exclusive gender identity, which ultimately leads to a gender dichotomy and the non-acceptance of transgenderism. Yet, the biological reality is that in every context of life, nature created the material basis for diversity: sexual orientation and gender diversities. Bagemihl (1999) acknowledged that the aforementioned types of diversity are universally found in both humans and animals. Therefore, should we not consider these diversities as archetypal, rather than create a pathology that produces conflict in the transgender individual?

Social and Theoretical Considerations

Gender is addressed in the methodologies of many theoretical frameworks, which has produced many exciting results. It should, therefore, not come as a surprise that there is little agreement and no unified theory on the origin of transgenderism. Gagnon and Simon (1973) found that human gender should be understood as a biological structure rooted in evolutionary limitations that directly translates into social institutions and, ultimately, social norms.

Throughout history, social norms have been correlated with "normal/natural" and "abnormal/unnatural" behaviour, and have put constraints on individuals' gender identity development. The perspective of symbolic interactionism, post-modernism, and learning theory provides a unique methodology for studying individuals and groups and their interactions with each other. Throughout a lifetime, an individual experiences change as new meanings are established through interactions with people and groups. Each group adheres to its rules; however, these rules are dominated by the values and norms set by the society. Consequently, these meanings are socially derived products. These meanings are a result of our social contacts and, therefore, the social world clearly influences the individual and his or her concept of self-identity.

Society is formed by human group life and, in these groups, people conform to set social norms that society outlines for the individual. Fausto-Sterling (1985, 2000) explained that gender development is accomplished through interaction with others and is not merely an individually achieved identity. The purpose of interactions is to socialize individuals to follow the discourse and the material relations embedded in interpretations of the "culture/group" they belong to. Children learn their gender roles and expectations from family, peers and society. According to children's biological makeup (male or female), a socially constructed mould is created. When the individual does not conform to socially accepted norms, he or she is labelled as an outsider. Being labelled as an outsider creates stigma. Goffman (1963) explained that stigmatized people are individuals who cannot conform to standards set by society. The consequences of a socially constructed gender dichotomy on a transgender person can be seen on a social as well as an individual level. The gender dissonance and social exclusion leads, in many cases, to problems in daily life and social functioning. Non-participation in human productivity might lead to the requirement for social assistance. When the individual is working, he or she often cannot reach his or her potential, as creativity is restricted and valuable energy is redirected into dealing with external as well as internal gender dissonance.

The conflict experienced by the transgender population was not created, as some might think, in the last decade; the historical influence on the formation of gender self-identity has to be taken into consideration when working with this population.

Historical Considerations

In the last century, great changes led to social movements and greater understanding of diversity. Yet, transgenderism did not benefit from these changes; society still has many myths and misconceptions about this population.

Transgenderism is not a new phenomenon; it is well documented throughout history and can be traced back at least to 621 BCE. The first written suggestion of transgenderism is found in Deuteronomy, the last of the five books of the Pentateuch. The translation of the word *deuteronomy* is "second law"; this book clearly established the socially accepted norms and laws of the time. The book states that "A woman shall not wear a man's apparel, nor shall a man put on a woman's garment; for whoever does such things is abhorrent to the LORD your God" (Deut. 22:5). Transgenderism was and still is forbidden in both Christian and Jewish doctrine. Islam also rejects transgenderism. "The Hadith in Sunan Abu-Dawud, (Bk. 32, No. 4087) stated that: Narrated Abu Hurayrah: 'The Apostle of Allah cursed the man who dresses like a woman and the woman who dressed like a man'" (Yik Koon Teh, 2001). These texts confirm that transgenderism clearly existed and was looked upon as a problem by society; otherwise, there would have been no need to address this issue in the laws of this time. Deuteronomy and Hadith encompass laws regarding obedience, status, strict class and gender divisions and, especially, socially accepted and non-accepted behaviours. Transgenderism has not always been perceived as negative or pathological, nor have transgender individuals been considered deviant and social outlaws; in some cultures, transgender individuals had the respect of the community. One can find great examples in North and South American native cultures. This changed with colonialization; the laws changed significantly and the church and later the medical community became the authorities for establishing socially accepted norms of normal and abnormal behaviour. Throughout colonialization, prohibition and oppression were used as tools to control and amalgamate people into one common, socially accepted norm. During this time, much native history and many original languages were lost. In 1833, Denig, a European explorer, settled among the Crow Indians and "found that some of the most important and respected individuals were men and women who in American and European societies would be condemned, persecuted, jailed, even executed" (Roscoe, 1998, p. 1). Transgenderism was not uncommon and each tribe had its own term for transgender individuals. Some of these were terms for a third and fourth gender; however, *berdache* appears to be the term most recognized by anthropologists. Yet, do we really know that this term originated in native language, or was this term implemented by explorers, since it existed pre-colonization, in languages spoken in colonizing countries such as France, England and Spain, to name a few? The 1680 edition of the *Dictionnaire français* gives the definition of *berdache* as "a young man who is shamefully abused" (Williams, 1986, p. 9). *Berdache* was used in a negative context long before it appeared in native language. We have to ask: how much did the usage of a negative term influence the change from respecting and accepting transgender people to viewing them as deviants, including them in a medical model of abnormality and mental illness? This latter development, furthermore, led to the internal and external conflict transgender individuals experience on a daily basis. Religious doctrines were not the only vehicle through which difficulties in understanding and accepting transgenderism were expressed. Transgender people were either treated as non-existent or became the fixation of the medical community, sexologists, psychologists and social workers. The goal of the medical profession was to treat transgender people and find a cure. Transgenderism was categorized and classified, various types were identified, and instead of normalizing the issue, transgenderism was declared a deviance – a mental health problem – and pathologized.

Categorization and Classification

As previously stated, there were many historical explanations and rationalizations for the transgender phenomenon and not all of them were negative. Yet, with the inclusion of transgenderism into a medical model in the late 19th and early 20th centuries, the positive view decreased rapidly and medicine did its part to pathologize the issue.

Transgenderism is placed into various categories by medical and counselling professionals, as well as by the transgender community itself. To understand the differences among transgender groups, we must be at ease with these categories. Common themes are found throughout the life narratives of transgender individuals, yet, at the same time, we know that every experience is unique and, therefore, no two transgender individuals are the same. We have to accept individual differences and work with these differences to resolve the conflict an individual experiences. On one hand, categorical classifications are necessary to help therapists in the process of diagnosis. Classifications also help transgender people to decrease isolation, normalize their feelings and find social group belonging. On the other hand, we also have to be flexible; therapists, and transgender clients themselves, cannot fall into the trap of "If the shoe does not fit, force it." Research has shown that transgender people are very aware of the treatment criteria and some, in order to get the right diagnosis of "true transsexuals," have actually falsified their life stories (Denny and Roberts, 1997; Walworth, 1997; Lev, 2004).

The standards of care created by the Harry Benjamin International Gender Dysphoria Association have guided approvals for hormone and surgical treatment for the last 40 years (Benjamin, 1966). Wheeler (1995) investigated the archived papers of Benjamin's case notes for 1,500 patients and found that the patients' descriptions of their experiences did not change much over the 42 years from 1948 to 1990. The guidelines went through several revisions, but the changes were small and did not reflect the changes we find in the makeup of today's society. Even Benjamin noted in one of his writings that transgender people would falsify their life stories in order to get the "proper" diagnosis. The inflexible guidelines contained in the *Harry Benjamin International Gender Dysphoria Standards of Care* (HBIGDSC) as well as the one in the *Diagnostic and Statistical Manual of Mental Disorders* (DSM 4 TR) do not allow therapists enough flexibility in the area of diagnosis and treatment, which might be one of the reasons why transgender clients falsify their life stories.

Many classifications have been developed and the majority of them are based on the medical model that views transgenderism as a pathology that, when possible, has to be treated and cured. Transgender people have been classified as "inverts," which was actually an early name for homosexuality (McKenzie, 1994); as having "metamorphosis sexualis paranoica," in which the individual experienced a severe mental illness (Krafft-Ebing, 1912); or as "autogynephilics" – individuals aroused by the thought or image of themselves as women (Blanchard, 1985, 1989, 1990, 1991). The pathologization is continuing in the work of Bailey (2003), who defends Blanchard's hypothesis of "autogynephilia." Some facts in this research might be right, and some people might fall into the categories identified by Blanchard and Bailey, but definitely not all. Being right with a diagnosis that pertains to a small group does not justify the pathologization of all transgender individuals. It is noteworthy that in earlier research transgender people were not asked to classify themselves, and even Blanchard admitted that he only asked in one of his extensive studies for "self-classification" from each individual (Lev, 2004); for all of the other studies, he classified according to the medical model, which was guided by the socially accepted standards of the time. The fact that the medical principles were always strongly influenced by the socially accepted standards of the time is clearly evident in the creation of a division between hermaphrodites. In the late 1830s, a physician named James Young Simpson classified hermaphrodites as either "true" or "spurious" (Faust-Sterling, 2000, p. 37). In 1896, the British physicians Blackler and Lawrence set new standards for the identification of hermaphrodites. When examining true hermaphrodites, they found that, out of 28 cases previously identified as true hermaphrodites, only 3 met the standards of the new classification, which left 25 as pseudo hermaphrodites (Faust-Sterling, 2000, p. 39).

As it was in the 19th century, diversities are classified today as pathologies or mental illness; however, as social change takes place, reclassifications come about. Homosexuality is an example of such reclassifications: it has gone from being classified as an abnormality and a mental health issue to being taken out of the DSM and normalized as part of the greater continuum of sexual diversity.

Under the current medical guidelines, transgenderism is still pathologized and the medical community proclaims that the only validity for the diagnosis of "gender identity disorder" is the strict criteria outlined in the DSM and the HBIGDSC. Again, the individual's knowledge of "self" is ignored.

Non-medical classifications that do not pathologize transgenderism take into account the needs of the various groups under the transgender umbrella. Bollin (1988) refuted some medical assumptions and identified that not all transgender people were effeminate in their childhood or exclusively gay. Others, such as Wilchins (2002), Boswell (1998), Feinberg (1998) and Namaste (2000), went even further away from the common clinical classifications to demand trans-liberation, greater inclusiveness, acceptance of diversity and political activism.

Several new group identifications have emerged since then: gender-blending (Devor, 1989) is one of them, others are gender-benders, bi-gender and gender-variant people, to name only a few new categories that opt for greater inclusiveness and call for greater flexibility and changes in clinical guidelines for diagnosis and treatment. Definitions are continuously changing and the following classifications address only some of the categories under the transgender umbrella.

Definitions

Transgender individuals experience varying degrees of "gender incongruence." In some people, the social conflict with their gender is greater than their internal conflict, while others experience social conflict as well as severe internal dissonance. The former group needs gender fluidity, whereas a gender binary structure is important for the latter group. The degrees of incongruence lead to the various categories of transgender expression. The reality is that there is an increasing number of groups that do not want to be labelled according to the socially constructed gender norms and expectations, and therapists need to listen to their clients and accept their decisions. The following definitions are suggested guiding principles for transgender identification.

Transgendered

The expression "transgendered" is given to people who know themselves and live full time in the gender opposite to the one assigned to them on the basis of their anatomy. They are individuals who have decided to live the life of the opposite sex without sex reconstruction surgery (SRS). Some might select hormone replacement therapy (HRT) to "pass" and be credible as either a female or a male in society.

Transsexual

For transsexuals, their physical body is in direct conflict with their internal, cognitive knowledge of their true gender. In most cases, they have an intense hatred of their physical sex, which creates a gender identity disorder or gender dysphoria. These individuals desire modification of their physical body through HRT and SRS to match their gender identity.

Cross-dresser/Cross-gender

Cross-genders are people who for emotional and psychological reasons, wear the clothing, and perhaps the makeup, assigned by society to the opposite sex. Cross-genders experience transgender feelings; however, they maintain their gender identity in accordance to their physical sex and they do not have the need to change their gender through HRT and SRS. The cross-gender is able to accept both genders and would be able to live a successful and satisfied life if he or she gained acceptance. It is a healthy form of self-expression and there is a clear difference between the cross-gender and the transvestite.

The gender identity of transvestites corresponds to their anatomical sex, but they dress in the clothes assigned by society to the opposite sex for erotic pleasure. Transvestites, like cross-genders, do not desire SRS or HRT. Many reject the term *transvestite*, since it evokes the concept of a psychological pathology, sexual fetishism and obsession. As long as transvestite do not harm themselves or others, this form of achieving erotic pleasure should be considered only another form of expressing diversity.

Clinical Considerations

The nature/nurture debate is still strong in research seeking to prove the cause of transgenderism. Essentialist theories argue that identity is inherent within human beings, as is suggested by the statement "I was born gay." For transgenderism, some proof of this is provided in the research of Zhou, Hofman, Gooren & Swaaab (1995, 1997), La Vay (1993) and Leo (1987), which supported the hypothesis that gender identity develops as a result of the interaction between the developing brain and sex hormones. This might support the transgender person's notion that he or she was "born in the wrong body." It is undeniable that biology sets the blueprint for the development of the physical sex organs (Jones, 2002). But the extent to which biological development influences gender expression is not known.

Social constructionists (Gergen, 2000) argue that gender identity is a social construct; it is characterized and experienced differently depending on the historical and social disposition of the time, which, as previously stated, has a crucial impact on the medical point of view and the description of transgenderism as a pathology. The social forces over time changed gender into a mutually exclusive binary system, not only excluding transgendered as a normal attribute of the gender continuum but also shifting transgendered into a pathological illness affecting "only" a small number of individuals. Transgenderism is misconstrued, and clearly transgender individuals are ostracized by society in general, as well as by health care professionals. The dominant discourse on gender might be one factor affecting transgender individuals, but this discourse also affects health-care professionals. We cannot ignore the fact that transgenderism remains controversial and this might be one of the reasons why it is either ignored in health-care professionals' education or only thought of in the context of pathology and mental illness. Yet, transgenderism is part of a universal gender continuum; it is real for some individuals, and as health-care professionals we have to get over our own transphobia. We have to be responsible and get educated so we can help members of this population overcome their internalized conflict, as well as the externalized conflict created by social non-acceptance of transgenderism. Currently, there is a new wave of being politically correct, which translates into being able to accept and work with all diversities. This is definitely an admirable notion, but how can we help people if we do not understand their, and our own, conflict about accepting transgenderism as part of a normal gender continuum and not as a pathology?

It is of the utmost importance that during our assessment we listen carefully to clients' "self-classification" and take the time to learn about the reality of their psycho-social environment. When working with transgender individuals, a client-centred approach is vital. This allows clients to obtain the therapeutic and psycho-educational services they need. Transgender individuals come from all walks of life and present with a range of issues. It is necessary, however, to point out that not all transgender people possess psychological problems; some might only need guidance to make well-informed decisions and to guide them through the developmental stages of "identity re-formation" (Seidl, 2000).

Based upon my experience, I have identified the following groups among transgender individuals who embark on therapy for the first time. (a) The individuals who know something is not right: they do not fit in and feel socially inept, and yet they do not know or identify with transgenderism. Members of this first group need help to self-identify and to work through internal conflicts of shame, identity confusion and guilt. (b) The individuals who clearly know who they are and that they are transgendered. People in this group usually want to deal with external conflict caused by the social non-acceptance of transgenderism (macro level) and, sometimes, non-acceptance by their family and friends (micro level). (c) The individuals who have self-diagnosed, often with the help of the Internet or through transgender groups in their community; they speak the jargon and tell the therapist what they think the therapist wants to hear, yet they will change their self-label according to group belonging. The constant changes do not indicate that these people are not transgendered; rather, it is an indication of the severity of the internal conflict they experience. (d) The individuals who know they are different but do not want or need a label; however, they want to express their gender diversity and, with the help of the therapist, reach self-acceptance and find meaning in their life. Generally, members of this group deal more with internalized conflict of self-acceptance, even though they usually will tell you that they have no problem; instead, it is society that has a problem. (e) The individuals who have gone through the mill of the mental health system, experience a lot of anger, and see the therapist as the enemy, the gatekeeper who they need to convince to get their letter (for HRT and/or SRS). Individuals in this group are often the most challenging; they often tell a story to satisfy the requirements and not their needs. (f) The final group is the fetishist transvestites, who do not experience gender incongruence but look for diagnosis to get acknowledgment and justification of their behaviour. But the diagnosis of transgendered also will facilitate the person's entrance into the transgender community, which brings much sought after acceptance. In my experience, the latter group (f) mostly comprises males.

Some transgender clients arrive with internalized transphobia as well as externalized transphobia produced through the socially created discourse of a mutually exclusive gender binary and the learned social assumptions of masculine and feminine gender roles and expectations. The socially imposed gender norms and expectations need to be deconstructed before the true gender identity can be constructed (self-identity re-formation). Each client group has to go through various stages, and doing so is a unique process for each individual (see the sections below, on individual therapy). Couple and family therapy is often another important step in the coming-out process of the individual. Of course, there are some transgender individuals who show signs of mental health disorders that began prior to or concurrently with the gender identity issue they present. The disorders have to be acknowledged and treated. In my experience, with acknowledgment of the gender issue, most other disorders can be addressed and treated concomitantly. Some transgender individuals have been treated for mental health issues but the gender issue was never addressed, and their need for HRT or SRS was ignored or outright refused, as evidenced by the following case.

> Since I can remember, I knew that I was born in the wrong body. I tried very hard to conform and accept my biological sex. I suffered with depression. Then in my early adulthood, I was ready to talk about my gender identity. I found a therapist associated with a hospital. It was not easy to make the first step and seek out therapy, but after reaching this decision I promised myself to be open with him, since I was sure about my transgenderism, and what I wanted and needed was HRT and SRS. I was assessed and at this point he suggested the best way to help me would be by dealing with my depression. Regarding my gender identity, he felt that I was only confused and we never talked about it again. After several months of daily therapy I felt exposed, vulnerable, depressed and swore to myself I would try to live my life according to my biological sex and never seek out help again. But ten years later, I could not ignore my true self any longer. I had only two choices: seek out help or ...

Many transgender people talk about the negative experiences they had with therapists. One of the reasons for these experiences might be that therapists do not receive adequate training on transgenderism or, the information they received was outdated and classified transgenderism as a mental illness. Another reason might be transphobia. Transgender individuals clearly experience various degrees of gender incongruence, which further explains the range of levels of conflict they live with and their need for gender fluidity or gender-reassignment. They need clinicians who look at the larger picture. What comes first, the chicken or the egg? Mental health issue or gender issue? We might never know the answers to these questions, but we should always put the well-being of the client first and, therefore, help the transgender individual cope during a difficult transitioning process, which in some cases might be combined with mental health issues. "It is possible that an individual with a history of depression or psychiatric hospitalization would continue to experience these problems postoperatively, but still be considered better off after reassignment" (Carroll, 1999, p. 133).

Another problem that is not uncommon in this population is alcohol and drug abuse. Valentine (1998) found that 27 per cent of those seeking therapy reported abusing alcohol and 23 per cent testified to having problems with drug abuse. Other commonly reported issues are increased risk for suicidal thoughts, depression, anxiety or panic disorder – issues that often lead to low self-esteem, unemployment and other conditions that clearly affect the quality of life of transgender individuals. Many of these intrapsychic problems are illustrated in case studies (Cohen, 1991; Burgess, 1999; Denny, 1995; Ettner, 1999; Feinberg, 1996, 1998). In a recent study, I found that feeling that one belongs to a group is not enough to overcome the internal and external conflict transgender individuals experience before they are able to find their true self; transgender individuals have to get professional help or they will continue to suffer from isolation, suicidal thoughts and depression. The study demonstrated that 73.3 per cent of the trangendered group under investigation experienced isolation even though they belonged to a transgendered support group, 67.7 per cent suffered from suicidal thoughts, and 58.1 per cent indicated living with depression (Seidl, 2003).

Lev (2004) says that everyone has the right to their own gender expression, to make informed decisions about their body and gender expression, and to access medical, therapeutic and technological services and information in order to gain knowledge to help them make the necessary decisions about their body and life. Yet, the reality is that not everybody has access to these resources and, most of all, only a small percentage of professionals have experience or interest in the area of transgenderism. Transgender people's experience of external conflicts can be candidly or clandestinely expressed. We hear about the difficulties of finding a doctor, being refused treatment by the medical profession in hospitals, being fired from a job, being denied housing, including parents or partners telling them to leave immediately, which results in them being homeless, refused service in a grocery store, ridiculed, harassed, threatened and sometimes even killed for being transgendered. These narratives are not exceptions or tales from the past; these stories are actual and current. This reality is the cause of the internalized conflict the transgender individual experiences, as well as the fear, shame, guilt, devastation, isolation, depression, anxiety and panic – to name only a few. Other issues might include financial difficulties and social isolation. According to the transgender community in Ottawa and environs, 77.4 per cent of therapists and health-care professionals have no or minimal experience or knowledge of transgenderism (Seidl, 2003). In working with transgender individuals, it is imperative to help them make well-informed decisions, but also to let them know that transgenderism should be identified as a normative component of human diversity.

Individual Therapy

As previously mentioned, clients seek treatment for many reasons, which must be recognized in the therapeutic process. In my experience, an eclectic therapy approach is the best way to deal with the wide variety of issues brought forth. Psychotherapy is beneficial for clients dealing with transgenderism, transsexualism or gender expression. It helps individuals examine their options and make well-informed decisions. Gender identity is not all about HRT and SRS. Primarily, it is about the internal process and identity re-formation during the transitioning process. It is not about becoming another persona; the individual allows parts of himself or herself to come out and be present as the primary self. The life the individual lives before transitioning is a make-believe world that may well be compared to theatre: "I'm wearing a mask." "Nothing is true about myself." "I don't feel real." or "I'm not real." During transition, individuals learn to be themselves, which is known as self-actualization. Transition also addresses isolation, feelings of shame (Anderson, 1998; Goffman, 1963), guilt, trauma, and, when present, current comorbid disorders.

During the transitioning process, the individual goes through the developmental stages of childhood, adolescence, adulthood and middle age. During these times, developmental stage and chronological age are not in sync, which often causes internal as well as external conflict. The external conflict can be experienced at work or home and in social situations, whereas the internal conflict is experienced in terms of the needs, wants, learned behaviour and social pressure perceived by the individual or the social pressure actually experienced on a daily basis. During this time, the individual might think he or she is doing a great job at work, and yet his or her supervisor has constant complaints. However, the individual's interest is often not at work; he or she is so self-absorbed (part of "adolescent behaviour") that it is not possible to perform to potential. Childlike behaviours are also seen; individuals want their "candy" and they want it now. Since they have had to hide their true self, they often become narcissistic, demanding and manipulative, which in turn creates conflict. In social situations, at family gatherings, with their spouses or partners, employers and co-workers they act inappropriately and demand acceptance, as if to say, "I am transgendered, in your face, and if you don't like it, deal with it." Feelings of having missed out during primary development lead to wanting to experience certain aspects of being an adolescent. This is often expressed in clothing, makeup, a desire for dating and other typical adolescent behaviours. Steiner (1990) reported that a therapist has to be prepared to see some of his or her clients "looking somewhat bizarre, either flamboyantly or inappropriately dressed, or looking like a man in 'drag'" (p. 96). Female-to-males pass more easily, so the issue of inappropriate dressing is not as prevalent as with male-to-females. The former get away with androgynous dressing, but the latter may go overboard, buying clothing or arrive in the office for their morning appointment in an evening dress, or in a miniskirt and a light short jacket on a cold winter day. Therapists cannot be judgmental; we have to be understanding and honest and help our clients, since these are all normal stages of identity development that individuals have to go through. During this time, they need role models and guidance, as does any child growing up, to learn to make sound judgments about themselves and their behaviour. Hormone therapy may lead to depression and aggression. Clients may also try to get hormones from friends or via the Internet. Female-to-males may experience early menopause, while all transgender individuals on hormones have puberty issues. All of these things might lead to many challenges for both the client and the clinician.

Furthermore, the internal conflict often comes from guilt, shame and psychosocial traumas, and often leads to fluctuations between emotions of depression, sadness, hostility, self-hatred, resignation and acceptance. Individuals' self-acceptance has an enormous impact on the creation or resolution of the internal as well as the external conflict, affecting their relationship with their families, work and society in general, and having a great influence on the stages of self-actualization and identity reformation. Transgender individuals need to be able to make mistakes from which they can learn, as every growing child does.

Transgender individuals guide the therapeutic process; they decide where and how far they need to go in their transitioning process. The therapist helps them to self-identify, to make informed decisions and to overcome the internal and external conflicts they experience. As a result, the therapist needs to meet transgender individuals where they are, inquire about their conflicts and ask them what they think they need to overcome these difficulties. Giving them the choice and control empowers them, helps them to take control of their own life, and changes and deconstructs socially constructed thinking patterns and self-destructive behaviours. Being themselves allows these individuals to grow and develop their self-identity. Furthermore, in the process of therapy we need to reframe the discussion of transgenderism away from pathology to a natural aspect of human diversity – along a continuum instead of as a binary. This will help transgender individuals to gain not only self-acceptance but also social acceptance and, in many cases, allow them to draw on their creativity and potential.

Group Therapy for Transgender Individuals

Group meetings arranged by transgender organizations are often the first and only connection for a transgender person to other transgender individuals. These groups are discussion and peer support groups only and, therefore, have no therapeutic aspect to them.

According to research, 80.6 per cent of those attending support groups reported that they still suffer from isolation, suicidal thoughts and depression (Seidl 2003). This high number might be an indication that peer support groups alone are not enough. For this particular population, group work might only be helpful when combined with individual therapy. Groups help with belonging but, too often, groups also bring peer pressures that force the transgender individual to conform to the group's gender expectations and stereotyping. How individuals perceive themselves, the roles they play and the expectations about those roles to which they conform are all influenced by what they learn through their interaction with others. During certain stages in the transitioning process the individual is especially vulnerable to conform to peer pressure. This vulnerability is encountered during the initial stage of coming out and finding a place on the gender continuum, and again in the later stage of self-actualization; therefore, individual therapy during this time is essential. However, individual therapy is not always available or affordable, so group therapy facilitated or co-facilitated by a therapist would be a good choice. Groups often provide their members with great information about resources and advocacy. Yet, inappropriately facilitated groups can have many negative effects on their members; transference and counter-transference are only two examples. When the transgender individual facilitating a discussion or peer support group has not worked through his or her own problems, he or she might project unresolved feelings onto group members – counter-transference. In transference the group members project their issues/feelings onto the group facilitator. A vicious cycle that spins out of control might result. Group facilitators need to be accountable for their actions, being aware that the group is for the group members and not for their own healing; they need to reflect and assess their own strengths and weaknesses before taking on the responsibility of being a group facilitator. Only then can groups be an effective tool for the transgender individual. Naming the group according to its function – discussion group, peer support group, social group, psycho-educational, or therapeutic group – and openly identifying the facilitator's credentials will help transgender individuals make an informed decision about what they can expect from a group.

With therapeutic groups, group members need to be encouraged to challenge the various conflicts (shame, guilt, transphobia) one by one. To help group members stay focused on working towards their goal(s), a contract is established and clarifications, redefining and renegotiating of their goals are done on an ongoing basis, always keeping their needs and wants in mind. Monitoring and evaluating group members' progress are important in order to help them resolve the conflicts they experience.

Couple and Family Therapy

Spouses, partners and families of transgender individuals are often ignored. There is very little literature on treatment and support for the families of transgender people. The existing literature often tells the spouse or partner to abandon the transgender individual, since staying with him or her might cause harm to the partner or the couple's children. According to Clemmensen (1990), "the marriage must be dissolved" (p. 130), since it is unavoidable that the relationship will end. The families' feelings are totally ignored and, therefore, the possibility of saving the relationship is not even taken into consideration. Appropriate support and psycho-education might help the transgender individual as well as his or her spouse or partner and family.

During the transitioning process, the transgender individual is very self-absorbed and often ignores the feelings of loved one(s). Also, therapists often do not discuss the consequences for and feelings of the family. Spouses or partners often feel betrayed, angry and confused, and ask themselves, "Who am I?" "What do others think about me?" "Why did I not see this?" Yet they also ask, "Can I change?" "Can we stay together?" "What does it mean for me and my family?" They are angry with the therapist(s), since the transgender individual is receiving all the attention while the family is left out. Other relationship issues might emerge, and blame and guilt are often used to cover the hurt. Spouses or partners may question their own sexuality. Spouses or partners of male-to-females are often viewed as lesbians; in the case of female-to-males, partners in previously same-sex relationships might now be considered straight. As a result, they might also lose the support of their friends, since the couple would no longer fit into their circle of friends or community. When a partner is a lesbian and has issues with males resulting from previous trauma, the internal conflict for the partner might be too severe and staying in the relationship might be impossible. Yet, in many cases, sexual orientation is often no hindrance in deciding to continue a relationship.

The survival of transgender relationships depends on several factors. Spouses or partners need to be given equal time to talk and to express their feelings and concerns. Time needs to be given for them to understand the process, to learn about transgenderism, to mourn the loss of their spouse or partner, father or mother, or child, as they perceived them, and to understand that many of the characteristics they love will not be the same after transitioning. Time also has to be allocated to explore who they are regarding sexual orientation, when they decide to continue in the relationship, or simply to figure out terms for the new relationship they will have. Also, the therapist has to help them to embrace transgenderism as normal and to say that it is okay for them to find their transgender spouse or partner sexually appealing. Most couples and families struggle with transgenderism, especially the dissonance during the transitioning process, but, when they accept it the transitioning process becomes much easier for the transgender individual and it also signals that the survival and strengthening of relationships is possible. With therapy, education and a lot of understanding, couples and families can overcome the conflicts transgenderism can create in a relationship or family; in the end, if understanding is achieved, relationships can survive. I believe Henry Van Dyke said it best: "Happiness is inward and not outward; and so it does not depend on what we have, but on what we are" (in Rudd, 2000, p. 65).

Group Therapy for the Partner and Family of the Transgender Individual

Group therapy for a transgender individual's loved ones is almost non-existent. As previously stated, the partner and family of the transgender individual experiences different conflicts, some of which can and should be addressed in individual therapy. Other conflicts can best be addressed in group therapy, since this is a safe and understanding environment to resolve issues such as isolation, feeling like an outsider, and expressing both anger and love for the transgender person. The spouse or partner or family member meets others and has the opportunity to talk, express concerns, build friendships and get the social and psycho-education they need. When the group therapy is facilitated by a therapist, they also get therapeutic support.

The resolution of the internal as well as the external conflict is vital for healthy transgender identity development. Transgender individuals and their partner or family can achieve personal growth and move forward only if they are equipped with the proper information, the tools to solve their conflicts and the right to make their own decisions.

Conclusion

Transgendered is not a new issue; however, the non-pathologicalization of transgendered is a new paradigm. Understanding the issue and normalizing it will, with hope, lead to including transgenderism in the larger gender continuum, leading toward internal as well as external conflict resolution and toward inclusion instead of exclusion of this population. To achieve change, we need to educate society as well as the medical community, psychologists, pastoral counsellors and social workers. Only then can we guarantee the resolution of conflict and give appropriate support and services to the transgender community.

Further research is needed to investigate the influence that the socially constructed gender binary has on the creation of internal conflict and the restriction of healthy transgender self-identity development. Further research will also be needed to determine whether a non-pathological therapy, which views transgenderism in a positive way and as part of a larger gender continuum, can influence or reverse the effects that the socially created conflicts have had on healthy transgender self-identity development

References

American Psychiatry Association (2000). *Diagnostic and Statistical Manual. (4th ed. TR).* Washington, DC: American Psychiatric Association Press.

Anderson, B. (1998). Therapeutic issues in working with transgender clients. In D. Dallas (ed.), *Current concepts in transgender identity* (pp. 215–226). New York: Garland.

Bagemihl, B. (1999). *Biological exuberance.* New York: St. Martin's Press.

Bailey, J.M. (2003). *The man who would be queen: The science of gender-bending and transsexualism.* Washington, DC: Joseph Henry Press.

Benjamin, H. (1966). *The transsexual phenomenon.* New York: The Julian Press.

Blanchard, R. (1985). Research methods for the typological study of gender disorders in males. In B.W. Steiner (ed.), *Gender dysphoria: Development, research, management* (pp. 227–257). New York: Plenum.

Blanchard, R. (1989). The concept of autogynephilia and the typology of male gender dysphorias. *Archives of Sexual Behavior, 18,* pp. 315–334.

Blanchard, R. (1990). Gender identity disorder in men. In R. Blanchard and B.W. Steiner (eds.), *Clinical management of gender identity disorders in children and adults* (pp. 49–76). Washington, DC: American Psychiatric Association Press.

Blanchard, R. (1991). Clinical observation and systematic studies of autogynephilia. *Journal of Sex and Marital Therapy, 17(4),* pp. 235251.

Bollin, A. (1988). *In search of Eve: Transsexual rites of passage.* New York: Bergin & Gravey.

Boswell, H. (1998). The transgender paradigm shift toward free expression. In D. Denny (ed.), *Current concepts in transgender identity* (pp. 55–56). New York: Garland.

Burgess, C. (1999). Internal and external stress factors associated with the identity Development of transgender youth. In G.P. Mallone (ed.), *Social services with transgender youth* (pp. 35–48). Binghamton, NY: The Haworth Press.

Carroll, R. (1999). Outcomes of treatment for gender dysphoria. *Journal of Sex Education and Therapy, 24,* 128–136.

Clemmensen, L.H. (1990). The "real-life" for surgical candidates. In R. Blanchard and B.W. Steiner (eds.), *Clinical management of gender identity disorders in children and adults* (pp. 121–135). Washington, DC: American Psychiatric Association Press.

Cohen, Y. (1991). Gender identity conflicts in adolescents as motivation for suicide. *Adolescence, 26(101),* pp. 1929.

Denny, D. (1995). The paradigm shift is here! *Current concepts in transgender identity: Towards a new synthesis,* New York: Garland Press.

Denny, D. & Roberts, J. (1997). Results on a questionnaire on the standards of care of the Harry Benjamin International Dysphoria Association. In B. Bullough, V.L. Bullough, and J. Elias (eds). *Gender blending* (pp. 320–336). Amherst, NY: Prometheus Books.

Devor, H. (1989). *Gender blending: Confronting the limits of duality.* Bloomington, IN: Indiana University Press.

Ettner, R. (1999). *Gender loving care: A guide for counseling gender-variant clients.* New York: W.W. Norton & Company.

Fausto-Sterling, A. (1985). *Myths of gender.* New York: Basic Books.

Fausto-Sterling, A. (2000). *Sexing the body: Gender politics and the construction of sexuality.* New York: Basic Books.

Feinberg, L. (1996). *Transgender warriors: Making history from Joan of Arc to Dennis Rodman.* Boston: Beacon Press.

Feinberg, L. (1998). *Trans liberation: beyond pink or blue.* Boston: Beacon Press.

Gagnon, J.H. & Simon, W. (1973). *Sexual contact: The social source of human sexuality.* Chicago: Aldine.

Gergen, K.J. (2000). *An invitation to social construction.* Thousand Oaks, CA: Sage.

Goffman, E. (1963). *Stigma: Notes on the management of spoiled identity.* New York: Touchstone.

Jones, S. (2002). *Y: The descent of men.* London: Little, Brown and Company.

Krafft-Ebing, R. V. (1912). *Psychopathia Sexualis.* 14. Alfred Fuchs Stuttgart: Ferdinand Enke.

La Vay, S. (1993). *The sexual brain.* Cambridge, MA: Massachusetts Institute of Technology.

Leo, J. (1987). Exploring the traits of twins: A new study shows that the key characteristics may be inherited. *Time 129.* p. 63.

Lev, A.I. (2004). *Transgender emergence: Therapeutic guidelines for working with gender-variant people and their families.* Binghamton, NY: The Haworth Clinical Practice Press.

McKenzie, G. O. (1994). *Transgender Nation.* Bowling Green, OH: Bowling Green State University Popular Press.

Namaste, V. K. (2000). *Invisible Lives: The Erasure of Transsexual and Transgender People.* Chicago: The University of Chicago Press.

Roscoe, W. (1998). *Changing Ones: Third and Fourth Gender in Native North America.* New York: St. Martin's Press.

Rudd, P. J. (2000). *Crossdressers: And those who share their lives.* Katy, Texas: PM Publishers Inc.

Seidl, H. (2000). *Post-Traumatic Stress Disorder Associated with Transgenderism and "Self-Identity" Re-Formation.* Unpublished master's thesis, McGill University, Montréal, Quebec.

Seidl, H. (2003). *Counsellor/Therapist Educational Knowledge and Qualification Survey.* Unpublished research paper, McGill University, Montréal, Quebec.

Steiner, B.W. (1990). Intake assessment of gender dysphoric-patients. In R. Blanchard and B.W. Steiner (eds.), *Clinical management of gender identity disorders in children and adults* (pp. 95–117). Washington, DC: American Psychiatric Association Press.

Valentine, D. (1998). *Gender identity project: Report on intake statistics, 1989–April 1997.* New York: Lesbian and Gay Community Services Center.

Walworth, J. (1997). Sex reassignment surgery in male-to-female transsexuals: Client satisfaction in relation to selection criteria. In B. Bullough, V.L. Bullough, and J. Elias (eds.), *Gender blending* (pp. 352–373). Amherst, NY: Prometheus Books.

Wilchins, R. (2002). A certain kind of freedom: Power and the truth of bodies-Four essays on gender. In J. Nestle, C. Howell and R. Wilchins (Eds.) *GENDERqUERE.* New York: Alyson Books.

Williams, W. L. (1986). *The spirit and the flesh: Sexual diversity in American Indian culture.* Boston: Beacon Press.

Yik Koon Teh (2001). *Mak Nyahe (Male Transsexuals) in Malaysis: The influence of Culture and Religion on their Identity. International Journal of Transgenderism 5(3) July-September 2001.* The Haworth Medical Press.

Zhou, J. N., Hofman, M. A., Gooren, L. J. & Swaab, D. F. (1995). A sex difference in the human brain and its relation to transsexuality. *Nature 378(2).* pp. 68–70.

Zhou, J. N., Hofman, M. A., Gooren, L. .J, & Swaab D. F. (1997) *A Sex Difference in the Human Brain and its Relation to Transsexuality, International Journal of Transgenderism 1(1). July-September 1997.* The Haworth Medical Press.

Part III

The Application of Conflict Resolution Models

Introduction

Conflict resolution includes specialized areas of knowledge about procedures, skills and techniques. The conflict resolver uses these for undertaking the mastery of diverse areas of application in the various settings that conflict resolution is practised: schools, families, neighbourhoods, organizations, and all levels of government. Specialists in conflict resolution today include, among others, negotiators, therapists, chaplains, training consultants, community mediators, academic mediators, multi-party public policy and environmental mediators. It is important to determine when the parties are able to resolve the dispute themselves, when they need assistance, and what form any assistance should take. Conflict resolution consists of a set of methodologies that can be applied to virtually any strategic conflict that could arise across the entire spectrum of human activities.

Part III explores current intervention models in the field of individual and couple counselling. Susan Ford demonstrates how Virigina Satir's Human Growth Model can be integrated with Sandtray Therapy in the resolution of intrapsychic conflicts. The author suggests that the emotional distress of childhood can be carried on into adult life in the form of "survival stances" such as placating, blaming, super-reasonable, and irrelevant. The author applies the integrated technique to help a client make a decision regarding a significant other in his life.

Martin Rovers demonstrates how concepts from attachment theory can be integrated with Bowen's system theory of couple therapy and used effectively, especially with difficult clients. Rovers's article suggests that disagreements are essential aspects in any intimate relationship, and can challenge us to deepen our inner healing journey of trust and acceptance in life. The author demonstrates how these concepts are useful to the therapist and to the couple in understanding and working through the strong emotional and relational problems. The author illustrates the therapeutic process by the use of excerpts from actual therapy sessions.

10

Satir in the Sand Tray: An Integrative Method for Resolving Intrapsychic Conflict

Susan Ford

This chapter presents a case study in which a client was helped to resolve an intrapsychic conflict. The therapeutic intervention used was an integrative method created by adapting and combining methods from two well-established and respected therapy models. Working within the conceptual framework of Virginia Satir's Human Growth Model, Satir's method for integrating the self, the Parts Party, was adapted and combined with methods adapted from Sandtray-Worldplay Therapy, created by Dr. Gisela Schubach DeDomenico.

The chapter begins with a discussion of the origins of emotional distress and how this distress contributes to the later development of intrapsychic conflict, which Satir termed *non-congruence*. The main concepts of Satir's Human Growth Model, including a discussion of a Parts Party, are then presented, as well as an explanation of the origins and theory of sandtray therapy focusing on DeDomenico's Sandtray-Worldplay Therapy. A case study in which this method was used to resolve an intrapsychic conflict is then discussed, followed by an exploration of reasons for success.

Emotional Distress

Whatever the reason one chooses to enter psychotherapy, the search for relief of emotional distress is an almost universal driving force (Korman and Greenberg, 1996). For many clients, emotional distress is the result of abuse or neglect in childhood. Briere (2002), who categorizes childhood maltreatment into acts of omission and acts of commission, notes that "... child abuse and neglect are unfortunately prevalent in North America. ... it is now becoming clear that childhood victimization is a substantial risk factor for the development of later mental health problems" (p. 1). Whether the maltreatment was an act of omission or of commission, it is certain that one or more childhood psychological needs were not met. As Maslow (1970) notes, our needs for acceptance, belonging and protection from fear and chaos are among our most basic. The ways in which these needs were met – or ignored – in infancy and childhood will have a major influence on behaviours, attitudes and relationships in adulthood.

Melanie Klein, an early object relations theorist, was a Hungarian psychiatrist and a contemporary of Freud. One of her core theories is that the foundation for the construction of the child's inner world is inextricably linked to the quality of the mother-infant relationship (Cashdan, 1988, p. 5). Bowlby (1988) notes that when a parent is not able to meet the child's biopsychological needs for contact comfort, nurturance and love, the child is vulnerable to acute psychological distress in adulthood. Satir expands Klein's concept of the mother-child dyad to include the relationship with the father; the primary triad of the family (mother, father and child) is the system that exerts the most influence on the development of one's sense of identity.

> Within the primary triad ... children learn the family rules about safety, about their bodies, their lovability, and their ability to love. Parents expect and frequently say what and how their children should be, showing them approval for certain acts and punishing them for others. ... So the infant whose survival depended on others becomes the child whose identity depends on others ... (Satir, Banmen, Gerber and Gomori, 1991, pp. 20–22)

Childhood relationships with parents and other caregivers also set the stage for relationships developed in later life. "These relationships also provide a basis for the formation of their interpersonal style, so it makes sense that infants who adapt to hostile or unavailable caregivers by withdrawing or being constantly on alert will use similar methods with peers and other adults" (Wolfe, 1999, p. 37).

Gold (2000) notes that children who grow up in a family system with a pattern of conflict and control can be expected to develop an interpersonal style marked by unassertiveness, deference and appeasement or, to use the terminology of the Satir Model, to develop the survival stance of "placating" (Satir's four survival stances are described in more detail below).

Intrapsychic Conflict

The emotional distress of unmet childhood biopsychological needs creates intrapsychic conflict that can be difficult to resolve. Meier and Boivin (2001) have defined *intrapersonal conflict* as "... a split wherein the person feels divided between two partial aspects of the self or tendencies which are experienced as in opposition" (p. 99). Redekop (2001) says this about deep-rooted intrapsychic conflict.

> Deep-rooted conflict is that which implicates the core of our identities. This identity core has cognitive, emotional, physiological and spiritual dimensions to it. It is complex, carrying within experiences that we have had as well as cumulative experiences past [sic] on from our ancestors. [It] is complex, ubiquitous, intractable and long-lasting. (pp. 11–12)

In Satir terminology, intrapsychic conflict occurs when an individual is in a state of non-congruence or, in other words, when there is an absence of harmony, clarity and emotional honesty (Lum, 2002, p. 191). One of the Satir Model's therapeutic beliefs is "The problem is not the problem; coping is the problem." Instead of viewing the symptoms of intrapsychic conflict as pathology, the Satir Model considers symptoms as the client's attempts to cope with emotional pain.

From her work with thousands of families in crisis, Satir described four "survival stances" – behaviours developed as a way to survive, or to cope with, intrapsychic conflict. It is important to note that these stances – which she called placating, blaming, super-reasonable and irrelevant (or distracting) – describe behaviours; they do not describe personality characteristics.

A brief description of each of these coping stances and their associated behaviours, dominant affect and self-concept, appears in Table 1.

Table 1. Satir's Four Survival Stances

Coping Stance	Behaviour	Dominant Affect	Self-concept
Placating	Apologizing, begging, dependent, overly nice and cheerful	Hurt, sadness, anxiety, resentment, suppressed anger	Lack of self-worth, lack of confidence, focus on expectations of Self
Blaming	Yelling, intimidation, judging, controlling	Anger, frustration, resentment, loneliness, suppressed hurt	Lack of self-worth, unsuccessful, lack of control, focus on expectations of others
Super-reasonable	Serious, manipulative, seems insensitive, boring	Shows little emotion, sense of isolation, empty, fear of losing control	Lack of self-worth, lack of confidence, can't show feelings
Irrelevant/ Distracting	Hyperactive, restless, inappropriate, silly, superficial, attention-getting	Shows little real emotion, lonely, isolated, empty, misunderstood, confusion	Lack of self-worth, out of touch with Self, no sense of belonging

(Satir Communication Workshop, John Banmen and Kathlyne Maki-Banmen, 1998)

Satir's Human Growth Model

While Satir is best known for her contributions to the field of family therapy, she has also added to our understanding of the principles of interaction between individuals and among groups. She was an advocate of equality and value, not only in personal relationships, but also in the therapeutic relationship. As with all therapy models, Satir's is grounded in certain beliefs, assumptions and hypotheses. She believed all individuals have the potential and the desire to learn new ways of being, to change unhealthy patterns and to reach their full spiritual potential. The discovery of feelings and the ability to express them are integral to her approach. The following assumptions guide the Satir Model.

1. Change is always possible, even when change can only take place inside the person. These changes might include feelings, perceptions and expectations.

2. Therapy sessions need to be experiential in order to bring about second level change. This involves a change in being, not only in doing or feeling.

3. The problem is not the problem; coping is the problem. Therefore, therapy focuses on improving one's coping instead of just solving one's problems.

4. Feelings belong to us and, therefore, we can learn to change them, manage them and enjoy them.

5. Therapy sets positively directional goals and resolves the impact of negative experiences.

6. Therapy is systemic, both intrapsychically and interactively.

7. People have the internal resources they need to cope and grow. Therapy is one vehicle to harness these resources to help people change.

8. Most people choose familiarity over the discomfort or fear of change, especially during times of stress (Banmen, 2002).

The Satir Model focuses on three primary systems: intrapsychic, interactive and family of origin. Intrapsychic human experience is conceptualized through the metaphor of the iceberg, an interactive system comprising eight elements: behaviour; coping stances; feelings; feelings about feelings; perceptions; expectations; yearnings; and the Self, or life force. The eight elements affect and interact with each other: e.g., feelings can influence behaviour, yearnings can influence expectations. Changes in one of these eight areas often result in change in other areas (Banmen, 2002).

The "Parts Party"

The Satir Model assumes that each person has all the resources needed in order to become emotionally and spiritually healthy and whole, and that the therapeutic task is to connect the individual with those resources, which are the following:

the capacity for being spiritual,
for inspiration and imagination,
for sensing and feeling,
for awareness,
for learning and changing,
for feeling,
for expressing,
for compassion,
for wholeness,
for intuition,
for being rational,
for wisdom,
for self-acceptance and the acceptance of others,
for hope,
for esteem,
for positive energy,
for making choices,
for connecting,
for loving and being loved,
for being creative and productive,
for taking charge of one's impulses, feelings, parts, and behaviours,
for being cooperative,
for admitting and correcting mistakes,
for trusting,
for understanding,

for making and carrying out decisions,
for perspective,
for breathing and getting centered,
for asking for what one needs,
and for courage to take action.
(Loeschen, 1988, pp. 14–15)

Congruence is the goal. When one is congruent, one is honest with oneself in terms of feelings, thoughts, expectations, wants and dislikes. Congruent behaviour is confident and competent, alive and loving, responsible and accepting. A congruent individual has high self-worth, appreciates and celebrates his or her own uniqueness and accepts the equality of value of all persons. The method Satir described to integrate these resources and resolve intrapsychic conflict is the Parts Party.

Most of us can recognize that we have many facets or parts; we may have an "Internal Censor," a "Rebel," or a "Little Kid" within us. We may have certain beliefs about these parts and their role in our lives, about whether they are "good" or "bad." They may "make" us do something that contradicts a previously stated intention, such as eating a piece of chocolate cake when we have started a weight loss program. We may associate a voice or particular words – often reminiscent of a parent or teacher – with different parts. We may feel ashamed of the "bad" parts and try to ignore or deny them. But this is counterproductive, as Satir, Banmen, Gerber and Gomori (1991) argue: "When we try to hide the parts we consider bad, we eliminate possibilities of growth. Our inner Manager organizes our other parts to fit our perception of ourselves, not necessarily our inner wisdom" (p. 177). The Parts Party is a way to accept our "bad" parts, to come to appreciate their strengths and purpose in our lives, to transform them – or our perception of them – when necessary and to integrate them into a congruent whole.

Satir used to conduct a Parts Party with groups of people. The "host" of the party would choose members of the group to act as the various identified parts of himself or herself, with Satir as the facilitator or guide. Today, the Satir therapist uses this method in a one-on-one setting.

A Parts Party has five steps: the client identifies, describes and categorizes each part as positive or negative; the parts meet each other and interact, through questioning by the therapist; any conflict between the parts is explored; the parts interact and co-operate with and accept each other; and integration is achieved: each part describes its many resources and is accepted by the client; the client takes charge of the parts, with new choices and new energy.

When using the traditional Parts Party method in a one-on-one therapy session, a flip chart is used in the first step, divided into two columns, for "positive" and "negative" (Satir, Banmen, Gerber and Gomori, 1991, pp. 175–204). The therapist acts as recorder of the information the client gives. The client is asked to identify the parts, to give each part the name of a person from fiction or history or a celebrity that represents that part for the client, to ascribe a "positive" or "negative" to the part, and to provide three adjectives for each part. Eight to twelve parts are usually identified. The "positive" column should contain as many or more parts than the "negative" side.

A typical client-therapist interaction at this stage might include the following statements.

We're going to start by identifying parts that you are aware of and give them some adjectives.

Remember that each one of your parts might be attached to a certain body part so we might want to be aware of that. Let's start by putting the parts into positive and negative columns. They may not end up there, but that's where we'll start. (Client identifies an angry part.) Who would you like to have represent the angry part of you? Do you want this part on the positive or negative side? If you could describe this part, what adjective would you give it? (Elicits three.) So let's think of another part of you. We're just gathering information now.

The process continues in this manner until the client is satisfied that all the necessary parts have been identified.

This can take up to an hour or longer. When the usual session is one hour in length, it is important for the therapist to leave enough time before the session ends to process the Parts Party to that point – the client's feelings, perceptions and expectations of the process (Satir, Banmen, Gerber and Gomori, 1991, pp. 175–204). An example of the completed first step of a traditional Parts Party appears in Table 2.

Table 2. Example of a completed first step of a traditional Satir Parts Party

Positive	Negative
Bob – sympathetic – aware of others – caring	**George** – anxious, nervous – stressed – tired, blocked thinking
Biff – image conscious – healthy – fit	**Wendy** – sees the possibilities – unrealistic – unfocused
Al – angry – energetic – motivated, focused	**Little Dog** – worried – wants to please – sometimes hopeful but scared because he always gets disappointed
Steve – confident – risk taker – adventurous	**Dan** – afraid – feels hopeless – no control

Once the client indicates satisfaction with the number of parts and their adjectives, the therapist then works with the parts. Typical therapist statements or questions include the following.

Just have a look at these many parts of you that you've identified, and see what happens when you see the many parts of you in one place. What's going on for you right now? (Client answers.) And as you look at them all there together, what happens inside? (Client answers.) And how is that, to know that? When you look at these parts, which seems to be the most powerful, to have the most energy for you? (Client answers.) Is there any one that seems to be more powerful than the others?

It is important to pay close attention not only to the answers but also to the client's body language and other indications of deeper emotional affect.

In effect, the therapist uses the elements of the iceberg metaphor (noted above) to help the client explore each part, noting especially the resources of each. The Parts Party is a strength-based approach, in which the client identifies, explores and resolves intrapsychic conflict. Resolution is attained when all the parts are working together in harmony, or are integrated. Typical integration statements and questions include the following.

Check in with all of the parts and with what each is bringing to the core now. How will your life be different now? How are you going to be different with yourself? And how about the people in your life, what will be different? And how is that for you?

Sandtray Therapy

Therapy that encourages clients to honour an experience, build a world or make a pattern by arranging miniature figures in a flat-bottomed container filled with sand and water has a number of names: sandplay, sandtray therapy, sandplay technique, world-play and World Technique. It is a multi-dimensional medium that lends itself to a multilevel analysis (Davenport, 2001). Dr. Margaret Lowenfeld first used what she called World Technique in the 1920s with children in her London Play Therapy Clinic. Inspired by H.G. Wells' 1911 book *Floorgames*, she adapted his idea of using miniatures on a cleared floor space by adding a container, sand and water to allow children to capture, contain and make sense of their experiences using tools other than language (Davenport, 2001).

There are two schools of modern sandtray therapy: Kalffian and Sandtray-Worldplay (ST-WP), each of which claims the other lacks the merits of its method. Both claim to be experience focused, to honour the natural process of the unconscious or depth of consciousness, and to be non-interpretive (Davenport, 2001).

Dora Kalff, a Swiss Jungian analyst, adapted many of Lowenfeld's methods but used them differently. In fact, it was not until the mid-1980s that she and her followers credited Lowenfeld as the originator of sandplay. Kalff shifted the emphasis from the personal realm of the child to the larger archetypal psycho-mythological realm of human experience. She used silent interpretative methods. Whereas in the Lowenfeld technique the client's story is clearly told, in Kalff's method the story is not told but observed and witnessed by the therapist. Kalff believed that this "silent understanding" created a link between the therapist's conscious mind and the client's unconscious mind (DeDomenico, 1988). She applied the principles and practices of Tibetan Buddhism in her sandplay sessions, "holding" the client's sandplay process by providing a container for silence and for the spirit. She extended the use of sandplay to adult clients. She saw sandplay as a technique that "... allows for the expression of spirit as an 'inner picture made visible in the sand' " (DeDomenico, 1988, p. 34).

Sandtray-Worldplay therapy, as created by Dr. Gisela Schubach DeDomenico, is based on principles of Dynamic Expressive Play Therapy. DeDomenico (1988) notes:

Play refers to the idiosyncratic (original/primordial) manner in which expressive, creative acts occur. Play is always dynamic. It is always "correct". Play is not "deep" or "shallow". Play is not "meaningful" or "meaningless". Play is not "pathological" or "healthy". Play is the spontaneous expression of existence. It is the expression of the life force using spirit, mind, soul, body, heart, and memory to give energy, sound, form or movement to experiences of life, self, and other. (p. 38)

ST-WP is a phenomenological method of sandplay. As such, it focuses on the wholeness of experience. Some of its pre-suppositions include the following:

1. Consciousness is the innate quality of the life force.

2. Play is the universal language of consciousness.

3. The unconscious is a social construct that has allowed for the widespread use of interpretation and authoritarianism. ST-WP therapy believes that the unconscious is, in reality, withheld or taboo consciousness, used to pathologize real experience and to undermine the freedom of creative expression.

4. Play cannot be "unreal" or "symbolic"; it needs to be experienced by both player and facilitator.

5. The psyche is the core consciousness. ST-WP allows the player to experience the interconnectedness of the psyche and the universe.

6. In discussions of whether the "I", the "ego", or the "psyche" plays, ST-WP therapy takes the position that it is always the psyche that directs the play, which comes from the central core of consciousness.

7. The psyche reveals the growing edge of the player, which is where growth, healing, transformation and learning can take place.

8. The therapist is the guardian of the client's growing edge. The ST-WP therapist encourages the play process without changing the direction of the play, or by interpreting what appears in the sandtray. (DeDomenico, 1988, pp. 37–40)

DeDomenico describes three types of sandtray session: the "builder psyche directed" world, in which a client builds without any particular agenda and with no specific instructions from the therapist; the "builder ego directed" world, in which the client builds a world around a specific issue or problem to be solved; and the "therapist-directed" world, in which the therapist assigns a specific topic to be explored or makes a suggestion that limits the complexity of the world. DeDomenico discourages ST-WP therapists from directing the client's play (1988, p. 194).

Case Study

The client, John (not his real name), was a 35-year-old white male, employed as a computer programmer. His stated objective in seeking therapy was "to be able to accept uncertainty without feeling overly anxious." He described himself as having been anxious and nervous all his life. In the previous three months, however, anxiety levels had risen to the point of panic attacks. Motivating him to enter therapy were problems in his relationship with his girlfriend, whom he had been dating seriously for about a year. At her urging, they each sought individual counselling with different therapists.

John's anxiety had increased significantly in recent months due in part to the purchase of a house – his first – of which he would take possession in two months. Although he had researched the purchase thoroughly and believed he was confident in his decision, the reaction of his parents had caused him to second-guess the decision. Most of his feelings of anxiety, however, stemmed from the fact that his girlfriend expected to move into the house with him. He, on the other hand, did not feel ready to take this step but was unable to tell her so. (This was the uncertainty he wanted to be able to accept without anxiety; he stated he was unsure whether he really felt this way.) He wanted to be able to go ahead with the move because he thought he "should." Further exploration revealed that he did not want to face his parents' expected reaction if his girlfriend did *not* move in with him. They had expressed disappointment at the break-up of two previous long-term relationships and had said on every possible occasion that "this is the right girl for him."

The client was born into a stable middle-class family in which the mother was a nurse until marriage and the father was a self-employed skilled tradesman. Both parents had emigrated, separately, from Europe and met and married in Montréal. John's sister is three years younger. He described his father as "explosive," "energetic," "loud" and "conservative." Mother was described as "quiet but opinionated" and "uneducated." He described a close relationship with his mother and said that as a child he "idolized" his father, who was often impatient with and critical of him.

He said that as a child he often felt afraid, guilty and never good enough.

John found it difficult to describe his strengths, but was able to list many self-perceived faults, some of which were "I have trouble staying with things." "I have no self-confidence." "I think I will never measure up to others."

Over the course of several sessions – which involved an eclectic range of therapeutic approaches and methods, but not the one that is the subject of this article – the client addressed and gradually began to transform most of his negative self-concepts. This brought the problems with his relationships with his girlfriend and his parents into clearer focus. When he took possession of the house, he invited his girlfriend to move in with him in spite of the fact he "didn't really want to do so." He continued to struggle with two opposing forces: his desire to end the relationship and his inability to do so.

Integrative Method: "Satir in the Sand Tray"

The therapy session in which the "Satir in the Sand Tray" method was used for the first time is described in this section. Permission to publish this case study was obtained from the client.

After being welcomed and reviewing any issues carried over from the previous session, the client indicated he was still having trouble deciding what he should and should not do. He noted that he is aware that he constantly second-guesses himself in his interactions with others – his girlfriend, his friends, his work colleagues.

It was apparent to the therapist that the concepts of the Parts Party method could be applied to this situation, but with a slight twist: the client could choose figures to place in the sand tray instead of providing information that the therapist would record on a flipchart. After eliciting the client's consent to explore the conflict between "should" and "shouldn't" using the sand tray, the following emerged.

> Therapist: Can you find one figure for the "should" part of you and one for the "should not" part of you?

Client: (Chooses a dog and an eagle.)

Therapist: As you hold them in your hands, what comes to you?

Client: This one [the dog] represents what I should do. I have to be responsible all the time; I can't let myself be me. This one [the eagle] is freedom.

Therapist: Where would you like to place them?

Client: (Places them in the tray, facing each other, about 3 inches apart)

Therapist: What would you like to name them?

Client: Should and Freedom.

The therapist begins to explore each part, using the iceberg metaphor. As the discussion proceeds, it is apparent that a third part is exerting its influence. The therapist explores this with the client.

Therapist: So am I hearing guilt? Does guilt need to be part of this discussion?

Client: Yes! (He searches for a few minutes, finally chooses the figure of a priest and places it in front of the two other figures, which are still apart.)

The therapist now continues the discussion among Should, Freedom and Guilt. The feelings, perceptions and expectations of each part are explored, which eventually leads to the following exchange.

Therapist: So are you saying that Should and Freedom could work together?

Client: Yes, I guess they could.

Therapist: How do you think you would feel if you moved Should and Freedom closer together?

Client: It would feel good. I think they would be strong together. (Client moves Should and Freedom closer together.)

Therapist:	How do Should and Freedom feel now as they look at Guilt?
Client:	Well, Guilt is still really strong. You can't argue with him. It's like he has an army or something on his side.
Therapist:	It sounds as though Guilt is well defended. What about Should and Freedom? Is anyone protecting them?
Client:	(Client finds an army soldier with a rifle and places it in front of Guilt. He gets a knight and places it in front of Should and Freedom. The two defenders are facing each other.)

The therapist continues to explore the feelings, perceptions and expectations of the different parts, then introduces the yearnings element of the iceberg.

Therapist:	So what do Should and Freedom really want?
Client:	Well, they want to know where they're going. They want to be sure of themselves.
Therapist:	Is there something that would help them know where they're going, to be sure of themselves?
Client:	(The client finds a policeman figure and holds it in his hand, hesitating to place it in the sand tray.)
Therapist:	What's happening for you now?
Client:	Well, I want to take out the Defenders and Guilt and put this one in.
Therapist:	(Allows the silence to build.) But ...?
Client:	(Begins to display deep sadness; tears fall.)
Therapist:	Can you thank those parts for all that they've done for you in the past, but let them know they're not needed any more?

Client: Yes, I can do that. (Removes the defenders and Guilt, puts the policeman figure in, facing Should and Freedom.)

Some time is taken to process the deep emotions emerging from this exchange and to allow the client to experience the beginnings of change. The session then continues.

Therapist: What is the name of this part?

Client: This is Questioning. You can't question Guilt. It is always right. But you can question an officer of the law; they're supposed to be there to help you.

The session continues, involving Should, Freedom and Questioning. The depth of the discussion is deeper now, shifting between the perceptions, expectations and yearnings of the parts. At one point the therapist interjects as follows.

Therapist: It sounds as though another part wants to join this party. Is there another part who needs to be here?

Client: Yes. (Goes to the shelves and takes the sea captain figure. He returns to the sand tray, turns Questioning around so that it is facing in the same direction as Should and Freedom, and places the sea captain figure, who is holding a compass, at the head of the line. All the figures are pointing in the same direction. He assigns the name Confidence to this figure.)

The therapist then begins the integration ritual of the Parts Party. She recalls that the client had used this particular figure on several occasions in the past in different sandtray sessions (which were conducted according to traditional ST-WP methodology). The client is encouraged to acknowledge that he possessed the resource Confidence all along, but was unaware of it. He is asked to speculate about how things will be different in his life, in his relationships. What does he think might happen? How might he feel?

At the next session, two weeks later, the client reports to the therapist that he has taken the initiative to have a discussion with his girlfriend and he has been able to tell her how he really feels. He reports that although the conversation was difficult, he knows he is making the right decision in ending the relationship. In the intervening two weeks, they have begun the process of separating possessions and determining a mutually convenient date for her to move out.

Contra-indications

Both ST-WP and the Satir Model are powerful therapeutic modalities that tap into our own unique ways of perceiving the world and the defences we may have built as a result. Each method has the ability to evoke powerful emotions in the client, and the therapist must not only be comfortable with these but also confident in his or her competence to manage them. As a result, it is imperative that the therapist be aware of his or her use of self in the therapy session. The therapist's use of self has been acknowledged as being the single most important factor in developing a therapeutic relationship (Lum, 2002, p. 181).

As their clients do, therapists carry negative impacts from past events that may need to be healed. The Satir Model advocates the congruent use of self in all therapy sessions. Lum (2002) states:

> It is important that therapists resolve unfinished family of origin issues.... If therapists have not resolved these issues, there is a strong possibility that they will have a variety of reactions to clients' problems, for example, getting stuck, avoiding the issue, skewing the information, or losing focus. (pp. 181–182)

ST-WP therapy also requires the therapist to be self-aware. The "success" of a sandtray therapist, according to DeDomenico (1988), must be measured in the ability of the therapist to explore his or her own psyche, and not in the number of clients healed through the use of this medium.

> The therapist needs to be capable of exploring the greatest depths and heights of his/her own psyche when utilizing

this medium. ... Only when intimately familiar with their own journeys in the tray can therapists help teach their clients to respect and honor their own personal creative healing potential. (pp. vii–viii)

As long as these conditions are met, it is difficult to identify a client who would not be able to benefit from this integrative method. Working in the sand tray is an effective way to create an open, trusting relationship between client and therapist. As with the Parts Party, sandtray play helps clients identify and acknowledge their inner resources and strengths, thus facilitating change. Sandtray play helps clients who suffer from depersonalization and low self-esteem to reconnect with their inner self, thus setting the stage for deeper transformation. Clients do not need a rich vocabulary to work in the sand tray; the therapist relies on image language, which is innate (DeDomenico, 1988, p. 14). Also, I have found that clients self-select in terms of sandtray work; those who are not comfortable with it will indicate this, either in words or through body language. This offers an opportunity to explore what the client is experiencing at that moment, thus preparing the ground for sandtray work at a future date.

Discussion

What are the processes at work with this method that allowed the client to act congruently rather than continue his placating stance?

First, it must be acknowledged that the client was ready to make a change in his life. He had made much progress in previous therapy sessions, which were conducted either within the Satir Model framework or using the Sandtray-Worldplay method. The client had not hosted a traditional Parts Party before this session.

This integrative method, "Satir in the Sand Tray," is an effective tool for resolving intrapsychic conflict because the two methods are compatible on a number of levels. Each is an experiential method, providing an opportunity for multi-dimensional application and interpretation. Each operates from a strength-based approach and assumes that individuals have within them the key to the potential transformation and resolution of their problems.

Both the Satir Model and Sandtray-Worldplay allow the therapist to tailor the healing journey to fit the client, rather than trying to fit the client into a particular school of psychotherapy. Both methods require the therapist to possess a high degree of self-awareness. In addition, both methods use an externalization and symbolization process to help individuals work on what is often hard to articulate and to make contact with, namely, their intrapsychic processes and conflicts. As therapeutically powerful as the traditional Parts Party method is, moving it from a two-dimensional to a three-dimensional medium, using figures that the client can choose, hold and move, perhaps strengthens the anchoring aspect of the therapeutic process.

Having the therapist assist a client to host a Parts Party in the sand tray, which constitutes a more directive intervention than the Sandtray-Worldplay protocol calls for, in no measure detracts from its effectiveness. Using this integrative method, the client is still "... at all times in total control over the situation; ... the prime mover; ... the mind, the body and soul" (DeDomenico, 1988, V. 3, p. 11). DeDomenico says that the "intrapsychic housecleaning" afforded by sandtray therapy allows individuals to become properly aligned and to bridge the intrapsychic and interpsychic realms (1988, V. 3, p. 10). Satir describes the "essentials of congruent living" as, *inter alia*, "... to communicate clearly; to empower rather than subjugate; to love, value, and respect (oneself) fully, to use problems as challenges and opportunities for creative solutions" (1988, pp. 369–370).

Thus, the "Satir in the Sand Tray" method provides a clear path to congruence, because of the power of the creative intrapsychic housecleaning that the client uses. The Satir Model sees the different parts of an individual as possibilities, rather than as a "good versus bad" dynamic that so often leads to intrapsychic conflict. The objective of a Parts Party is to provide an opportunity for the client to choose to transform negative beliefs by considering the positive intention of the part, thus allowing the client access to the resources of that part. In the case under review, the client was able to appreciate the roles that defenders and Guilt had played in his life until then, and also to recognize that these roles were no longer beneficial. He transformed them into Questioning, which was an important step in his resolution of the conflict with which he had been struggling for some time.

References

Banmen, J. (2002). The Satir model: Yesterday and today, *Contemporary Family Therapy, 24*(1), 7–22.

Bowlby, J. (1988). *A secure base: Parent-child attachment and healthy human development.* New York: Basic Books.

Briere, J. (2002). Treating adult survivors of severe childhood abuse and neglect: Further development of an integrative model, in J.E.B. Myers et al. (eds.), *The APSAC handbook on child maltreatment, 2nd Edition.* Newbury Park, CA: Sage Publications.

Cashdan, S. (1988). *Object relations therapy: Using the relationship.* New York: W.W. Norton & Company.

Davenport, M. T. (2001). Mythprints in the sand: Comparing the mythographical approaches of sandplay and sandtray-worldplay, *Sandtray Network Journal, Summer 2001.* http://www.sandtray.org/mythprints.html

DeDomenico, G. S. (1988). *A comprehensive guide to the use of the sand tray in psychotherapeutic and transformational settings*, Vols. 1, 2 and 3. Oakland Park, CA.

Gold, S. N. (2000). *Not trauma alone: Therapy for child abuse survivors in family and social context.* Philadelphia, PA: Brunner-Routledge.

Innes, M. (2002). Satir's therapeutically oriented educational process: A critical appreciation," *Contemporary Family Therapy, 24*(1), 35–55.

Korman, L.M. and L.S. Greenberg (1996). Emotion and Therapeutic Change, in *Advances in biological psychiatry, 2,* 1025, JAI Press Inc.

Loeschen, S. (1998). *Systematic training in the skills of Virginia Satir.* Pacific Grove, CA: Brooks/Cole Publishing Company.

Lum, W. (2002). The Use of Self of the Therapist, *Contemporary Family Therapy, 24*(1), 181–197.

Maslow, A. (1970). *Motivation and personality,* second ed. Harper and Row.

Meier, A., and M. Boivin (2001). Conflict resolution: The interplay of affects, cognitions and needs in the resolution of intrapersonal conflicts. *Pastoral Sciences*, 20(1), 93–119.

Redekop, V. (2001). Deep-rooted conflict theory and pastoral counselling: Dealing with what one sees," *Pastoral Sciences*, *20*(1), 9–24.

Satir, V., J. Banmen, J. Gerber, and M. Gomori (1991). *The Satir model: Family therapy and beyond.* Palo Alto: Science and Behavior Books, Inc.

Wolfe, D. (1999). *Child abuse: Implications for child development and psychopathology.* Thousand Oaks, CA: Sage Books.

11

Couple Therapy with Severely Conflicted Partners: A Synthesis of Bowen and Attachment Theory

Martin Rovers

The goal of life is to become a mature adult who has achieved a sense of differentiation of self (Bowen, 1976: 1978) – that is, who has learned how to balance the two life forces of individuation and togetherness (McGoldrick & Carter, 2001; Titelman, 1998; Rovers, 2000). Differentiation of self in couple relationships can also be defined as a secure attachment pattern (Bowlby, 1969, 1973, 1980, 1988). The opposite of differentiation of self is emotional reactivity that can be expressed in family-of-origin "wounds," such as fusion or emotional cut-off, as well as insecure attachment patterns, such as preoccupied and avoidant. This journey to a mature balancing of individuation and togetherness begins within one's family of origin and is best expressed yet most complicated in a couple relationship. Each partner brings both gifts and wounds into the couple relationship. When these wounds are severe, couples often enter therapy for help. How does a therapist handle a couple that is highly emotionally reactive as expressed in conflictual cycles of fusion and cut-off? What concepts and techniques can be taken from Bowen and attachment theory to guide the marital therapist?

Bowen Theory

Bowen theory views the family as an emotional unit consisting of interlocking relationships best understood within a multi-generational and historical context. These relationships are governed by the need to counterbalance the life forces of individuation and togetherness that operate in all natural systems (Kerr & Bowen, 1988). Bowen theory provides a conceptual structure for recognizing the impact of relationships between partners and family members, and within society as a whole, especially factors that influence the health and direction of family relationships.

According to Bowen, the couple, like the family, constitutes a relationship system conceptualized by eight clinical concepts: differentiation of self, triangles, nuclear family emotional system, family projection process, multi-generational transmission process, emotional cut-off, sibling position and societal emotional process (Kerr & Bowen, 1988). Several main concepts of Bowen's theory are relevant when couple therapists begin dealing with highly reactive partners: differentiation of self, family emotional and projection system, multi-generational emotional unit and triangles.

Differentiation of Self

The cornerstone of Bowen theory is differentiation of self. In the interpersonal realm, differentiation of self can be understood to be the degree to which a person develops into a distinct and thinking individual, while interacting and connecting with significant others. More differentiated individuals are thought to be able to establish greater autonomy in a significant relationship and to achieve emotional togetherness or intimacy at the same time than less-differentiated individuals. In other words, greater differentiation of self permits one to maintain secure connections with those who hold different opinions and to resist the use of emotional cut-off or fusion to maintain one's sense of self (Skowron, 2000). Differentiation of self is the lifelong process of balancing the forces of togtherness, intimacy and individuation, rather than a state of being or a goal that can ever be achieved.

On an intrapsychic level, differentiation of self involves being able to distinguish between emotional and intellectual functioning. Greater differentiation is thought to allow for thoughts and feelings to be separated (differentiated) enough to enable the individual not to be dominated by the automatic emotional system. These individuals are less emotionally reactive and are able to maintain a sense of self in an intense emotional relationship such as marriage, family or friendship. In other words, they are able to take an "I" position in important relationships (Bowen, 1978). At the other end of the differentiation of self continuum, emotional and intellectual processes are enmeshed to the point that the people are dominated by automatic emotional system responses. These individuals are highly emotionally reactive to the positions or reactions of others. Emotional reactions are most present in times of high anxiety and can set either partner off into a fight or flight mode: these reactions can be mannerisms, words, tones or facial gestures that are probably reminders of old family-of-origin wounds and cause a deep knee-jerk reaction in the other partner, who reacts emotionally.

Bowen assumes that to some degree everyone has unresolved attachment to his or her family of origin; however, the well-differentiated individual has more resolution and is therefore better able to maintain a mature connection with family members. The opposite of differentiation of self is the interrelated and interlocking process of cut-off and fusion. Fusion refers to the individual's tendency to fuse with his or her family of origin despite overwhelming stress associated with family interaction. Poorly differentiated or fused people depend on the acceptance and approval of others and tend to lose themselves emotionally in intimate relationships (Kerr, 2003). *Fusion* and *enmeshment* are often given similar meaning (Bogard, 1988) and both words are used interchangeably in this article. Emotional cut-off relates to the ways family members manage their unresolved emotional issues with other family members by either minimizing emotional distance or completely cutting off contact. This concept deals with the way people separate themselves from their past family attachments to begin a new life in the present generation. This distance does not mean that one is more differentiated, for maturity comes only after an orderly differentiation from one's family of origin. Cut-off is the reverse side of enmeshment and occurs when individuals are unable to manage unresolved issues with family-of-origin members (Kerr, 2003). Bowen assumes that there is a correlation between the degree of differentiation and/or fusion in relationship(s) in one generation and the degree of differentiation and/or emotional cut-off in relationships in another. For instance, high levels of fusion within one family generation tend to be associated with high levels of anxiety and emotional tension in the next generation. In an attempt to resolve or avoid this tension, the next generation may respond by cutting off or distancing itself from the family, or by increased fusion. Ironically, however, this process of emotional reactivity typically results in further anxiety and emotional tension.

Enmeshment and cut-off are our family-of-origin wounds, the areas in which partners can struggle in significant relationships. Wounds are born within the family of origin so as to be old habits that are fully functional within couple relationships. These wounds are not our fault, but they are now our responsibility to repair. Partners may pretend not to see them or take a long time to deal with them. Differentiation is characterized in the couple relationship as the patterns in which each partner exhibits emotional individuality and the means used to balance the need for intimacy and individuation concurrently.

Bowen (1978) formulated a scale of differentiation as a theoretical framework to describe the differentiation people attain from their families of origin. The scale of differentiation is a continuum with arbitrary numbers from 0 to 100. A high score represents better differentiation, when a person has fully resolved emotional attachment to his or her family. A lower score represents undifferentiation from her or his family. There are two ways to manage undifferentiation: fusion and emotional cut-off. They are very different, indeed, opposite expressions of undifferentiation and extremes in terms of relational patterns. Emotional cut-off can be described as the flip side of fusion (Titelman, 1998; Rovers, 2004). Relationship patterns vary: "At one extreme are members who are very distant from or in conflict with each other ... at the other extreme is what is called emotional fusion or stuckness"

(McGoldrick & Gerson, 1985, p. 7). In the process of balancing individuation and intimacy, people can be viewed as operating on a continuum of fusion or emotional cut-off to differentiation (McGoldrick & Carter, 2001). Therefore, the scale of differentiation can be reconceptualized to look like this.

Differentiation		
Intimacy	(balancing)	**Individuation**
Enmeshment/Fusion		Emotional Cut-off
0..........25..........50..........75..........100..........75..........50..........25..........0		

Bowen (Kerr & Bowen, 1988) divided his scale of differentiation into four ranges of functioning. Bowen suggested that most people probably function within the 50–75 range on either side of the scale. These people can make choices and are secure enough to move back and forth between relationships and goal-directed activity. They are able to balance individuation and togetherness. People in the 0–50 range are described as people who have difficulty differentiating between thoughts and feelings and tend to be either fused or cut-off. Bowen suggested that few people function in the 75–100 range and set the 95–100 range as the ideal.

Family-of-origin theory sets out a continuum of attachment or belonging patterns, ranging from enmeshed or cut off to differentiated. These attachment patterns are learned within the womb of the family and function throughout life. Therefore, the foundation stones of present-day couple attachment patterns can be discerned and better understood by assessing family-of-origin experiences.

Attachment Theory

Bowlby's (1969, 1973, 1980, 1988) attachment theory has increased awareness of the importance of early attachment experiences on interpersonal relationships throughout life. Bowlby described the process of intergenerational transmission of attachment from parent to child. Attachment theory rests on the concept of an attachment behavioural system, "a homeostatic process that regulates infant proximity-seeking and contact-maintaining behaviors with one or a few specific individuals who provide physical or psychological safety or security" (Sperling & Berman, 1994, p. 5). Attachment behaviour is activity that promotes closeness to one's attachment figure. This "secure base" or at least "felt security" (Sroufe & Waters, 1977) is the primary purpose for attachment behaviour. There are common variations, patterns and working models to explain the way attachment is learned or bred into us. The internal working model is a representation based on experiences of attachment from family of origin in conjunction with current interactions between self and significant others. For the secure attachment pattern, a delicate balance is sought between seeking proximity to the caregiver and exploration, between connectedness and autonomy. This is similar to Bowen theory, in which the concept of differentiation is characterized by the "balance/imbalance of two life forces or instincts: the force of togetherness and the force of individuality" (Titelman, 1998, p. 14). Differences in individual attachment behaviour are grouped into two categories: secure and anxious/insecure (Bowlby, 1973).

Attachment and Couple Relationships

Bowlby's attachment theory provides the theoretical model to account for adult love relationships and concentrates on such issues as emotional bonds, as well as adaptive needs for protection, security and connectedness with significant others (Hazan & Shaver, 1987; Johnson, 1996; Dankoski, 2001). Recent literature has begun to examine the relationship between attachment patterns learned in childhood and adult attachment patterns in couple relationships. Important differences exist between parent-child and couple attachments, such as the more reciprocal nature of the couple and the role of sexuality. The work on adult attachment by Hazan and Shaver (1987) draws parallels with the work of Bowlby.

Hazan and Shaver (1987) used attachment patterns as descriptors for adults. They contend that romantic love can be viewed as an attachment process and that the three major attachment styles of childhood are manifest in romantic love. Adults who identified themselves as secure got closer to others and were more comfortable being dependent upon others. They had little worry about abandonment. Adults who saw themselves as avoidant acknowledged their discomfort with closeness and difficulty trusting others. These adults got nervous when love came too close. Adults with a preoccupied pattern worried that their partner did not really love them and thus wanted to get very close and hold onto their partners.

Past attachment behaviours can be transferred to current relationships (Main & Hesse, 1990, 1999). Turned around, present relationship patterns can be better understood by uncovering experiences or working models of childhood and characteristics of past attachment figures, especially parents, by observing, researching and realizing unfinished business of childhood that still organizes present processes (Simpson & Rholes, 1998). Clients' current and past family climate can be quite predictive of present attachment styles (Diehl, Elnick, Bourbeau & LaLouvie-Vief, 1998).

Family-of-origin Theory and Attachment Theory: A Synthesis

To illustrate attachment patterns, Bowlby borrowed a schema from the biologist Waddington's theory of epigentic developmental pathways (Simpson & Rholes, 1998). This schema of attachment patterns pictures a wide range of normal development in the centre of the pathways and more dysfunctional development on both extremes.

In Bowlby's theory of development, there is no single route to normality or secure-enough attachment pattern. Development is not blocked by particular experiences of deficits but rather rerouted or constrained into increasingly particular pathways over the wide range of normal to abnormal development (Caperton-Brown, 1992). A full classification schema, suggested by Goldberg's (1991) research, found that attachment classifications can range from secure to marginally secure to insecure. Even the "normal" or secure range is made up of numerous pathways, branches or clusters. The road to security is not a primrose path, but a process involving risks, choices and anxieties. This schema conceives a continuous measure, moving away from set categorical traits of attachment patterns. In addition, this schema leaves space for changes and healing as one experiences new attachment figures in adolescence and adulthood. Falling in love or the birth of a child can necessitate conscious re-evaluations of relationship patterns. Therapy, such as a re-examination of one's family-of-origin attachment patterns or emotionally focused couple therapy, can also fashion changes in current attachment patterns.

Figure 1. Schema of Attachment Patterns

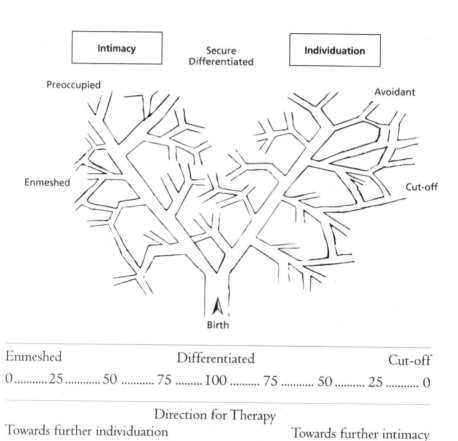

Enmeshed	Differentiated	Cut-off
0..........25...........50 .... 75 .... 100 .... 75 .... 50 .... 25 0		

Direction for Therapy

Towards further individuation →   ← Towards further intimacy

Family-of-origin theory demonstrates a continuum of relationship styles from enmeshed or cut-off to differentiated. Attachment theory offers three attachment patterns for adults, ranging from preoccupied or avoidant to secure. A full range of possible attachment patterns, based upon both family-of-origin theory and attachment theory, can be illustrated by means of Bowlby's multipathway schema. In this way, the normal development in the centre of the pathways presents the healthy range of blends of intimacy and individuation that can operate in one's life. In a similar vein as Knudson-Martin (1994, 2002), this schema enables people to live and relate while leaning more toward one side of the pathways than the other, be that with preference for intimacy or for individuation, according to their own life experiences, and still reach the goal of secure/differentiation. This schema more clearly accents these various pathways to secure/differentiated and both forces of intimacy and individuation are given equal, reciprocal importance. On the one hand, there is a want for autonomy, freedom and individuation; on the other hand, there is a need for intimacy, closeness and togetherness.

These apparently opposite needs are a necessary and healthy part of life and may change in their intensity and function, depending upon one's stage of life and experiences on the way. The zipper model (Horne & Hicks, 2002) depicts a coming together of individuation and togetherness, but achieving this differentiation of self does not fit as nicely in the centre as the zipper metaphor suggests. Each person has a natural preference towards intimacy or individuation, but the other side will also be solidly present for the secure/differentiated person. The pathways taken through life can have some leeway, depending upon life experiences, and the pathways travelled can be redirected or rerouted somewhat as a result of life experiences or therapy. In this schema, there is room for growth and change and the possibility to better balance oneself towards the middle secure/differentiated attachment position.

If one's attachment patterns are located towards the outsides of the schema of attachment patterns, one begins to experience more dysfunctional expressions of attachment, such as preoccupied and enmeshed on the one side, and avoidant and cut-off on the other side. Enmeshment and cut-off would be seen as most dysfunctional, as described by Bowen (1978). Enmeshed and cut-off people live in a feeling world and are unable to differentiate between thoughts and feelings. Enmeshed people are suggestible and quick to imitate others to gain acceptance or to seek out the ideal close relationship, while, at the other end of the continuum, cut-off people may be fearful or dismissive of relationships, sometimes seen as lone rangers. Enmeshed and cut-off people are both in the realm of insecure/undifferentiated. Many highly enmeshed or cut-off people can shift from an enmeshed attachment pattern to a cut-off one quickly or reactively, a sort of need-you-desperately or dump-you-quickly knee-jerk reaction (Bowen, 1978). Secure/differentiated people tend to be more uniform and regular in their attachment patterns, treating people in a similar and consistent manner.

It is strongly noted, however, that all these attachment patterns lie on a descriptive continuum and that exact diagnosis is not always possible or desirable. The Bowen scale of differentiation allows graphic, albeit more theoretical, assessments to be made that may help clients find a possible place to position and know themselves on the range of attachment patterns. Within this range of possible attachment patterns, and since no one scores a perfect secure/differentiated 100, there can be a variety of relationship expressions that probably tips each individual's attachment pattern either towards secure or insecure, towards greater emphasis on intimacy or on individuation. This schema helps choreograph the couple's dance of attachment/differentiation more distinctly. By depicting potential placement on the schema of attachment patterns for clients, the picture can well be worth a thousand words both for their past and present attachment patterns and for direction in their therapy.

There are many possible attachment patterns on this schema but four clusters are noted: the more functional middle clusters of secure/preoccupied and secure/avoidant and the more dysfunctional outer clusters of enmeshed/preoccupied and cut-off/avoidant.

Figure 2. Four Attachment Clusters

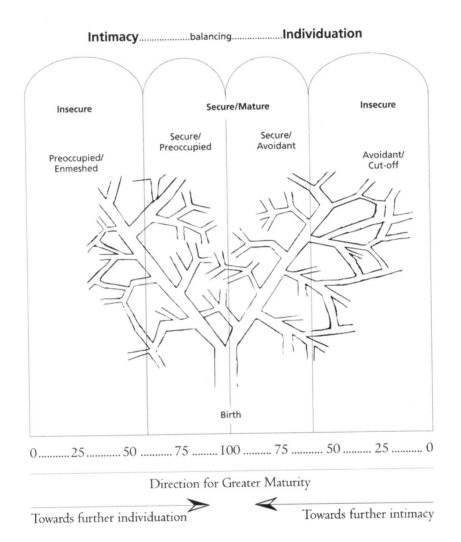

Although perhaps at first perplexing to the client, the various clusters illustrated enable clients and therapist to talk about movement towards a more secure/differentiated centre and possible areas of insecurity in relationships, and to mutually arrive at some attachment descriptors for both partners.

Pathways taken in life depend on many past experiences, but especially the legacy of the family of origin. Some childhood experiences may have caused a person to incline or move further into the direction of enmeshed/preoccupied. Other experiences within the family of origin may have had the effect of swaying a person into the direction of avoidant/cut-off. A detailed family-of-origin history, using instruments such as the genogram, would expose childhood attachment patterns and enable both partners and therapist to become more aware of antecedents of present relationship problems, thus gaining a more complete picture of present attachment patterns. By means of this schema of attachment patterns, the partners would have more self-knowledge and a better foundation upon which to engage in their relationship.

Therapy is also delineated on this schema. The person whose attachment pattern leans toward the enmeshed/preoccupied side would be seen as being fearful of further individuation; therefore, more individuating steps would be the direction of therapy. On the other hand, the person who prefers the cut-off/avoidant side would be seen as being fearful of intimacy, and so steps towards a deeper connectedness would be called for in therapy. Implications for therapy are elaborated later in this chapter.

Couple as an Emotional System

The family is seen as a multi-generational emotional unit or system in which each partner is characterized by his or her level of differentiation and functioning position as well as by the multi-generational transmission process. The latter presupposes that family dysfunction results from the transmission of undifferentiation over several generations. As parents project onto their children, three things can happen. Some children emerge more involved in the parental triangle and with a lower level of differentiation, other children might be more minimally involved and emerge with a similar level of differentiation, and some children might be more free of the family emotional system and emerge with a higher level of differentiation (Kerr, 2003). Functioning position assumes that certain functions are generated in every family emotional system and that each individual's personality is shaped according to his or her functioning position in the family (Kerr & Bowen, 1988). Values, beliefs, feelings, attitudes and behaviours are influenced by one's functioning position, which operates in a reciprocal relationship. The multi-generational transmission process assumes that each family member is both unique and shares characteristics with all other family members.

The nuclear family emotional system assumes that people choose partners who are equally differentiated. Therefore, the undifferentiated person will choose a partner who is "equally fused to his or her family of origin" (Goldenberg & Goldenberg, 1991). The undifferentiated and fused married couple will likely produce a family with similar characteristics, resulting in an unstable nuclear family emotional system that seeks means and ways of maintaining stability and reducing tension. High levels of fusion within the couple relationship increase the likelihood of high levels of anxiety and instability as well as the partners' propensity to seek resolution through conflict and distancing. Other results may be the impaired functioning of one partner; the couple becoming overly concerned about a child; or symptomatic patterns such as chronic and overt marital conflict, emotional distance, physical or emotional dysfunction in one spouse or psychological impairment of one or more children (Goldenberg & Goldenberg, 1991).

Triangles

The triangle is the "basic building block" (Bowen, 1978) of the family's emotional system. In times of stability and calm, a two-person system can remain relatively stress free. A triangle is formed when anxiety or emotional tension threatens the couple relationship and one or both partners involve a third person, activity or addiction. When tension within the triangle becomes too high, it spreads to form a series of interlocking triangles that can include another person, such as a parent or child, or other distractions, such as alcohol or work (Goldenberg & Goldenberg,

1991). A triangle assumes a "rigid or fixed dysfunctional stability" characterized by a lack of differentiation and openness among members (Titelman, 1998, p. 12). Distancing or the fusion between two members occurs and, as a result, the relationship becomes unstable. Consequently, others become involved or triangled, and interlocking triangles are formed.

Functions of the Therapist

For Bowen, the role of the therapist is like that of a coach. When working with both partners, the coach has the following functions:

- engaging the couple: bringing down emotional reactivity;

- system mapping: defining and clarifying the relationship between the spouses, especially helping partners become thoughtful about their own wounds or emotional triggers;

- keeping oneself de-triangled from the family emotional system; and

- demonstrating differentiation of self by using "I statements" and constructive talking and listening during therapy as a means of mentoring the partners.

In Bowen theory, teaching about family systems, helping partners become more thoughtful about their place in the system and their own contribution to the problem, and helping couples plan new modes of interaction take precedence over interpretation, insight or emotional engagement.

The learned patterns of attachment and emotional expressiveness typically learned within the family of origin affect every other relationship within and outside the family system, especially with one's chosen partner. Therefore, it makes sense, when troubles come to a couple relationship, to look in two places for a better understanding of the causes of these troubles as well as for the solution. These two places are within oneself, especially within the couple relationship in the here and now; and within one's relationship in the family of origin, in which these troubles probably started as childhood wounds. Not all people are able to be in touch with or articulate the here and now experiences and feelings that are present in couple relationships. Some people do not know what they are feeling or why they act as they do. Telling stories of what happened within their family of origin can be easier and safer – somewhat more removed. It provides a safer base and an experience upon which they can begin to comprehend their current relationship as well as their feelings. It offers partners a "why" to how the wounds are dancing in their relationship. Family-of-origin therapy, however, is not to relive an old memory or to blame parents for all that may have gone wrong in life. Rather, a review of family-of-origin relationship patterns can provide a working model or blueprint of current functioning and thus help partners obtain a better grasp of the here and now. Unfinished business of the past is probably one of the main issues partners trip over again and again. The old family-of-origin map and attachment patterns that have been followed most of one's life need adjustment and updating to better fit adult relationships. Knowing where one came from, in terms of family of origin and attachment patterns, enables one to seek pathways towards the middle ground of a more secure/differentiated relationship with one's partner. In other words, we can stand more solidly on the two feet of past and current attachment patterns by observing our family of origin functioning and by focusing on present emotional attachments with partners. Our family of origin is probably one of the most powerful, influential and formative influences on our life. So much happens with the family of origin within the first six to ten years of our life that one might say we are who our family of origin created us to be. Each one of us has a natural curiosity to know our past, our family of origin. Most of us go through phases of hating or being disconnected from our parents, only to realize at some point that we really are a little bit like each of our parents, and this too is a step on the road to self-integration.

As well, when partners can stand on the two feet of knowing themselves, their family-of-origin attachment patterns and wounds, and their emotional connectedness with their partner, both partners also have two places to go to heal these wounds and create a new dance of intimacy and individuation. Partners are strongly encouraged to do couple therapy together so that they can address the issues that dance between them; for example, emotional security and trust, communication, knowing themselves better and spirituality. Partners are also healing their couple wounds when they create an improved relationship with their respective parents and begin to practise new attachment patterns with their parents. In other words, as Bowlby stated, partners have to adjust their working models, and since these working models were created in a person's relationship with their parents, it makes sense to address the issues at their source. Doing an extended family map so that one can know oneself better, and talking over and communicating one's wounds as well as one's newly chosen attachment desires with parents, can only help to unpack and sort through the many steps each person needs to take to assume responsibility for their own dance of wounds. In other words, to change one's attachment patterns with parents is to change attachment patterns with all others, especially partners. This can be all the more essential when one partner is not yet open or willing to make changes in self or the relationship. Bowen suggests that couple therapy can be done with only one partner present, for when one partner changes, others around him or her will also have to change, because a more differentiated partner will no longer engage in the old dance of wounds he or she learned in childhood and used in the couple relationship. In other words, the goal of therapy is to get one or both partners to become thoughtful and change their own contribution to the couple relationship pattern, interrupting the couple interaction flow, and helping partners become more differentiated and mature.

Engaging the Couple:
Bringing down Emotional Reactivity

Couples often come into therapy in a heightened state of anxiety or emotional reactivity, with both partners blaming the other for the problem, while unable to see their own contribution. Therefore, the first task of the therapist is to connect with the couple and lower the couple's anxiety and each partner's emotional reactions to the other. In other words, it is to define and reduce the dance of wounds that happens between partners when most thoughtfulness seems to have gone out the window. This can mean to name and reduce blaming, anger, self-pity, aggressor/victim positions, and other "buttons" that partners can trigger in each other. It is for the therapist to begin to bring some calm and safety to the relationship and to assure both partners that he or she is present, and hears and values them, and that progress can be made when everyone calms down and begins to become more thoughtful and reflective. Bowen suggests that one way to accomplish this is to have both partners talk directly to the therapist as coach, and that the therapist become the mediator of the conversations at this stage. This can help decrease reactiveness in the session, encourage listening, stimulate thinking and demonstrate one-to-one interaction. This will be the crucial time for the therapist to demonstrate his or her own differentiation of self and keep himself or herself outside the couple's attempts to triangle the therapist in on their side. Worded another way, the task of the coach is to get the partners to think and talk about their relationship, their feelings and their expectations. Couples in therapy have been through this dance of wounds hundreds of times, reacting in their usual patterns and, most often, ending up in the same place. When partners tend to slip back into old reactive ways of interacting, the coach can gently but firmly call them back to talking to him or her.

Example: The Case of Mary and Joe

Mary and Joe presented in therapy with severe couple dysfunction and conflict. They have two teenage children who are in strong rebellion, often refusing to go to school, and who were in constant conflict with their parents and each other. Social agencies have become involved with the older daughter. Mary is the youngest child in her family and presents in an enmeshed/preoccupied attachment style, while Joe is the youngest in his family and tells stories of his childhood days alone in his room with his computer.

When Joe and Mary came to my office for the first session, they sat at opposite ends of the couch. As they shared the story of why they were here in therapy, they exchanged stares at each other to the point that they interrupted their story to comment on their partner's facial or bodily gestures. The following exchange took place near the end of the first session of therapy.

Coach: So I hear that you are both hurting and that you have expectations of your partner that are not being met. I was wondering what you think your own contribution to the couple problem might be?

Mary: I want Joe to change, get his head out of the sand and start taking responsibility for the kids. He never ... (she looks over at Joe) ... what are you saying by that face? See! There you go again, thinking that it is not your fault.

Coach (interrupting): Mary. I want you to look at me and tell me again what you see your contribution to be in this couple difficulty, not what you see Joe's problem to be. Mary, can you slow down a bit, look at me and tell me. I am listening.

Mary (taking a deep breath and a pause): I know that I am not perfect and that I have my faults in this, but Joe never helps out. He ...

Coach (interrupting): Mary, I want to know more about what you might see your contribution to be. I am of the opinion that when each of us becomes aware of and acknowledges our own contribution to the problem, then things can begin to change. I would like to move you and Joe from "you" statements to "I" statements. So please continue and tell me about yourself.

Mary: I can get so angry at times. I know that I lose it with Joe and with the kids. I just want them to become more responsible for themselves.

Coach: What things would you want them to begin doing or stop doing?

Mary: Well. I need Joe to finish his job of writing out our contract with the kids.

Coach (turning to Joe): Joe. What do you hear Mary saying?

Joe: She is trying to tell me that I never do anything around the house and that I don't care. She gets me so angry!

Coach: Joe. Slow down. That is not what I heard Mary say. (Turning to Mary) What I heard you say, Mary, was that you want

Joe to finish the job he promised to do, to write down the contract you both had negotiated with the kids. Is that right, Mary?

Mary: Yes.

Coach: Joe, can you hear just that request for the contract?

Joe: Yes, but ... (looks at Mary) ... See, she thinks that I never do anything!

Coach: Joe. Look at me. Let's just stick to the issue of the contract. Tell me again what you heard Mary say?

Joe: Well, she is right. I have not written it out, but ...

Coach (interrupting): Good, Joe. So I hear you saying that you have a job to do, to write out the contract with the kids. Is that correct?

Joe: Yes. I can do that.

Systems Mapping: Defining and Clarifying the Relationship Between the Spouses

The schema of attachment patterns is a good place to begin to have partners look at knowing themselves and understanding their role in the couple's difficulties. Partners can be shown the schema and, after it is explained to them, asked where they see themselves and their partner on it. Often partners are on the opposite ends of the continuum, with one partner more preoccupied and the other partner more avoidant. The dance of wounds between the partners can be one of pursue/flee, with neither partner's needs really being met. On the family system level, it would probably also be true that one partner is more enmeshed with his or her family of origin and the other is very distant from his or hers. This family-of-origin interference often can complicate a couple's difficulties.

Early in therapy, the coach begins to map out the couple relationships as well as their bigger family systems. The genogram or family map is an excellent way to do this. Gilles-Donovan (1991) writes that "the focus is on knowing the system, the structure and how it works" (p. 9). The genogram is a dynamic, evolving understanding of the family system and the coach can highlight patterns and share these with the couple to enable the partners to begin making connections between their family system and their current attachment patterns and conflictual problems. Bowen encourages clients to become researchers and observers of their own family dynamic and begin to see their role or function within it, as well as the dance of wounds that is happening between the partners. Having partners tell their family-of-origin stories can lead to insight into self as well as partner.

Example

The genogram for Joe and Mary follows. One of the highlights of therapy was when Joe began to observe and comment on the frequency of his distant relationships with most of the significant people in his life. Prior to that time, Joe was quite adamant that Mary was the real one at fault with her volatile ways of interacting, and if she were simply to change her voice and volume, all would be better. Now, Joe began to see that he is distant with most people, even his mother and brother, who are quiet people like himself. Joe started to describe himself as inclining to "be in his head" and acknowledged that he needed to connect more in relationships.

Couple therapy needs to focus on patterns rather than on content, so that partners may learn about their own couple system and the wider family system each comes from. This sets the stage for further differentiation of self.

De-Triangling: Learning to Stay out of the Family Emotional System

The high road to differentiation of self is to avoid the pitfalls of the family emotional process, especially triangles. A triangle is formed when anxiety or emotional tension threatens the couple relationship and one or both partners involve a third "person," such as work, addiction, children, an affair or the therapist. De-triangling is, first of all, necessary for the coach; it is crucial the coach not get emotionally caught up in one partner's story, or become focused on one issue. Bowen has suggested the use of humour and reversal as means to bring about thoughtfulness within the couple relationship, while remaining de-triangled.

Figure 3. Genogram of Joe and Mary

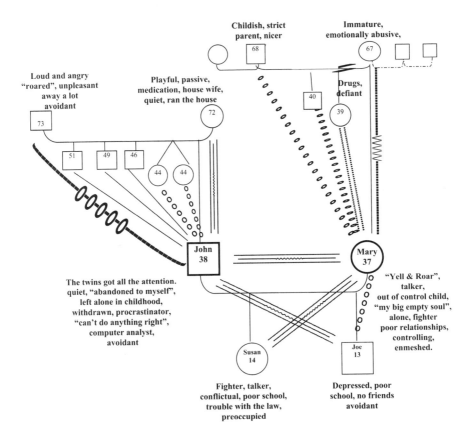

Example

After three sessions of couple therapy, having obtained stories of the couple's difficulties and begun work on constructing their genograms, there were two individual sessions with each partner. This is session four, with Mary alone.

Mary: We are thinking of having our older daughter stay with Joe's brother and his wife for a while. They have agreed to take her, and it might help in the house. But I was talking with Alice [Joe's brother's wife] yesterday and she began to rub it in my face, how I can't do anything right. I let her know exactly what I thought of her. She makes me so mad!

Coach: Mary, I have the impression that you act on the motto Fire! Ready! Aim! And that you do have a lot of firepower.

Mary (laughing): That is what my brother and sister use to call me when I was young: firepower.

Coach: Fire is a great thing: it gives off heat and light and is necessary for life. I wonder where all that firepower comes from?

Mary: I had to fight for everything I have. My dad was abusive and I had to fight for myself and my brother and sister.

Coach: Are you aware when your firepower gets too hot?

Mary (laughing): Often too late. I know that I have to work on that.

Coach: How do you think you might want to do that?

Demonstrating Differentiation of Self by the Use of "I statements"

As partners become more aware of and thoughtful about their place within the couple system, as well as their larger family systems, change can begin. By observing and listening to each other, partners can begin to see and think about themselves in systemic terms and grasp their own starring role in the couple conflict. Partners will need to make changes to their old dysfunctional attachment patterns and begin the joint couple reconstruction project of non-reactive communication and re-entry into relationship. Mc-Goldrick & Carter (2001) write:

> The basic idea of coaching is that, if you can change the part you play in your family, and hold it despite the family's reaction while keeping in emotional contact with family members, you maximize the likelihood that they will eventually change to accommodate your change. (p. 291).

Thus begins the main work of therapy which is making shifts in one's position, especially by taking responsibility for self and using "I statements." An "I statement" is a complete and engaging statement of one's thoughts, feelings and wants on a subject that is spoken nicely and honestly. The Dialogue Wheel (Rovers, 2005) is one model for expressing "I statements."

Figure 4. Dialogue Wheel

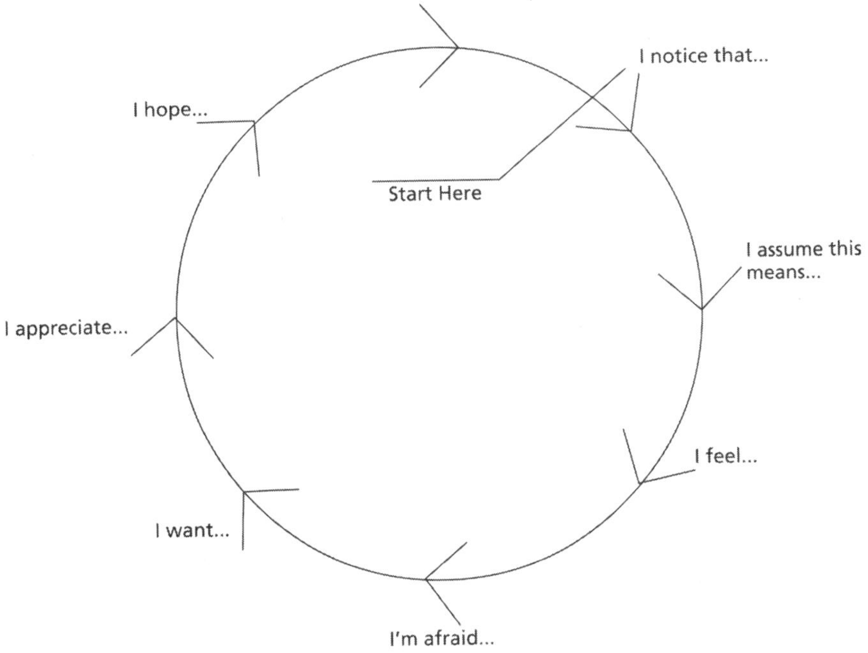

The Dialogue wheel is a communication tool that can be used to see the wounds and attachment patterns within couple relationships and to begin the process of talking about them.

Example

Session six is again a couple session. The coach introduces the Dialogue Wheel and asks Mary to tell Joe what she needs from him.

Mary: Joe, I notice that when we begin to talk to the children about something, you often have the habit of saying nothing at all and leaving it all up to me. I assume that you are afraid of these confrontations with them. This makes me feel uncomfortable, alone and, in the end, frustrated and angry. I am afraid that it too often ends up a fight between me and the kids and that you come in to take their side. I want us to have a contract with them so that everyone knows what to expect and what the rules are and then I want us to stand together when we need to enforce them. I appreciate that I am asking a lot of you and that you prefer to be left alone and out of these discussions. I hope we can work to reach agreement between you and me with the kids.

Coach: Thanks, Mary. Joe, what are you hearing?

Joe: I know that I need to get involved more when we deal with the kids, but I have always been afraid of confrontation, ever since I was a kid. I run from it.

Coach: Tell me more about that, Joe.

Conclusion

Differentiation is about learning to become more individuated, while remaining connected in one's significant relationships; it is about discovering that balance between intimacy and individuation and taking responsibility for self with one's partner and other significant people. Some of these conceptual tools and techniques from Bowen theory have a strong teaching component: schema of attachment patterns, attachment clusters, the genogram and the Dialogue Wheel. When integrated in therapy, Bowen theory can have a powerful effect on learning to find a new way to relate with one's partner and family of origin.

References

Bogard, M. (1988). *Enmeshment, Fusion or Relatedness? A Conceptual Analysis.* New York: Haworth Press.

Bowen, M. (1976). Theory and practice in psychotherapy. In P. J. Guerin (ed.), *Family Therapy: Theory and Practice.* New York: Gardiner Press, 42–90.

Bowen, M. (1978). *Family Therapy in Clinical Practice.* New York: Jason Aronson.

Bowlby, J. (1969). *Attachment and Loss: Vol.1: Attachment.* London: Hogarth Press.

Bowlby, J. (1973). *Attachment and Loss: Vol. 2: Separation.* London: Hogarth Press.

Bowlby, J. (1980). *Attachment and Loss: Vol. 3: Loss.* London: Hogarth Press.

Bowlby, J. (1988). *A Secure Base. Clinical Application of Attachment Theory.* London: Routledge.

Caperton-Brown, E. H. (1992). *Ethnic and Gender Differences in Intergenerational Family Processes.* Unpublished Doctoral Dissertation. Houston: University of Houston.

Dankoski, M.E. (2001). Pulling on the heart strings: An emotionally focused approach to family life cycle transitions. *Journal of Marital and Family Therapy*, 27, 177–187.

Diehl, M., Elnick, A.B., Bourbeau, L.S. & LaLouvie-Vief, G. (1998). Adult attachment styles: Their relations to family context and personality. *Journal of Personality and Social Psychology*, 74, 1656–1669.

Gilles-Donovan, J.(1991). Common misunderstandings. *American Family Therapy Academy Newsletter*, 81, 7–14.

Goldberg, S. (1991). Recent developments in attachment theory and research. *Canadian Journal of Psychiatry*, 36, 393–400.

Goldenberg, I. & Goldenberg, H. (1991). *Family Therapy: An Overview.* Pacific Grove, CA: Brooks/Cole Publishing.

Hazan, C. & Shaver, P.R. (1987). Romantic love conceptualized as an attachment process. *Journal of Personality and Social Psychology*, 52, 511–524.

Horne, K.B., & Hicks, M.W. (2002). All in the family: A belated response to Knudson-Martin's feminist revision of Bowen Theory. *Journal of Marital and Family Therapy,* 28(1), 103-113.

Johnson, S. (1996). *Creating Connections: The Practice of Emotionally Focused Therapy.* Levittown, PA: Brunner/Mazel.

Kerr, M.E. & Bowen, M. (1988). *Family Evaluation.* New York: Norton.

Kerr, M. (2003). *One Family's Story: A Primer on Bowen Theory.* Washington, DC: The Georgetown Family Center.

Knudson-Martin, C. (1994). The female voice: Applications of Bowen's family systems theory. *Journal of Marital and Family Therapy,* 20, 35–46.

Knudson-Martin, C. (2002). Expanding Bowen's legacy to family therapy: A response to Horne and Hicks. *Journal of Marital and Family Therapy,* 28, 115–118.

Main, M. & Hesse, E. (1990). Parents' unresolved traumatic experiences are related to infant disorganized attachment status: Is frightened and/or frightening parental behavior the linking mechanism? In Greenberg, M.T, & D. Cicchetti (Eds.). *Attachment in the Preschool Years: Theory, Research and Intervention.* Chicago, IL: The University of Chicago Press.

Main, M. & Hesse, E. (1999). Second-generation effects of unresolved trauma in nonmaltreating parents: Dissociated, frightened and threatening parental behavior. *Psychoanalytic Inquiry,* 19, 481–540.

McGoldrick, M. & Carter, B. (2001). Advances in coaching: Family therapy with one person. *Journal of Marital and Family Therapy,* 27, 281–300.

McGoldrick, M. & Gerson, R. (1985). *Genograms in Family Assessment.* New York: W.W. Norton.

Rovers, M. W. (2000). A family of origin workshop: process and evaluation. *The Family Journal: Counseling and Therapy for Couples and Families,* 8(4), 368-375.

Rovers, M.W. (2004). Family of origin theory, attachment theory and the genogram: a new paradigm for couple therapy. *The Journal of Couple and Relationship Therapy,* 3(4), 43–63.

Rovers, M.W. (2005). *Healing the Wounds in Couple Relationships.* Ottawa: Novalis.

Simpson, J.A. & Rholes, W.S. (1998). *Attachment Theory and Close Relationships*. New York: Guildford Press.

Skowron, E. A. (2000). The role of differentiation of self in marital adjustment. *Journal of Counseling Psychology*, 47(2), 229–237.

Sperling, M.B. & Berman, W.H. (1994). *Attachment in Adults: Clinical and Developmental Perspectives*. New York: The Guildford Press.

Sroufe, L.A. & Waters, E. (1977). Attachment as an organizational construct. *Child Development*, 48, 1184–1199.

Titelman, P. (Ed.). (1998). *Clinical Applications of Bowen Family Systems Theory*. Binghamton, NY: The Haworth Press.

Part IV

Empirical Studies and Ethics

Introduction

Conflict resolution needs to better engage in the discipline of research and use books and established journals to disseminate research findings. More and more articles on conflict resolution are finding their way into journals from other disciplines, such as psychology and education. The primary reason for limited research projects at this point has been the emphasis on the application of conflict-resolution skills. In arenas badly in need of new ways to resolve disputes – notably, schools, institutions, communities and courts – the conflict resolution practitioners have been busy. Equally important is research that brings the full knowledge of the intrapersonal processes to bear on conflict and conflict resolution. Now that conflict resolution is known at a national level, research needs to lead the field into new expressions and applications for practictioners. At this juncture, research should focus on assessing the effectiveness of the conflict resolution work of the past few decades.

In Part IV, two chapters offer up-to-date research on conflict resolution in practice. Seung Hee Kang, Thomas O'Connor and Suzanne Joyce present the results from a qualitative analysis of the transcribed interviews of a chaplain and nurse in resolving a conflict. Central to the management of this conflict was the realization that one party needs to stay calm, thoughtful and differentiated throughout the dialogue, as well as have the ability to manage frustration and pain. Augustine Meier and Micheline Boivin report their findings from a study using a conceptual model that integrates affects, cognitions and needs in the resolution of intrapersonal conflicts. It was observed that for those who resolve conflict, Need and Positive Feeling statements predominate immediately prior to the resolution of the conflict, and Judgment, Thought and Negative Feeling statements decrease immediately prior to the resolution of a conflict. The results suggest the necessity of simultaneously assessing many aspects of a client's inner experiences when studying the occurrence of significant in-therapy client events.

Peter Barnes offers a method of resolving ethical issues in organizations using a dialogue approach similar to that used in narrative therapy. The author cogently summarizes the negative effects of an adversarial approach to deal with ethical violations on the part of professionals. He proposes the steps that might constitute the dialogue process in resolving ethical issues between a complainant and a respondent.

12

Birth of a Star

Seung Hee Kang, Thomas O'Connor and Suzanne Joyce

Introduction

Is conflict a blessing or a curse? This question seems neither to encompass nor portray the experience of 21st-century postmodern conflict. Friedrich Wilhelm Nietzsche (1844–1900) once said, "Chaos gives birth to a dancing star." Now, when we only look at the star, we miss out on the process of "giving birth," which includes a labouring moment, and this process involves pain, suffering and endeavour. When we only look at the aspect of chaos, life can be nothing but confusion after confusion. This study captures the moments of chaos until the birth of a star. The study presents an incident of conflict, the process of conflict and a newly created reality of conflict that is raised with forgiveness, healing and reconciliation. The study shows in what way the experience of conflict between a nurse and a chaplain was psychologically and theologically entwined and how the conflict reached a different reality from where it began.

Review of the Literature

For the literature review, various databases, such as Medline (from 1966 to January 2004), CINAHL [Cumulative Index to Nursing & Allied Health Literature] (from 1982 to December 2003), AARP [Association for the Advancement of Retired Persons] Ageline (from 1978 to December 2003) and Healthstar (from 1975 to January 2004) were searched. English studies were all included in the literature review. The keywords used to capture the data were *pastoral care; pastoral counselling; conflict resolution; con-*

flict management in healthcare setting; chaplain and nurse; and conflict and problem solving in inter-professional relations.

The primary literature on conflict resolution and management is rich and provides theoretical approaches from various perspectives, such as psychophysiological, psychological, anthropological and sociological. Generally, the literature in this category speculates about what the most effective and constructive methods of conflict management and resolution might be (Deutsch, 1971; Littlejohn and Domenici, 2001; Deutsch & Coleman, 2000). Some directly related literature uses specific cases to show ways to manage conflict (Kellett & Dalton, 2001). These approaches view conflict as a problem to be solved.

Another approach that is quite different from the problem-solving one is called the narrative mediation approach. This approach is more focused on developing a relationship rooted in understanding, respect and collaboration. Before addressing the conflict, both parties are invited to reflect on its impact. By doing so, the parties move to resolution (Winslade & Monk, 2000). Both problem-solving approaches and narrative mediation approaches can be applied to any interpersonal relationship in various situations.

One group of relevant literature addresses how conflict and conflict resolution are viewed in a healthcare setting, exploring how conflict arises and what the problem areas are for conflict among nurses, medical doctors, pharmacists, dentists, social workers and those in other fields (Leininger, 1976); what the conflict resolution skills are for staff nurses (Baker, 1995); and what the principles and practices are for resolving conflict for physicians and other medical professionals (Hall, Jr. & Stong, 1993; Gill, 1995; Anonymous, 2000). Here, conflict is viewed as "an essential and expected part of human life and behaviour" (Leininger, 1976, p. 165; Baker, 1995). Conflict means, for Leininger, "opposing viewpoints, forces, issues and problems confronting individuals, groups and institutions, which have been generated from a variety of internal and external personal and group forces" (Leninger, 1976, p. 169). The concept of conflict is related to "antagonistic interests, misunderstanding, competition, logical irreconcilable interests and goals, opposing tensions, rivalry, political manoeuvres, and game behaviour" (Leininger, 1976, p. 169). Baker introduces Thomas' five behavioural approaches for conflict management: competing, compromising, avoiding, accommodating and collaborating. Among those approaches, the collaborating approach is considered an "open and insightful approach which leads to mutually satisfying decision making" (Baker, 1995, p. 296). Gill claims that competition limits conflict resolution and that effective problem solving would transform "win-lose approaches to win-win solutions," which come from mutual respect and collaboration. Conflict, for Gill, "stays resolved when the other parties feel acknowledged, informed, and involved" (Gill, 1995, pp. 13–14).

The related literature speaks about the conflict between hospital departments, specifically two hospital departments and an operating room, and how a systems approach can resolve the conflict (Pape, 1999). Also, Hall, Jr. and Stong describe how a mediation of "a neutral third person" can resolve a conflict not by imposing a resolution but by facilitating negotiation between the parties (Hall, Jr. & Stong, 1993, pp. 1–2). Davidhizar and Dowd do not view conflict as a negative event, but they do argue that patient care can be enhanced by a combination of conflict and collaborative techniques. Healthy disagreement is welcomed to improve patient care (Davidhizar & Dowd, 2001, p. 13). Rakley introduces the case of a female physician, in terms of how her self-improvement in the workplace results in a desirable working relationship with her colleague (Rakley, 1999). In this case, one individual's self-improvement contributed to the conflict resolution.

Other literature deals with spirituality as it relates to conflict in a hospital setting. This literature talks about the process of negotiation and how win-win negotiation (mutual victory) can be achieved among the nurse specialists (Laser, 1981; Beare, 1989). Negotiation is, for Beare, the process of reaching a satisfactory settlement of differences in a conflict situation (Beare, 1989, p. 138). Negotiating is also viewed as a "life process" and is considered central to growth and happiness (Laser, 1981, p. 24). Laser suggests four elements of negotiation: "1. Both conflicting and non-conflicting goals, 2. Variable values, 3. Mutual victory, 4. Incomplete information" (Laser, 1981, p. 25).

Literature on the subject of interaction between nurses and chaplains in a hospital setting is available. This literature is, however, highly focused on how staff nurses (or parish nurses) and staff chaplains (or hospice chaplains) can team up to work in a friendly and co-operative way to provide spiritual care for patients (Morris and Foerster, 1972; Wright, 1980; Eickhoff, 1982; Griswold, 1990; VandeCreek, 1997; Harris and Foerster, 1998; Greeding and Honn, 2001). This literature considers the relationship between various departments as "joint-ventures," derived from St. Paul's "separate parts into the body on purpose" (Griswold, 1990, p. 71). Fives portrays the chaplain's positive involvement by describing the ways the nurses learned from the chaplain in Emergency (Fives, 1977). VandeCreek specifically explores three ambiguities to spell out why the collaboration between the nurse and chaplain is inevitable. The first ambiguity is that the nurse and chaplain have the same concerns for the spiritual needs of the patient and this discussion is necessary; the second ambiguity is that the chaplain relies on the nurse's referral, which comes from the nurse's personal and professional experience of the patient; the third is the element of parish clergy. There is a tendency for the nurse to consult a colleague who is a chaplain, rather than one who is outside of the hospital community (VandeCreek, 1997, p. 279).

One literature resource recognizes and indicates collisions between the nurse and the chaplain in the process of collaborative work among parish nurses, healthcare chaplains and community clergy (Schumann & Vanduivendyk, 2001). Nevertheless, the discussion is limited to the reasons why the various philosophies, boundaries, priorities and the "desires, wishes and perceptions" of chaplains, nurses and parish clergy may collide when providing care for patients (Schumann & Vanduivendyk, 2001, p. 65).

In the two groups of related literature, the acknowledgment of the presence of emotions such as fear, rage, anxiety and anger in conflict is emerging (Gill, 1995) and uncontrolled emotion is considered a sign of loss in negotiation (Beare, 1989). Davidhizar and Dowd assert that anger is a spontaneous response to feelings of conflict, lack of power of being unfairly treated, and warn that anger can be a major obstacle to positive relationship. Davidhizar & Dowd suggest that it is better to wait until "calm and objective thinking" arises and not to respond in anger (Davidhizar and Dowd, 2001, p. 14). Despite the acknowledgment of the presence of emotion in conflict, conflict mostly seems to be observed as an external phenomenon on the basis of behaviour and is perceived as a problem, so that a win-win negotiation is suggested as a method of problem-solving. Greenberg, however, recognizes internal dynamics of emotions in conflict and values emotion. Emotion is, for Greenberg and Johnson, not a spin-off of the process of the conflict, but a valuable and useful ingredient of the transformation (Greenberg & Johnson, 1988). Emotions are, thus, not feelings to avoid in conflict but active feelings that could be worked on. Further, for Greenberg, for each dimension of the conflict the aspect of voice quality and depth of experiencing are deeply intertwined with resolution. The change of voice thus tends to generate internally a new meaning (Greenberg, 1986a, p. 7).

In spite of the recognition of the value of co-operative work between nurses and chaplains and the acknowledgment of possible collisions between these professionals, little has been written about the specific case of conflict management between the two professionals in a clinical setting. When the conflict is viewed as an "inevitable and essential" element in life (Leininger, 1976, p. 165) and when a conflicted relationship may enhance patient care (Davidhizar & Dowd, 2001, p. 13), the need for conflict management among the health professionals should be recognized and thoroughly explored. The literature indicates that conflict is recognized as an inevitable event in life. Nevertheless, the spiritual dimension of conflict in terms of how both parties move to the realization of learning through the transformation of conflict has not been investigated. The purpose of this research begins with the hope that the outcome of the research results in a positive impact on various working relationships.

Method

This research was born out of a conflict between a charge nurse and a chaplain on a clinical unit in a teaching hospital. The conflict had a positive outcome. The authors of this study wondered how the nurse and chaplain managed the conflict. Thus, the research question is, "How is the conflict between a nurse and a chaplain managed?" Since the conflict and resolution had already taken place, the research is based on the nurse's and the chaplain's recollection of and reflection on the conflict. Conversation analysis was chosen as the qualitative method to investigate the question. The hospital's ethics board gave its approval, ensuring informed consent, confidentiality, anonymity and no harm to participants. The nurse and chaplain were interviewed together and this interview was audiotaped and then transcribed.

Four questions were asked of the nurse and chaplain.

- How do the nurse and the chaplain remember the conversation in conflict?

- How are the turns of the conversation and the conflict differently perceived by the nurse and the chaplain?

- How is the conversation in conflict reflected upon by the nurse and the chaplain?

- How does the hostility and anger (initial encounter) move to the realization of conflict as a learning opportunity (transformation of conflict; spiritual aspect of conflict)?

The transcribed data were coded and thematically analyzed.

Conversation analysis is a discovery-oriented qualitative research method. It is concerned with the process, focusing on "how" questions and on the specific occurrence of shift in the conversation. Through this process of discovery, the method looks into where and how the various themes emerge and develop, and how the meaning is constructively formed (Gale, 1996; Gale & Newfield, 1992). Conversation analysis is a method of data analysis that describes how language is used to elicit new constructions of reality. It offers descriptive categories useful to both clinicians and researchers (Gale & Newfield, 1992).

During the conversation, the conflict reached a new reality. Several themes emerged during the data analysis, which ultimately constitute the therapeutic realities that brought the conflict to resolution. What this study provides is understanding of how "talk" may contribute to creating new "therapeutic realities."

Narrative of the Conflict

The conflict occurred one morning. A unit chaplain received a referral (a yellow note from the department secretary, which was written by a receptionist of the unit in charge the day before) and visited a patient. When the chaplain was visiting the patient, there was a nurse starting an IV for the patient. During the visit, the patient looked anxious and talked only a little with the chaplain. The chaplain went to the office after the visits on the unit and to the nursing station to do the charting. The chaplain entered the nursing station and asked the clerk where the chart was. The charge nurse turned to the chaplain, asking why the chaplain was looking for the chart. This is when the conflict began. After the incident, the chaplain attempted to talk over the conflict with the charge nurse, by inviting the nurse to lunch and coffee. Lunch took place the day after the incident and the nurse and chaplain met over coffee one or two weeks later. The charge nurse agreed to meet and was open to the conversation.

Results

The data consists of five themes. These themes are developed through the coding system based on content analysis. The various themes explain where the turn-taking occurs in the process of conversation and the process of conflict management. In this display of the data, **N** is the nurse and **C** is the chaplain. The subsequent number represents the person's turn in the conversation.

Theme 1: Nurse and chaplain have similarities and differences in remembering the conflict. Both nurse and chaplain thought the outcome was positive.

The interview shows *similarities* in how the nurse and chaplain remember a possible hurt to the chaplain. The interview also shows *differences* in perceptions of the conflict. The nurse frequently notes that the chaplain's perceptions were very succinct and did not encompass the whole picture of the conflict. The nurse's remembrance was focused on the cause of the conflict. During the interview, the nurse gave ample background information for the day of conflict. The nurse somehow sensed the chaplain's hurt by the look on the chaplain's face. The chaplain described the nurse's way of talking as abrupt – devoid of explanation or background. The nurse's initial talk was hurtful to the chaplain.

On nurse's part

First, the cause of the conflict is rooted both in a boundary issue between the nurse and chaplain and in a misunderstanding between the nurse, chaplain and patient.

N2: Two things, really. One [was] that she [a nurse] was busy trying to get the patient ready for surgery and you were chatting with the patient. And she had to start intravenous. You went to the other side of the bed and continued. It just didn't allow her to finish what she was doing. [The other was] she said that the patient asked why you had to come to see him, that he hadn't asked for a visit.

Second, the nurse was not aware that chaplains could write in charts. The nurse had not seen chaplains writing charts on the unit. Third, the nurse disagreed with the chaplain's understanding of the conversation:

N2: I don't remember saying it quite that way. Maybe I did. I would feel very badly if I answered so sharply as that.

N6 (lashing out and venting her anger continuously): Oh my goodness! That was a very bad perception, I think on your part. I don't think that I put it quite [so] succinctly ... I think we've left parts of this out, making it a lot worse ... Well, I think that that's the way you heard.

N21: I do think that some of [the] earlier conversation ... that doesn't quite give the whole picture. I do recognize that clearly if you were feeling overwhelmed, I didn't convey something in a very good way.

Fourth, the nurse did not remember that the chaplain said that there had been a referral from the secretary to see that patient.

C20: Oh. Right. I got a referral from our secretary to see that patient.

N20: You see, I don't remember you saying that. But anyway.

Fifth, the nurse sensed that the chaplain's feelings had been hurt.

N21: You can write the chart. It will be on the tray. After we are done with [the] patient, you may write the chart. You know, you are doing a great job. I did not mean to hurt your feelings.

On chaplain's part

First, the chaplain did not hear the nurse's full explanation when the nurse was talking to the chaplain. The chaplain felt stunned and speechless.

C21: Yeah, that's right. Somehow the way you talked to me was not ... it was just boom, boom, boom.

Second, the chaplain thought that the nurse's tone of voice went up during the conflict. The nurse was concerned that the chaplain was asking questions of patients that made them more anxious and fearful before their surgery. She challenged the chaplain. The chaplain found the nurse's speech abrupt. Then the tone went down after the chaplain asked the nurse what kind of question the nurse would ask if their roles were reversed. When the chaplain affirmed the nurse's question as part of the chaplain's approach, the tone and tension started to de-escalate.

C13 (accommodating the nurse's response and respecting her opinion): What do you think that I could ask?

N14: You might say, "I came to see how you are doing. What are your concerns and thoughts around the operation?" ("I think that that's perfectly acceptable": nurse's commentary)

C15: That's exactly what I am doing. (Nurse's attitude is changing.)

N16 (tone changes): Ah.

The audiotaped interview itself was helpful for conflict management. Even though there were similarities and differences in terms of both remembering and perceiving the conflict, the hearing of each person's perceptions was very helpful. Vulnerability was present in the conversation.

Theme 2: The similarities and differences in evaluating the turns of the conflict and chaplain's approach.

In the area of differences, the nurse perceived that the chaplain's invitation for lunch was an extended opportunity. The chaplain thought that the lunch was a turning point of the conflict.

C8: Right. And okay. What do you think? Was there any turn or turning point that you felt during the conversation. I approached and explained what happened ...

N9: You mean, prior to lunch?

N16: And we sort of resolved a lot later in our lunch meeting.

N20: That was new information to me. For me, I have to honest with you. There was no turning point for me as far as recognizing the value and importance of your presence there.

The chaplain thought that there were two turns in the management of the conflict. The first one was within the conversation of conflict. The chaplain thought that the nurse's tone changed after the chaplain explained what kind of questions the chaplain could ask during the visit. In terms of the whole conflict, the chaplain felt that both the nurse and the chaplain were in the same reality during the second meeting over coffee, when they debriefed the conflict, which came after the lunch. That was the second turn of the conflict.

C15: That's exactly what I am doing. (Nurse's attitude is changing.)

N16 (tone changes): Ah. (**C**: That was just the next door, you remember? We talked about it.) Yes. (**C**: I saw you somehow calmed down after you heard that. Somehow that there was understanding going on. Yes. So, (imitating tone change), is that what you are doing? That kind of feeling I received from you.

C37: And then after I suggested that coffee or lunch, you were quite open. That was a really graceful moment. And the most graceful moment was when we were having coffee. (**N**: Yes.) You saw something going on within me. (**N**: Yes...)

The chaplain dropped the boundary issue in the actual incident, while listening to the nurse's suggestion regarding the possibility of questions for the patient during the pastoral visit.

C13 (accommodating nurse's response and respecting nurse's opinion): What do you think that I could ask?

N14: You might say, "I came to see how you are doing. What are your concerns and thoughts around the operation?" ("I think that that's perfectly acceptable": nurse's commentary)

C15: That's exactly what I am doing. (Nurse's attitude is changing.)

The nurse did not frame the incident as a conflict, but as a learning opportunity. The chaplain saw it as a conflict and the learning arose in the process.

N34: Oh, absolutely, I think. Although I am distressed to think about the original incident referred to as a conflict.

N36: I hate to think of it as a conflict. I prefer to think of it as learning about others' roles and clarifying.

C37: There was a point that I felt speechless. I was wondering where it was from ... and then ... So there was a kind of a point that way your attitude changed. Wow. It's great that there was a change.

In the area of similarities, both the nurse and chaplain perceived that the chaplain's gentle, non-anxious and calm approach were crucial in managing the conflict.

C41: I place all my needs before the Lord to see where the Lord really leads this to. Without knowing, you were willing to help me. Wow. Where is this from? (Nurse laughing.) I am fine without it. It doesn't really matter. We wouldn't feel comfortable to go back. It's not a pleasant experience.

The nurse told the chaplain at the end of the interview that the chaplain was gentle. During the conflict the chaplain sought to be non-anxious and gentle. The chaplain was gentle in seeking an opportunity to continue the conversation with the nurse. During the talk, the chaplain's way of asking questions was neither argumentative nor abrupt. When the chaplain asked the nurse for help, the conversation changed. Later on reflection, the nurse noted:

N70: You are gentle, you know.

C1: Can you remember from the beginning and the conversation possibly too?

C3: And can you remember when after I finished my visit, I went back to the nursing unit and I was looking for the chart?

C18: What I am hearing from you is that the turning point was your awareness of what we are doing. Is that … ?

C21: Do you want to see how I (big laugh from both) … How do you feel. How do you feel now? Are you feeling okay?

C29: I guess based on what I remembered and … that's why I wanted to show you. Well, thank you for your reflection. Are you feeling okay?

C31: I hope that somehow my own perception wouldn't influence you badly.

Finally, the chaplain's invitation to lunch and coffee for extended opportunities to talk were good ingredients in the conflict management, without leaving the conflict behind.

N40: Very gratifying on my part, too. I think that it could have been left and we would have been left. We wouldn't have been at this point of, I would say, on a friendlier and more comfortable basis.

N56: You started to roll the ball, I guess. You did.

Theme 3: During the talk, mutual explaining, open listening, respect, understanding and acceptance were crucial. Both nurse and chaplain thought that they managed conflict well.

First, the nurse apologized to the chaplain.

N34: If that came out in such a way that you were feeling either offended or as I say less welcomed, my apologies certainly for that … I think that that's what you felt from what was said.

Because the nurse experienced the exchange as open listening, respect and understanding, she thought that the incident should be understood as learning, not as a conflict.

N36: I hate to think of it as a conflict. I preferred to think of it as learning each other's roles and clarifying.

Second, the nurse felt grateful for an extended opportunity to get to know the chaplain after the exchange through coffee and lunch. The nurse got to know more about the chaplain as a person and felt friendlier and more comfortable.

N40: Again, I am grateful, as I said, for extending the opportunity … But in fact, I think that it's much more than that now. I am very grateful for having the opportunity that you extended to me to meet and chat. There were each other's past experiences and how we got to where we are and what we are here doing for patients. So I think that was very enlightening on both of our parts (both chuckle) – certainly on my part.

N42: Again, I am grateful, as I said, for extending the opportunity. (**C**: Wow.) Thank you. It worked out really well. I hope you feel the same.

Third, the nurse felt that both the chaplain and the nurse managed conflict well.

N54: OK. That's good. I think that we did a good job (chuckle), coming to this point from how you felt from the beginning. (Both laugh.)

Fourth, the chaplain and nurse mentioned that mutual explaining, open listening, respect, understanding and acceptance were crucial. For the chaplain, this was a grace-filled moment.

C37: There was a point that I felt speechless. I was wondering where it was from ... and then ... So there was a kind of a point that way your attitude changed ... So ... Wow. It's great that there was a change. And then after I suggested that, you know, coffee or lunch, you were quite open. That was a really graceful moment. And the most graceful moment was when we were having coffee. (**N**: Yes.) You saw something going on within me. (**N**: Yes...)

C39: I was impressed while we were having coffee ... by you, your qualities within you. I told you when I asked you for lunch. It was the second time? (**N**: Yes.) Once I say it, there's nothing left there. It's all gone. That was grace, too. (**N**: Wow, that's good.) Having coffee and altogether ... the whole [process] was really wonderful.

Part of the mutual respect and understanding was the chaplain's invitation to lunch and coffee. These were the ingredients for the conflict management, without leaving the conflict behind. The nurse notes the importance of the informal atmosphere of coffee and lunch as part of the change.

N40: Very gratifying on my part, too. I think that it could have been left and we would have been left. We wouldn't have been at this point of, I would say, on more friendlier and comfortable basis.

N56: You started to roll the ball, I guess. You did.

In the transcript of the interview between the nurse and chaplain, there is a gentle tone that underscores the respect, understanding, open listening and acceptance. In remembering and reflecting on the conflict, both the nurse and the chaplain were mostly relaxed. During the interview, the tone of the voice was not high. During the interview, the nurse and chaplain chuckled often. According to the transcript, the nurse and chaplain laughed in ten out of seventy exchanges. There is more laughter at the end than at the beginning. This is a signal of the growing development of respect, listening and understanding.

Theme 4: Sharing honest feelings and clarifying the cause were vital.

Both the nurse and the chaplain shared honest feelings. That was a crucial element in the management of the conflict. By doing so, both the nurse and the chaplain were able to reach the same reality, which brought joy and a spirit of love to both of them.

N38: I am grateful that you wanted not to leave just the first conversation as it was. You reached out, because you were looking for resolution, not wanting to be at odds with one another. And ... I think that was very good. I have probably known more about you as a person and you probably have me, too. (**C**: Sure.)

C39: I was impressed while we were having coffee ... by you, your qualities within you. I told you when I asked you for lunch. It was the second time? (**N**: Yes.) Once I say it, there's nothing left there. It's all gone. That was grace, too.

The chaplain in the conflict felt like an underdog and the nurse a topdog. According to Greenberg's terminology (Greenberg, 1984a), one party feels like the underdog during the conflict. However, in the management of the conflict, underdog versus topdog seemed to disappear. This stage is what Greenberg calls "the stage of integration" (Greenberg, 1984a, p. 84). Similar intra-psychic dynamics are found in Meier & Boivin's research on conflict resolution (Meier & Boivin, 2001). The change happened when the topdog (nurse) became empathetic towards the underdog (chaplain) and then mutual understanding occurred, in sharing honest feelings.

In the process of the conflict, both parties strove to seek the cause of the disagreement. Later in the talk, the chaplain showed the nurse a referral note written by the unit clerk and given to the secretary of the spiritual care department. The nurse understood the awkward position that the chaplain was in. The cause of the conflict was clarified and listened to.

C50: I remember just a new thing came up in our conversation about that particular patient (showing the referral note to the nurse). I got a referral from your department. I guess that our secretary received that so she asked me to see that patient. I went to see that patient and he looked perplexed – What is [the] chaplain doing here? – and then he told me that he got anxious. He got quite anxious about the whole surgery. That was the greatest change happening in his life. Although the nurse came in, I stayed for a while. I felt that I had to stay for a while to care for the patient. I normally leave. I think that that's what happened on that day.

N51: Clearly you were in a bit of a quandary, too. Because on the one hand, you were being asked to see the patient and then you come in and the nurse was busy with the patient. So I guess the other part of this would be to communicate to the nurse ... I think that if you make the nurse aware that you have been asked to pay a visit. If you are there just to hold the hands if that's all they want. If she is not needing any response from the patient, then clearly you can stay and you know either [to] say a few words or have a prayer, whatever the patient really wants.

Theme 5: Transformation in emotion

Towards the end of the talk, the transformation of emotion took place. The negative emotion was transformed into positive emotion: from anger and hostility during the initial encounter to recognizing the conflict as a gift and a learning experience. The nurse's hostility and anger moved to affirmation and the chaplain's hurt feelings were healed and transformed. In hindsight, the chaplain realized that the conflict as a whole had been a blessing. The chaplain did not see that at the time of the conflict, but later realized it.

First, the nurse's respect for the chaplain grew.

N48: I think that you are absolutely right. It does not matter what was said or how it was said. But it's what happened in terms of since then. As I said, I have come to respect you a lot for what you are here doing and what we ought to do and the very value you have.

N52: Oh no, not for me. I certainly have no issues.

N54: I think that we did a good job (chuckle) coming to this point from where you felt from the beginning. (Both laugh.) I would have to say, had you not invited me to have lunch to open up ... to each other it would have been left there. Wouldn't it? I wouldn't have any hurt feelings and I would hope that you wouldn't. But that's less than the best it could be. We brought it far further than that ... If anything comes out of this, it would be to communicate, to not be afraid to bring this thing forward to say, "Do you think that we could sit down and just talk?" And a lot can come out from that, as we have seen here. I think that other people would like to find that that would be the better place, if they are having some issues.

It should be noted that after the conflict management, the chaplain has gained greater respect for the nurses, especially when the nurses are working on the patients before surgery. Second, the nurse acknowledged the significance of the chaplain's initiation of the conflict resolution.

N56: You started to roll the ball, I guess. You did.

Third, the nurse recognized the change and learning that resulted from the conflict management process and complimented the chaplain accordingly.

N68: It's been a good experience for me, too. It also makes me reflect on just because I want to clarify something with someone that I have to be very conscientious how it was perceived. My intention might be different from what the other person has taken it. I am certainly aware of that. So ... you can never not learn something like this. I am taking away something from it. (Both chuckle.)

Fourth, the chaplain experienced healing and that hurt feeling was transformed into an uplifting experience, and both the nurse and the chaplain affirmed each other, acknowledging that the conflict was resolved and transformation took place mutually.

C39: I was impressed while we were having coffee ... by you, your qualities within you. I told you when I asked you for lunch. It was second time? (**N**: Yes.) Once I said it there's nothing left there. It's all gone. That was grace, too. (**N**: Wow, that's good.) Having coffee and altogether the whole [process] was really wonderful.

C55: Again, I would like to emphasize that it is mutual and you were open to it.

C69: To me, every moment is a gift from God. This experience has been also a gift from God, though it was not a pleasant start. I have learned to confront things, by following my heart's desire.

Discussion: Theological Reflection and Limitations of Research

In the process of managing this conflict, four kinds of movements occurred. First, there was a movement from cognitive to feeling. Conflicted reality moved away from the cognition phase, and later was integrated by being holistic. Secondly, the beginning of the conflict was very intense in terms of emotion and the dimension of conflict made a gradual shift to gentle and relaxing reality, as the conflict management progressed. Thirdly, with respect to transformation of emotion, hostility and anger moved to affirmation. Initially, the chaplain felt that the nurse perceived the chaplain as a hindrance to the unit and this moved to the realization of the chaplain's presence as a gift in the unit. Finally, when the conflict was managed, both parts experienced forgiveness, healing and reconciliation. Forgiveness is, according to Powell, "not to bring us back to where we were as if nothing happened" (Powell, 2003, p. 203), but it is moving to a reality and its nature is quite different from where we were. This dovetails with what Jesus said about forgiveness, "Not seven times, but, I tell you, seventy-seven times" (Mt 18:21-22, NRSV).

Crucial to the management of conflict in conversation is that one of the parties remains fairly calm. In this case, it was the gentleness of the chaplain. With the rise in feeling, especially hostility and anger, it is easy for the conflict to run out of control. Edwin Friedman mentions that a non-anxious presence in ministry is important to a congregation in chaos (Friedman, 1985). Certainly, the chaplain believed that the chaplain visiting the patients before surgery and writing in their charts was a challenge to the nurse's role and place in the institution. The nurse noted feelings of chaos. However, the chaplain did not escalate the chaos by challenging the nurse and demanding the rights the chaplain is supposed to have. Rather, in the chaos, the chaplain remained calm and asked the nurse to suggest questions to ask patients before surgery. The gentle, non-anxious presence is crucial to the management of a conflict.

From the perspective of the chaplain, the conflict was a painful experience. In a situation of self-conflict, the chaplain's world was chaotic and confused with the wondering as well as wandering. For a brief moment, the chaplain felt a challenge in terms of identity and role as a chaplain. The stories of Job (Job 30:16-17, 20–21) and Jonah (Jon 1:3, 5-7) seem to capture the chaotic reality. Nietzsche's image of the dancing star born out of the chaos best describes the transformative experience for the chaplain, who experienced healing. Later, the chaplain felt grateful for the gift of the conflict and thankful to the nurse for being part of the journey of spiritual growth. In hindsight, the chaplain thought that the nurse was a gift from God for spiritual growth. The chaplain's understanding of God's love and grace has deepened, believing that nurse's role in the growth was as precious as the personal transformation. In a nutshell, both the chaplain and the nurse went through the chaos of a different kind and became dancing and sparkling stars.

The research has looked at a case study of conflict management. The data were coded and analyzed using a conversation analysis research method. The result of the research shows five themes that helped conflict management between a nurse and a chaplain. In this study, conflict was not viewed in a dualistic perspective but rather was approached from a postmodern angle which embraces the whole process of conflict as well as the beginning and the outcome. The process of conflict management was analyzed from a psychological and theological point of view.

Some limitations remain in this research. This research borrowed a conversation analysis research method to analyze a case study. The focus was mainly on "how" questions and turn-takings in the conflict management process. The study did not look into breathing, both inhalation and exhalation, in depth, as is the case in the actual conversation analysis.

This case does not intend to generalize about conflict management. In order for this case to work generally, more research concerning conflict management would be needed in the future.

References

Anonymous. (1998). Everyday spirituality can help healthcare professionals sustain their passion. *Health Progress*, July/August, 79(4): 32–33.

Anonymous. (2000). Overcoming difficulties in communicating with other professionals. *Nursing Times*, 96(28): 47–49.

Baker, K. M. (1995). Improving staff nurse conflict resolution skills. *Nursing Economics*, Sept./Oct., 13: 295–298, 317.

Beare, P. G. (1989). The essentials of win-win negotiation for the clinical nurse specialist. *Clinical Nurse Specialist*, 3(3): 138–141.

Cox, S. (2000). Improving communication between care settings. *Professional Nurse*, 15(4): 267–271.

Davidhizar, R. & Dowd, S. (2001). How to get along with doctors and other health professionals. *Journal of Practical Nursing*, Spring, 51(1): 12–14.

Dealing with conflict. Available at www.nsba.org/sbot/toolkit/Conflict.html. (Accessed April 25, 2006.)

Deutsch, M. (1971). Conflict and its resolution, in C. G. Smith (ed.) *Conflict Resolution: Contributions of the Behavioral Sciences* (pp. 36–57). Notre Dame: University of Notre Dame.

Deutsch, M. & Coleman, P. (eds.) (2000). *The Handbook of Conflict Resolution: Theory and Practice*. San Francisco: Jossey-Bass Publishers.

Eickhoff, A. M. (1982). The chaplain-nurse relationship. *Nursing Management*, 13(3): 25–26.

Emblen, J. D. & Halstead, M. (1993). Spiritual needs and interventions: Comparing the views of patients, nurses, and chaplains. *Clinical Nursing Specialist*, 7: 175–182.

Firth-Cozens, J. (1998). Celebrating teamwork. *Quality in Health Care*, 7 (Supp.): 3–7.

Fives, B. (1977). Support your patient's family – with a chaplain. *RN*, March: 58–59.

Franklin D., Piscolish, M. A. & Stephens, J. B. (2000). *Researching for Higher Ground in Conflict Resolution: Tools for Powerful Groups and Communities*. San Francisco: Jossey-Bass Publishers.

Friedman, E. H. (1985). *Generation to Generation: Family Process in Church and Synagogue*. New York: The Guildford Press.

Gale, J. E. (1991). *Conversation Analysis of Therapeutic Discourse: The Pursuit of a Therapeutic Agenda*. Norwood, NJ: Ablex.

Gale, J. E. (1996). Conversation analysis: Studying the construction of therapeutic realities in D. Sprenkle and S. Moon (eds.), *Research Methods in Family Therapy* (pp. 107–126). New York: The Guildford Press.

Gale, J. E. & Newfield, N. (1992). A Conversation analysis of a solution-focused marital therapy session. *Journal of Marital and Family Therapy*, 18: 153–165.

Gill, S. L. (1995). Resolving conflicts: principles and practice. *Physician Executive*, *21*(4): 11–15.

Gill, S. L. & Spence M. S. (1988). Five roadblocks to effective partnerships in a competitive health care environment. *Journal of Healthcare Management*, Winter, *33*(4): 505–520.

Goodwin, C. & Heritage, J. (1990). Conversation analysis. *Annual Review of Anthropology*, *19*: 283–307.

Greeding, D. M. & Honn, D. (2001). Modeling the wisdom of journeying together: parish nursing and chaplaincy, *Journal of Health Care Chaplaincy*, *11*(2): 69–80.

Greenberg, L. S. (1982) Psychotherapy process research, in E. Walker (ed.), *Handbook of clinical psychotherapy* (pp. 164-204). New York: Dorsey Press.

Greenberg, L. S. (1983). Toward a task analysis of conflict resolution in Gestalt therapy. *Psychotherapy: Theory, Research and Practice, 20*: 190–201.

Greenberg, L. S. (1984a). A task analysis of intrapersonal conflict resolution, in L. N. Rice & L. S. Greenberg (eds.), *Patterns of change: Intensive analysis of psychotherapy process* (pp. 67–123). New York: The Guildford Press.

Greenberg, L. S. (1984b). Task analysis: The general approach, in L. N. Rice & L. S. Greenberg (eds.), *Patterns of change: Intensive analysis of psychotherapy process* (pp. 124–148). New York: The Guildford Press.

Greenberg, L. S. (1986a). Change process research. *Journal of Consulting and Clinical psychology, 54*(1): 4–9.

Greenberg, L. S. (1986b). Research strategies, in L. S. Greenberg & W. M. Pinsof (eds.) *The Psychotherapeutic Process: A Research Handbook* (pp. 707–734). New York: The Guildford Press.

Greenberg, L. S. & Johnson, S. M. (1988). *Emotionally Focused Therapy for Couples.* New York: The Guildford Press.

Greenberg, L. S., Rice, L. & Elliott, R. (1993). *Facilitating Emotional Change: The Moment-by-Moment Process.* New York: The Guildford Press.

Greenberg, L. S. & Webster, M. C. (1982). Resolving decisional conflict by Gestalt two-chair dialogue: Relating process to outcome. *Journal of Counseling Psychology,* 29: 468–477.

Griswold, C. A. (1990). Pastoral partners. *Health Progress, 71*(2): 71–73.

Hall, Jr., J. L. & Stong, R. A. (1993). Alternative dispute resolution and the physician: The use of mediation to resolve hospital-medical staff conflicts. *The Medical Staff Counselor,* Spring, *7*(2): 1–8.

Harris, M. D. & Shatterly, L. R. (1998). Medicare and the nurse: The chaplain as a member of the hospice team. *Home Healthcare Nurse, 16*(9): 591–593.

Horvath, Adam O. & Greenberg, L. S. (eds.). (1994). *The Working Alliance: Theory, Research and Practice.* New York: Wiley.

Kellett, P. M. & Dalton, D. G. (2001). *Managing Conflict in a Negotiated World: Narrative Approach to Achieving Dialogue and Change.* Thousand Oaks, CA: Sage Publications.

Laser, R. J. (1981). I win–you win negotiating. *Journal of Nursing Administration,* 11: 24–29.

Leininger, M. (1974). The leadership crisis in nursing: A critical problem and challenge. *The Journal of Nursing Administration,* March–April, *4*(2): 28–30.

Leininger, M. (1976). Conflict and conflict resolutions: theories and processes relevant to the health profession. *Healthcare Dimensions,* 3: 165–183.

Littlejohn, S. W. & Domenici, K. (2001). *Engaging Communication in Conflict.* Thousand Oaks, CA: Sage Publications.

McGilloway, F. A. (1977). Religion and patient care: the functionalist approach. *Journal of Advanced Nursing,* 2: 3–13.

Meier, A. & Boivin, M. (2001). Conflict resolution: The interplay affects, cognition and needs in the resolution of intrapersonal conflicts. *Pastoral Sciences*, 20 (1): 93–119.

Morris, K. & Foerster, J. D. (1972). Team work: Nurse and chaplain. *American Journal of Nursing*, *72*(12): 2197–2199.

Pape, T. (1999). A systems approach to resolving OR conflict. *Association of periOperative Registered Nurses Journal*, *69*(3): 551–553, 556–557, 560–566.

Powell, E. (2003). *The Heart of Conflict: A Spirituality of Transformation*. Kelowna, BC: Northstone.

Rakley, S. M. (1999). When I stopped yelling, everybody started listening. *Medical Economics*, *76*(19): 131, 134 and 137-138.

Schumann, R. & Vanduivendyk, T. (2001). Connections, collisions, and complementarity: the dynamic of health care chaplain, parish nurse and parish clergy collaboration. *Journal of Health Care Chaplaincy*. *11*(2): 61–67.

Sussman, D. (2000). A spirited approach: nurses, chaplains team up to provide pastoral care. *Nursing and Allied Healthcare*, 5: 12–end.

Vandecreek, L. (1997). Collaboration between nurse and chaplains for spiritual caregiving. *Seminars in Oncology Nursing*, *13*(4): 279–280.

Winslade, J. & Monk, G. (2000). *Narrative Mediation: A New Approach to Conflict Resolution*. San Francisco: Jossey-Bass Publishers.

Wright, P. (1980). Nurse and chaplain: Administering to both a patient's physical and emotional needs can be a very difficult task. *Nursing Times*, July 24: 1314–1316.

13

Intrapsychic Conflicts, Their Formation, Underlying Dynamics and Resolution: An Object Relations Perspective

Augustine Meier and Micheline Boivin

In their published study on the process of resolving intrapsychic conflicts, Meier and Boivin (2001) reported data that they interpreted in terms of the interplay among client cognitive, affective and need statements. The aim of their study was to demonstrate the significant role that need statements play in the resolution of conflicts.[1] The purpose of the current study is to re-examine this data from the perspective of object relations theory and determine how this perspective can add to the understanding of the process of resolving intrapsychic conflicts.

The first part of this chapter presents the theoretical aspects of object relations theory pertinent to the understanding of intrapsychic conflicts. The second part summarizes the empirical literature on the resolution of intrapsychic conflicts. The research method of the original study is presented in the third part and the

---

1   Meier and Boivin (2001) provide a rationale for the inclusion of needs, wants and desires in a theoretical model regarding the understanding of human phenomena, including conflicts. They refer to the contributions by Freud (1938), Murray (1938), Maslow (1954), Perls (1969), Blanck & Blanck (1979), Zajonc (1980), Benesh & Weiner (1982), Lazarus (1982), Yalom (1989) and Stumpf (Reisenzein et al., 1992), all of whom argue for the integration of needs, wants and desires in a model of human behaviour. Meier and Boivin provide a four-phase model of conflict resolution: opposition, empathic, collaboration and resolution phases.

findings summarized in the fourth.[2] The last part discusses these findings in terms of object relations theory.

Object Relations Theory

Resolving intrapsychic conflicts is very different from resolving interpsychic (interpersonal) conflicts. In interpsychic conflicts, the parties at war with each other are known. The stance that each takes towards the other(s) is apparent. Often the warring parties can be described as the "oppressor" and the "oppressed," the "controller" and the "controlled," and so on. The parties in conflict speak from a voice that is consistent with their perceived position in the relationship.

In the case of intrapsychic conflicts, the warring parties are within the person's psychic structure. So how do intrapsychic conflicts begin and how are they resolved?

An object relations theory of the development of intrapsychic conflicts and their resolution rests on the pillars of Freudian psychoanalysis and on the contributions made by Klein, Fairbairn, Winnicott, Mahler et al. and Kernberg.

Freudian Contribution

Freud (1938) defines splits (conflicts) as "two mental attitudes [that] have been formed instead of a single one – one, the normal one, which takes account of reality, and another that, under the influence of the instincts, detaches the ego from reality. The two exist alongside each other" (p. 73). Freud assumed that underlying an intrapsychic conflict is a psyche that is divided and at war with itself. Freud (1923) conceptualized the psyche in terms of three structures or agencies, namely, the Id, Ego and Superego. Psychic structure refers to the dynamic internal organization of the mind. According to Freudian theory, both the Id and the Ego emerge from the potentials of an innate inheritance described as an undifferentiated matrix (Hartmann, 1939), with the Id representing instincts,

---

2   The editors of *Pastoral Sciences* granted permission for the inclusion of the literature review, research methodology and findings from the article published by Meier & Boivin (2001). It was decided to include most of this information, since the journal does not have a wide readership and is not available in every library.

urges and drives (innate inheritance) and the Ego representing the rational component of the psyche. The Superego is the product of socialization and enculturation and represents the prolongation of parental influence (social inheritance) (Freud, 1938). Intrapsychic conflicts are the result of the unconscious demands of two or more agencies (e.g., the innate inheritance versus the social inheritance) that are at war with each other or with reality. The Ego acts as the mediator between the instinctual urges of the Id and the internalized social forces of the Superego (Freud, 1938). When not mediated and harmonized, the urges of the Id and the forces of the Superego lead to intrapsychic (internal) conflicts.

Object relations theorists elaborated on Freud's model and added a conceptual sophistication to the formation of psychic structure and to the development of conflicts.

Concepts central to this elaboration are primary motives, formation of internal object representations, formation of internal self-representations, development of psychic structure, and development and resolution of intrapsychic conflicts.[3] These concepts are presented below, with particular reference to the contribution of Fairbairn.

Primary Motives

According to psychodynamic theory, personality, psychic structures and conflicts are the products of the interaction of a person's primary needs, wants and desires with significant others and with reality. Freud (1938) conceptualized the primary motives in terms of two instincts, namely, the life instinct (eros) and the death instinct (thanatos). The push to actualize these instincts is considered to be the primary motivating force within a person that leads to personality development and influences interactions with others.

Object relations theorists (Klein, 1936, 1959; Fairbairn, 1943/1954, 1944/1954; Winnicott, 1962/1965) reject Freud's notion that a person is primarily driven by instincts and suggest that the

---

3   Since object relations theory, its concepts and the linkages of its concepts are not that well known to the readers, this section will be presented in somewhat greater detail than others.

drive towards relationships is the most fundamental motive, that is "libido is object-seeking" (Klein, 1936, 1959). This drive towards relationships is expressed in terms of two forces or strivings, the force to be connected and the force to be separated (Mahler, Pine & Bergman, 1975). "The force to be connected" means to be bonded with a significant other (e.g., mother) for the purpose of physical nourishment, emotional nurturing, safety, security and protection. "The force to be separated" means to take distance from the loved object (e.g., mother) to become one's own person and to become individuated. These two forces have also been referred to as the striving for "oneness" and the striving for "separateness" (Kaplan, 1978). For healthy development, it is important that these two forces find expression in a balanced and harmonious way within oneself and in relationships.

Within the context of seeking out relationships and then separating from them, the infant also seeks affirmation regarding his or her ambitions and successes and his or her goodness as a person (Kohut, 1977). The need for affirmation of the child's ambitions is organized around his or her narcissistic needs for omnipotence and grandeur, while the need for affirmation of his or her goodness is organized around his or her ideals (idealized parental image). These two stivings are referred to as "nuclear ambitions" and "nuclear ideals," respectively (Kohut, 1979). The infant relies on "good enough parenting" (Winnicott, 1962/1965, p. 57) to have these needs responded to within the context of the relationship.

A child's specific relational needs and self needs change as he or she moves from being intimately bonded with his or her mother to becoming a separate and an individuated person (Mahler, Pine & Bergman, 1975). The basic relational and self needs are reworked each time the person goes through a major phase in life, such as the initial separation from the love object and leaving parents and home during adolescence (Meier & Meier, 2004). The manner in which the needs or strivings are responded to within the primary relationship (e.g., mother) will influence the bonding and separating/individuating processes, the formation of internal object- and self-representations, the development of a child's personality and the integration of his or her psychic structure. The inability to achieve these development tasks could lead to emotional problems and to intrapsychic conflict.

Formation of Internal Object Representations

The more radical object relations theorists (e.g., Fairbairn, 1944/1954) dispensed with Freud's Id as a constituent of the psychic structure and opted for a purely psychologically derived psychic structure. Fairbairn explicitly stated that "the infant from the start is a whole, is primitive, dynamic ego with a unitary striving, at first dim and blind, towards the object relationships he needs for further ego-development" (Guntrip, 1969, p. 55). There is no Id, only Ego. All libido resides in the Ego. The Ego at first is unitary; there are no divisions in the Ego. Eventually, because of the experience of frustration with external objects, the Ego becomes divided through the process of splitting to form a psychic structure.

Psychic structure, according to object relations theorists, is formed from the internalized object- and self-representations and the affects that link them (Fairbairn, 1944/1954; Kernberg, 1986). The quality of these representations, the nature of their interaction and the associated affects determine how the psychic structure is formed and how it functions. According to object relations theory, internal object-representations are built up in the following way.

In the normal course of the infant's interactions with the mother (or principal caregiver), the most important of all relationships (Klein, 1959/1975; Winnicott, 1962/1965; Mahler, Pine & Bergman, 1975; Bowlby, 1988), the infant has both pleasant and unpleasant experiences. Pleasant experiences originate from the infant having its needs met (e.g., love), whereas unpleasant experiences originate from feeling frustrated about not having its needs met. Due to the infant's immature ego and perceptual processes, it perceives the mother who responds positively to its needs as being a different person from the one who frustrates the infant. The person who responds to the infant's needs is perceived as being the "good-mother" whereas the person who frustrates the infant is considered as being the "bad-mother" – that is, as a mother who withholds love or who rejects. The infant is not able to express its hatred towards the mother because this might lead the mother to rejecting her or him even more. Nor can the infant show its need for the mother, since this might lead to greater humiliation and depreciation of his or her feelings. To deal with this situation, the infant mentally separates or splits the mother into two part-objects. In so far as the mother satisfies the infant's needs, the mother is good and in so far as the mother frustrates the infant, she is bad (Grotstein, 1981, p. 3).

Second, despite splitting the mother into two part-objects, the infant is powerless to change things in the outer world. The infant then tries to transfer the problematic factor in the interpersonal relationship with his or her mother to his or her own inner reality. The infant internalizes the mother as a good object and as bad object (Klein, 1936; 1959, p. 248). The simple internalization of the good and bad object, however, does not solve anything, since the bad object continues to be unsatisfying. It continues to have power over the infant's inner world; the infant feels possessed by it (Fairbairn, 1943/1954, p. 67). As was the case with the external object, the inner or unsatisfying object both allures and frustrates the infant. The infant, however, continues to need the alluring and frustrating object.

Third, the infant attempts to resolve the situation with the inner bad object by splitting it into an exciting (needed) object and a frustrating (rejecting) object (Fairbairn, 1944/1954, p. 89). Attached to each of these inner part-objects is a split-off and repressed part of the ego. Associated with the exciting object is the Libidinal Ego and associated with the frustrating object is the Anti-Libidinal Ego. The Libidinal Ego is the needy aspect of the ego and the Anti-Libidinal Ego is that part of the ego that identifies with the rejecting object.

Lastly, to ensure the love of the mother and to maintain a relationship with her, the infant represses the negative representations and negative affect. That is, the infant represses the exciting object with its attached Libidinal Ego and the rejecting object with its attached Anti-Libidinal Ego and associated negative affects. The infant copes with the negative experiences by splitting-off a part of the ego that becomes attached to the perceived bad object.

However, the repressed objects and ego states continue to influence the child's feelings and behaviours.

Formation of Internal Self-Representations

Parallel to forming internal representations of the mother, the infant also forms representations of self. When the mother responds positively to the infant's needs, the infant experiences pleasure and feels good about self and when the mother fails to respond to the infant's needs, the infant experiences displeasure and feels bad about self. The infant therefore forms two representations of self, the "good self" and the "bad self." In similar fashion to negative images of mother, the infant represses negative images of self – unwanted aspects of self – and stores them in the unconscious, where they continue to exercise an influence on the person's psyche. The process of forming object- and self-representations, together with the affects, leads to the organization or structuring of the psyche.

Development of Psychic Structure

According to object relations theorists, psychic structure is formed from the internalized object- and self-representations and the affects that link them (Fairbairn, 1944/1954; Kernberg, 1986). Consequently, the inner objects (good object, exciting object, rejecting object) give rise to a psychic structure that comprises three ego states: (infantile) Libidinal Ego state, Anti-Libidinal Ego state, and Central Ego state (Fairbairn, 1944/1954).

The Libidinal Ego state is that part of the self that feels needy as well as attacked or persecuted. The child dominated by this ego state feels perpetually frustrated and deprived, and thirsts for more but its thirst is never quenched (Cashdan, 1988, p. 11). In the adult, this ego state manifests itself as chronic overdependency, craving for appreciation and compulsive sexuality (Guntrip, 1973, p. 98). This ego state arises due to the alluring and enticing aspects of the mother (e.g., unkept promises) and corresponds to the "exciting object."

The Anti-Libidinal Ego state is identified with the "rejecting object" from which it arises (Guntrip, 1973, p. 98). It is the internal saboteur (attacking ego) and functions in a way similar to the Superego. This part of the ego is aggressive and attacking, especially against the needy part of the self (Libidinal Ego). It is hateful, vengeful and bitter, and rails against the denial (rejection) that it has experienced. It is controlled by an ever present fear that it is unwanted and unloveable. Yet it desperately yearns for acceptance, union and the connectedness it feels it deserves. The child dominated by this ego state is enraged and feels hateful most of the time.

The Central Ego state derives from the "ideal ego" and is still connected to those parts of the mother that were once gratifying. It relates to the environment and comprises conscious and unconscious elements. When the disturbing parts of the Libidinal and Anti-Libidinal Ego states have been split off and repressed, the Central Ego conforms with the idealized parents. Because of its compromising, the Central Ego becomes depleted (Guntrip, 1973, p. 75). This ego state alone is available for relationships with real people in the real world.

The development of object- and self-representations and their splitting into good and bad representations and the formation of the psychic structure are summarized in Figure 1.

Development and Resolution of Intrapsychic Conflict

With continued maturation and differentiation, and in the presence of "good enough parenting," the negative and positive images of the mother and self become integrated to form a representation of a "whole" mother and "whole" self that are seen as being both good and bad. These internal representations become the internal working model (Bowlby, 1988) by which the person interprets information and events, and interacts with persons. In the same manner, the internal psychic structures (Libidinal, Anti-Libidinal and Central Ego states) become integrated and harmonized. The child who has developed positive representations of mother and self is able to turn to these positive representations in times of emotional hurts and stress to seek comfort, and is able to manage with minimum conflict the Libidinal and Anti-Libidinal demands and live productively at work and in relationships.

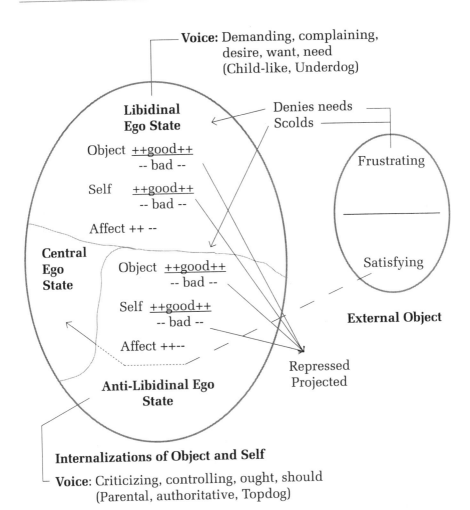

Voice: Demanding, complaining,
desire, want, need
(Child-like, Underdog)

Libidinal
Ego State

Denies needs
Scolds

Object ++good++
-- bad --

Self ++good++
-- bad --

Affect ++ --

Frustrating

Central
Ego
State

Object ++good++
-- bad --

Self ++good++
-- bad --

Affect ++--

Satisfying

External Object

Repressed
Projected

Anti-Libidinal Ego
State

Internalizations of Object and Self

Voice: Criticizing, controlling, ought, should
(Parental, authoritative, Topdog)

Figure 1. Interpersonal conflict according to Object Relations Theory

(Extrapolated from M. Klein (1959/1975). Our adult world and its roots in infancy. In *Envy and gratitude and other works, 1946-1963* (pp. 247–263). New York: Delta & W.R.D. Fairbairn (1944/1954). Endopsychic structure considered in terms of object relationships. In *An Object-relations theory of personality* (pp. 82–136). New York Basic Books.

When "good enough parenting" is interrupted in a major way (e.g., violence, parental emotional illness) or when the child is not able to avail itself of "good enough parenting," the process leading to the integration of the three ego states is halted. The three ego states remain at war with each other, with each pressuring the others for the fulfillment of its demands. The infantile Libidinal Ego, for example, craves appreciation, recognition and love and becomes overdependent, whereas the Anti-Libidinal Ego attacks the neediness of the weak and undeveloped Libidinal Ego, enforces rules and regulations, assumes a rigid control, and is angry and hateful (Guntrip, 1969, p. 195). The Central Ego, for its part, is depleted and not able to resolve the conflict between the two ego states. The child is in a state of conflict that, unless resolved, can continue into adulthood. Unlike in the Freudian model, in which the conflict resided among the Id, Ego and Superego, in object relations, the conflict resides within the Ego itself (Fairbairn, 1944/1954; Kernberg, 1986).

An object relations approach to resolving intrapsychic conflicts aims at strengthening the infantile Libidinal Ego and making it more independent of the Anti-Libidinal Ego. This means "helping the patient to become reconciled to accepting help for his weakness, so that the Libidinal Ego may become re-endowed with the energies that had been turned to anti-libidinal ends" (Guntrip, 1969, p. 195). Psychotherapy, therefore, "must aim, not simply at the resolution of specific conflicts, but at the fundamental regrowing of the basic ego, the whole personal self ... the need for a rebirth and regrowing of a 'whole person'" (Guntrip, 1969, p. 317).

In summary, a failure on part of the principal caregiver to respond to the primary needs of the infant leads to the development of split representations of objects and self that, in turn, leads to a psychic structure that is unbalanced, out of harmony and at war with itself. This situation leads to deep-seated intrapsychic conflicts. When resolving these conflicts, it is necessary not just to resolve the specific conflict, but to strengthen the infantile Libidinal Ego and make it more independent of the Anti-Libidinal Ego. It is necessary that there be a regrowing and rebirth of the basic ego, the whole person. The resolution of an intrapsychic conflict, therefore, rests upon the reformation and reintegration of ego structures.

Review of Literature and Research Hypotheses

Two major research programs have studied in depth the resolution of intrapsychic conflicts. (These programs are by Greenberg and associates and by Meier, Boivin and associates.) For a more detailed summary of this research, see Meier & Boivin (2001).

Greenberg and associates conducted a series of research projects investigating the resolution of splits (Greenberg, Rice & Elliott, 1993). Among their findings were that there was a deepening of experience as the resolution of a split (conflict) was approached (Greenberg, 1979; Greenberg & Rice, 1981) and that there was an expression of "felt wants" in the Experiencing Chair and a softening of the harsh critic in the Other Chair as resolution was achieved (Greenberg & Webster, 1982; Greenberg, 1991). "Felt wants" were operationalized as comprising both feelings and wants (needs); feelings and wants remained merged (Greenberg, 1984). Feelings and wants were regarded as occurring when a want appeared in the context of feelings (Greenberg, 1984, p. 112). Greenberg and associates' conflict resolution studies were designed within an experiential (Gestalt) theoretical framework (Greenberg, 1984) that focused primarily on the depth of experiencing – that is, on affective and not on cognitive and need dimensions.

Meier, Bovin and associates carried out a series of research projects to study the process of conflict resolution from an experiential and psychodynamic perspective that argued for the inclusion of client needs, wants and desires statements together with client cognitive and affective statements (Meier, 1984). The first of their studies (Furmanzyk & Kenyon, 1981) produced unexpected results, with needs, wants and desires and positive affect client statements occuring immediately prior to the resolution of intrapsychic conflicts. The study was replicated twice (Boisvenue, Chen, Colman, Driscoll & MacIver, 1982; Bernatchez, Bradley, Buis, Estabrooks & Fillion, 1984) with similar results. An intrapsychic conflict was operationally defined as a split wherein the person feels divided between two partial aspects of the self or tendencies (e.g., being devilish versus being angelic) (Greenberg, 1979, p. 317) experienced in opposition. The Gestalt Two-Chair dialogue (Perls, 1969, pp. 81–85) was used to help clients resolve conflicts and the client verbal responses were categorized using the Client Verbal Response Category System (Meier & Boivin, 1984a, 1984b, 1986, 1990). These early studies did not include a control group of Non-Resolvers. The results from these investigations were as follows: (a) Need statements when compared to Feeling and Cognitive (Thought and Cognitive) statements predominate immediately prior to the resolution of a conflict, (b) Positive Feeling statements when compared to Negative Feeling statements predominate immediately prior to the resolution of a conflict; and (c) there is an increase in Need statements and a decrease in Cognitive statements as resolution is approached.

In a subsequent study on the resolution of intrapsychic conflicts, Meier and Boivin (2001) used an experimental group (Resolvers) and a control group (Non-Resolvers). Resolvers and Non-Resolvers were operationally defined using the Criteria for Identifying Conflict Resolvers (described below). The purpose of the study was to evaluate the presence of cognitions, emotions and needs in the resolution of intrapsychic conflicts, as worked through in a therapeutic context. It was hypothesized that the resolution of intrapsychic conflicts entails accessing blocked off needs, wants and desires, reclaiming and expressing them, and harmoniously integrating them within the context of one's intrapsychic structures (e.g., Libidinal, Anti-Libidinal and Central Ego) and real relationships. The specific research hypotheses were that for Resolvers alone and immediately prior to the resolution of an intrapsychic conflict:

1. client Need statements predominate,

2. client Positive Feeling statements predominate,

3. client Negative Feeling statements decrease,

4. client Thought statements decrease,

5. client Judgment statements decrease,

6. When client statements are divided into those arising from the Experiencing Chair and those emerging from the Other Chair, there will be an increase in client Need statements from both the Experiencing Chair and the Other Chair immediately prior

to the resolution of a conflict. There will be no significant differences in client Cognitive and Feeling statements. The same pattern is not expected for the Non-Resolvers.

Method

The sample, instruments and procedures for selecting participants and coding the interview material of Meier & Boivin (2001) are presented here.

Data Base

The material used to test the research hypotheses consisted of 20 transcribed one-hour audiotaped interviews with 20 clients in which the Gestalt Two-Chair dialogue (Perls, 1969, pp. 81–85) was used to resolve an intrapersonal conflict. None of the clients had been in therapy before. More specifically, the subjects for the study and the criteria for their inclusion were as follows.

1. There were ten clients divided equally for gender who met the criteria for "Resolvers" and ten clients divided equally for gender who met the criteria for "Non-Resolvers," as defined by the Criteria for Identifying Conflict Resolvers (see Table 1, below).

2. The clients were young adults between the ages of 25 and 35 at date of requesting outpatient therapy.

3. The clients were diagnosed with definite anxiety disorders and adjustment disorders (triggered by mild stressors) by the intake worker using the *Diagnostic and Statistical Manual of Mental Disorders* (DSM-IV) criteria.

4. The clients did not have a secondary diagnosis of any of the DSM-IV diagnostic categories

5. The Gestalt Two-Chair dialogue was administered to resolve an expressed conflict.

6. The Gestalt Two-Chair dialogue was administered between the fifth and tenth interview.

7. The Resolvers and Non-Resolvers were matched for age and educational background using years of schooling as the criteria to assess the latter.

The Gestalt Two-Chair dialogue is a therapeutic technique wherein the client takes both sides in a conversation between himself or herself and another person (e.g., son and father), or between two aspects of self (e.g., being devilish and being angelic). To facilitate the dialogue, an empty chair is used and the client is asked during the course of the dialogue to move back and forth between the two chairs. This technique facilitates the emergence, demarcation and resolution of interpersonal and intrapersonal conflicts (splits) (Greenberg, 1979, 1983). Generically, Perls (1969) construed these splits or conflicts in terms of the underdog and the topdog. Greenberg operationalized these respectively as the Experiencing Chair and the Other Chair (Greenberg, 1979, 1983). The dialogue was partitioned into statements, according to whether the client was in one chair or the other.

Interviews that used the Gestalt Two-Chair dialogue were selected because empirical data supports its effectiveness for resolving conflicts (Greenberg, 1979, Greenberg & Higgins, 1980). The Gestalt Two-chair dialogue portion of the interview comprised from 30 to 40 minutes of the one-hour interview.

Instruments

One instrument was designed to identify and select Resolvers and Non-Resolvers and two instruments were used to categorize the interview material.

Criteria for Identifying Conflict Resolvers

Five criteria similar to those of Greenberg and Webster (1982) were used to measure the extent of opposition between the psychic parts, their degree of empathic understanding, and their willingness to work together and collaborate to resolve their conflict. Each of the criteria is scored on a five-point scale, with a score of 1 indicating a total absence of the criterion and a score of 5 indicating a definite presence of the criterion (Table 1). Resolvers were those who scored four or higher on each of the criteria, whereas Non-Resolvers were operationally defined as those who scored four or higher on the first criterion and two or lower on the remaining four criteria. The first criterion assessed whether the groups commenced the Gestalt Two-chair dialogue in a state of conflict and opposition and the remaining four criteria assessed the degree of empathic understanding and collaboration.

Table l. Criteria for Identifying Conflict Resolvers

Criteria and Rating Scale
a. At the beginning of the dialogue, the two parts are in conflict and in opposition to each other
1) not at all 2) likely not   3) sometimes 4) most of the time 5) definitely
b. The two parts empathically understand each other's feelings, needs, thoughts, concerns, etc.
5) definitely 4) most of the time 3) sometimes 2) likely not   1) not at all
c. The two parts offer to work together to resolve the conflict
1) not at all 2) likely not   3) sometimes 4) most of the time 5) definitely
d. Each part feels that the other is collaborating to resolve the conflict.
5) definitely 4) most of the time 3) sometimes 2) likely not   1) not at all
e. The client feels a sense of inner freedom, a relief in that a weight has been lifted, and is more energetic following the Two-chair dialogue.
1) not at all 2) likely not   3) sometimes 4) most of the time 5) definitely

Counselor Verbal Response Category System (HCVRCS)

The Hill Counselor Verbal Response Category System (HCVRCS) (Hill, 1978) was employed to assess consistency of counsellor behaviour across the interviews. This system contains fourteen nominal and mutually exclusive categories for judging counsellor verbal behaviour among which are the following: Minimal Encouragers, Direct Guidance, Open Question, Restatement, Reflection and Interpretation (Hill, 1978). Recent refinement of this instrument has led to the collapse of several categories to produce an eight-category system. For example, restatement, reflection and non-verbal referrent are regrouped under the general category, Interpretives (Hill, 1986). Studies demonstrate that the HCRCS is both a reliable and valid research instrument (Hill, 1986, Hill et al., 1979).

Client Verbal Response Category System (CVRCS)

The conceptual model of feelings, cognitions and needs has been operationalized by the Client Verbal Response Category System (CVRCS) (Meier & Boivin, 1984a, 1986, 1990). This four-dimensional research instrument comprises criteria to classify client verbal responses according to Subject, Temporal, Experiential and Direction categories. The categories and their sub-categories are nominal and mutually exclusive. Of importance to this project is the Experiential category, thus it alone will be described.

The Experiential category classifies client responses according to the components of his or her inner psychic experience. Three of these categories are Affective State, (e.g., I love my mother), Cognitive Process state (e.g., I am aware of my options) and Needs (e.g., I need to spend a quiet vacation). Sub-categories of Affective States are Positive/Pleasant, Negative/Unpleasant, Ambivalent Feelings, and the expression of Physical Sensation. The client's expressions of Need States are scored as being either Physical, Social, Affectional, Psychological or Spiritual. Sub-categories of the Cognitive Process include client responses that may be classified as Perception, Thought, Judgment, Interpretation, Awareness, Decision or Fantasy (Meier & Boivin, 1984a, pp. 11–17; 1990, pp. 30–51).

Studies using the CVRCS have produced high kappa coefficients, which indicate excellent interrater agreement (Meier & Boivin, 1986; Bernatchez et al., 1984).

The HCVRCS was used to code therapist's interventions and Meier and Boivin's CVRCS was employed to code client responses, which were divided into those coming from the Experiencing Chair (Self) and those coming from the Other Chair (Other).

Therapist and Therapy

The therapist was male and experienced (ten years of practice) and used the Gestalt Two-chair dialogue as one of the counselling strategies. The therapist's orientation integrated psychodynamic and experiential approaches. The therapist was unfamiliar with the research project and its hypotheses. Even though the ideal would have been to use two or more therapists to rule out the effect of the therapist on the outcome, this was difficult to implement because the researchers chose to use the interviews of actual clients. The interviews for this project were randomly selected from the bank of stored audiotaped interviews.

The consistency of the therapist's verbal behaviour across the sessions for both the Resolvers and Non-Resolvers was assessed using HCVRCS (Hill, 1978). The data indicate that the therapist's interventions were similar for both the Resolvers and the Non-Resolvers.

Both the therapist and the clients consented in writing to the use of the interview material for research purposes.

Procedure

Selecting Subjects

Two steps were taken to identify and select subjects. First, the therapist, using records kept of therapy sessions, identified potential Resolvers and Non-Resolvers with whom the Gestalt Two-Chair dialogue was used. The therapist labelled them as such using as a basis his clinical judgment and the client's statement indicating that a resolution took place (e.g., "I feel something happened," "I feel relieved," "Things are different now").

Next, two research assistants using the Criteria for Identifying Conflict Resolvers independently coded the Two-Chair Dialogue portion of the selected interviews that were classified as being with either Resolvers or Non-Resolvers. The interviews on which both coders agreed formed a pool of interviews from which ten Resolvers and ten Non-Resolvers were randomly selected.

The Resolvers and Non-Resolvers obtained the same means (4.45, 4.45) and standard deviations (.43, .44) on the first criterion, but differed significantly on the remaining four criteria. The means on the four remaining criteria ranged from 4.4 to 4.5 for the Resolvers and from 1.4 to 1.5. for the Non-Resolvers. All t-scores (12.63, 9.72, 7.57 and 9.77 for criteria b to e, respectively) were significant beyond the .001 level. The two groups therefore began the Gestalt Two-Chair dialogue in a state of conflict and opposition but differed significantly from each other in their empathic understanding and collaboration to resolve the conflict.

The Resolvers and Non-Resolvers did not differ significantly on the session number during which the Gestalt Two-Chair dialogue was administered (M=7.1, 7.2; SD=1.52, 1.32; T=.23; p.=.82), on the number of client statements for the complete interview (M= 94, 96; SD=41.12, 19.00; T=-.10, p.=.92), and on the number of client statements for the dialogue portion of the interview (M=32.50, 29.13; SD=5.62, 8.80; T=1.78; p.=.09).

The unit of analysis for this project was a client statement, which is essentially a grammatical sentence. Rules and procedures for unitizing were adapted from Auld and White (1956) and are included in the manual (Meier & Boivin, 1990, pp. 70–76).

Transcribing Interviews

Each of the 20 audiotaped interviews was transcribed by a research assistant unfamiliar with the research project. The interview material was divided into therapist interventions and client responses, using rules, procedures and standards adapted from Auld and White (1956) and Mergenthaler and Stinson (1992) and then numbered sequentially. For the Gestalt Two-Chair portion of the interview, the client statements for the ten Resolvers and for the ten Non-Resolvers were coded for those arising from the Experiencing Chair and for those coming from the Other Chair.

Coding Interviews

The transcripts were independently coded, using the Hill (1978) and Meier and Boivin (1984a, 1990) classification systems, by two raters trained by the principal author. The raters scored practice protocols until the interrater kappa coefficients were .75 or higher (Cohen, 1960), which indicates excellent interrater agreement (Landis & Koch, 1977).

To secure one classification for each therapist intervention and client response, the following procedures were used. When the raters agreed on their classification, the category on which there was agreement was accepted. When the raters were not in agreement, a third rater was asked to independently rate the intervention and/or response. When this failed to bring about agreement, the three raters were asked to discuss their ratings with each other to determine the most appropriate category. In reality, the third rater was seldom used, as the high interrater kappa coefficients reported above suggest.

Analysis of Data

For purposes of analysis, the section of the transcript containing the Gestalt Two-Chair dialogue was divided equally into three segments (called Time Segments), using the number of the client responses as the criterion for partitioning. An alternative procedure would have been to divide the Gestalt Two-Chair dialogue section of the interview into three equal parts using time as measured by the clock. Both systems of partitioning have limitations, in that there might not be a correspondence between the number of client statements and actual time. Thus, there might be an unequal distribution of client statements across time. To assure an equal distribution of client statements for each segment for purposes of statistical analysis, the Gestalt Two-Chair portion of the interview was partitioned using the number of client statements as a criterion.

For each Time Segment, the specific client response category was identified and coded, and separately summed for frequency of appearance. The responses spoken when the client was in the Experiencing Chair and those when the client was in the Other Chair were summed separately for the ten Resolvers and for the ten Non-Resolvers. These data were utilized for all of the analyses.

Interjudge Agreement

The kappa coefficients for the Counselor Verbal Response Categories range from .67 for Open Question to .88 for Direct Guidance. The mean kappa coefficient across the fourteen categories was .80. These kappas are somewhat higher than those reported by Hill (1978) but somewhat lower than the .89 reported by Bernatchez et al. (1984, p. 69).

The Client Verbal Response Categories obtained a kappa coefficient of .90 across the combined Experiential categories. The kappa coefficients for Positive Feeling, Negative Feeling, Needs, Judgment and across the combined Cognitive categories were .91, .88, .88, .83 and .92, respectively. These results are similar to those reported by Meier & Boivin (1986) and Bernatchez et al. (1984). The high kappa coefficients indicate that the Client Verbal Response Category System can be used reliably by trained judges.

The rate of agreement for the two raters on the use of the Criteria for Identifying Conflict Resolvers was .91 (Pearson's correlation coefficient).

Results

The hypotheses were tested by applying a 2 (Group: Resolvers and Non-Resolvers) x 3 (Time Segment (TS): TS1 [beginning], TS2 [middle], TS3 [end]) Multivariate Analysis of Variance (MANOVA) Repeated Measures procedure separately to each of the dependent variables (Positive Feelings, Negative Feelings, Needs, Judgments, Thoughts). Level of significance was determined by Wilks criteria (Tatsuoka, 1971, p. 197). Univariate Fs for main effects and interactions were computed. When significant differences were observed, the Tukey post hoc procedure was applied to identify the significant mean scores. Of importance to this study are not the main effects, that is, Group and Time Segment difference, but Group x Time Segment interactions, since the latter permit comparison of conflict resolution patterns for the Resolvers and the Non-Resolvers. The statements the clients made in the Experiencing Chair and the Other Chair were combined to test the first five hypotheses but were separated to test the sixth hypothesis.

Need Statements

To test the first hypothesis, Group (Resolvers, Non-Resolvers) Time Segment (TS1, TS2, TS3) classes were formed using the frequency of client Need statements as the dependent variable. The Group x Time Segment means and standard deviations for the Need Statements are summarized under Need in Table 2 and the Univariate Repeated Measures F-value and level of probability are summarized in Table 3 in the row labelled Need Statements.

The MANOVA statistic was significant for both Time Segment ($F(2,17)=26.49$; $p=.00$) and for the Group x TS interaction ($F(2,17)=13.84$; $p=.00$). The Univariate table indicates that there is a significant Group x TS interaction. When a Tukey post hoc procedure was applied to the Group x Time Segment means it was observed that the TS3 mean for the Resolvers was significantly greater than all of the other means and that the TS3 mean for the Non-Resolvers was not different from its TS1 and TS2 means. However, the TS3 mean for the Non-Resolvers was greater than the TS1 and TS2 means for the Resolvers. The data support the hypothesis that for Resolvers alone there is an increase in Need statements immediately prior to the resolution of the conflict.

Positive Feeling Statements

To test the second hypothesis, Group x Time Segment classes were formed using as dependent variable the frequency of client Positive Feeling statements. The means and standard deviations for these Group x Time Segment classes are summarized in Table 2 under P-Feeling. The MANOVA statistic was significant for Time Segment ($F(2,17)=5.07$; $p.=.01$) but not for Group x TS interaction ($F(2,17)=2.30$; $p=.13$). The Univariate data (Table 3, in the row labelled Positive Feeling Statements) indicated that there is a significant Group x TS interaction. The application of a Tukey post hoc procedure indicated that TS3 for the Resolvers was significantly greater than all other mean scores. No significant differences were observed among the TS mean scores for the Non-Resolvers. The results of the statistical analysis support the hypothesis that for the Resolvers alone, there is an increase in

Positive-Feeling statements immediately prior to the resolution of the conflict.

Negative Feeling Statements

The third hypothesis was tested using the same procedures as above, with the exception that the dependent variable was the frequency of client Negative Feeling statements. The means and standard deviations for the Negative-Feeling statements are summarized in Table 2 under N-Feeling, and the Univariate Repeated Measures F-value and level of probability are presented in Table 3 in the row labelled Negative Feeling Statements.

Table 2. Means and Standard Deviations for Resolvers and Non-Resolvers on Need, Feeling and Thought Statements for Three Time Segments (N=20)

Group Category	Time Segment (TS)					
	TS1		TS2		TS3	
	M	SD	M	SD	M	SD
Resolvers						
Need	.90	.88	1.00	1.16	4.90	1.20
P-Feeling	.30	.48	.50	.53	1.60	1.08
N-Feeling	3.20	1.93	2.20	1.32	.90	.74
Judgment	2.10	1.79	1.50	1.08	.40	.70
Thought	3.90	2.60	2.80	2.70	2.20	1.99
Non-Resolvers						
Need	1.90	.88	2.20	1.40	2.70	1.77
P-Feeling	.10	.32	.20	.42	.40	.97
N-Feeling	1.80	1.88	2.10	2.30	1.37	1.63
Judgment	2.20	1.99	1.70	1.60	.70	.68
Thought	1.10	1.66	2.00	1.41	2.20	1.32

Legend: P-Feelings = Positive Feeling Statements; N-Feelings = Negative Feeling Statements

Table 3. F-Values and Levels of Significance for Group x Time Segment Interactions for Categories of Client Statements Obtained by Univariate Repeated Measures Analysis

Client Statement	df	F	p
Need Statements	2.36	21.84	.000
Positive Feeling Statements	2.36	6.60	.004
Negative Feeling Statements	2.36	3.60	.009
Thought Statements	2.36	3.25	.050
Judgment Statements	2.36	.03	.967

The MANOVA statistic was significant for both Time Segment ($F(2,17)=10.53$; $p=.00$) and for Group x TS interaction ($F(2,17)=6.90$; $p=.00$). The Univariate table indicates that there is a significant Group x TS interaction. The application of a Tukey post hoc procedure to the Group x Time Segment means indicates that the TS3 mean for the Resolvers is lower than all other mean scores and the Non-Resolvers' TS3 mean is not different from all other means. No other significant differences were observed. These findings support the hypothesis that for the Resolvers alone, there is a decrease in the number of client negative feeling statements immediately prior to the resolution of a conflict.

Thought Statements

The fourth hypothesis was tested by forming Group x Time Segment classes using as dependent variable the frequency of client Thought statements. Thought statements refers to the combined Cognitive statements (e.g., perception, awareness, interpretation, decision, reasoning) minus the Judgment statements. The means and standard deviations for these classes on Thought statements are summarized in Table 2 under Thought, and the Univariate Repeated Measures F-value and level of probability are summarized in Table 3 in the row labelled Thought Statements.

The MANOVA statistic was significant for both Time Segment ($F(2,17)=3.51$; $p=.05$) and for the Group x TS interaction

(F(2,17)=3.49; p=.05). The Univariate table indicates that there is a significant Group x TS interaction. A Tukey post hoc procedure found that TS3 was significantly smaller than TS1 for the Resolvers alone. No differences were observed among the Non-Resolvers' TS mean scores. It was also observed that TS1 for Resolvers was greater than all of the other TS mean scores. The results of this analysis support the hypothesis that there is a decrease in Thought statements for the Resolvers alone immediately prior to the resolution of the conflict.

Judgment Statements

To test the fifth hypothesis, Group x Time Segment classes were formed using as dependent variable the frequency of client Judgment statements. Judgment statements are a sub-class of Cognitive statements. The means and standard deviations for these classes on Judgment statements are summarized in Table 2 under Judgment, and the Univariate Repeated Measures F-value and level of probability are presented in Table 3 in the row labelled Judgment Statements.

The analysis of the data failed to produce any significant Group x Time Segment interaction. The data, therefore, do not support the hypothesis that the Resolvers when compared to Non-Resolvers become less judgmental as they approach conflict resolution.

Experiencing versus Other Chair

The sixth hypothesis was tested by forming Participant (Experiencing Chair, Other Chair) x Time Segment classes using as dependent variables the frequencies of client Cognitive, Affective and Need statements for the Resolvers and Non-Resolvers taken separately. A Multivariate Analysis of Variance, Repeated Measures, was applied to each of these groups. The means, standard deviations, MANOVA F-values, and levels of probability derived from these analyses are summarized in Table 4.

The analyses provided only one significant MANOVA F-value (F(1,13)=6.47; p=.007), which is for Resolvers on the variable Need. When the performance of Experiencing Chair and Other

Chair were compared on this variable, there was a significant Univariate F only for Experiencing Chair (F[1,13]=7.12; p=.008). The data indicate that the performance of the Other Chair across the three time segments remained constant, but for the Experiencing Chair, there was a significant increase in the number of Need statements in the third time segment when compared to TS1 and TS2. Another interesting observation is the decrease for Revolvers in the number of cognitive statements for the Experiencing Chair. When the performance of the Experiencing Chair and the Other Chair were compared on TS3, the difference between the mean scores just failed to reach significance (F[1,14]=4.31; p=.057).

Although no significant Participant x Time Segment differences were found for the Non-Resolvers on the three variables (Affect, Need, Cognition), there is one interesting observation. The Experiencing Chair, when compared to the Other Chair, expressed significantly more affect on TS1 (F[1,14]=8.07; p=.013) and on TS3 (F[1,14]=5.76; p=.031). This means that the Experiencing Chair was more emotional than the Other Chair throughout the dialogue designed to resolve the conflict. Put another way, the Other Chair was less emotional than the Experiencing Chair. The performance of the Resolvers' on Affect would support this finding.

Discussion

When applying object relations theory to the interpretation of the data, reference is made to the concepts of the Libidinal, Anti-libidinal, and Central Ego states and their characteristics. For this discussion, the Experiencing Chair is viewed as corresponding to the Libidinal Ego and the Other Chair to the Anti-Libidinal Ego. Both the Libidinal Ego and the Experiencing Chair are described as complaining, whining, frustrated and neglected, etc., whereas the Anti-Libidinal Ego and the Other Chair are described as controlling, harsh, attacking and inconsiderate, etc. It can be said that deep-seated intrapsychic conflicts are the outcome of repressing libidinal needs and desires (Libidinal Ego) and accepting and internalizing parental prohibitions (Anti-Libidinal Ego) and rationale for the prohibitions.

*Table 4. Means, Standard Deviations, MANOVA F-Values, and Levels
of Probability for the Resolvers and Non-Resolvers on Each Dependent
Variable Divided into Experiencing Chair (Self) and Other Chair (Other)
(N=20)*

	Time Segment (TS)						MANOVA	
	TS1		TS2		TS3			
	M	SD	M	SD	M	SD	F	p
Resolvers								
Affect:								
Self	2.13	2.03	2.00	1.60	1.38	1.77	1.94	.18
Other	1.38	1.30	1.00	.76	.88	.84		
Need:								
Self	1.63	2.20	1.00	1.31	3.75	1.58	6.47	.007
Other	.13	.35	.88	1.13	1.50	1.20		
Cognition:								
Self	2.25	1.75	1.88	1.46	.63	.74	1.89	.19
Other	3.25	2.32	3.38	1.60	2.38	2.26		
Non-Resolvers								
Affect:								
Self	2.38	1.85	1.38	1.19	2.13	1.12	2.88	.08
Other	.38	.74	1.38	1.19	.75	1.17		
Need:								
Self	1.38	1.19	2.00	1.07	1.50	.93	1.19	.36
Other	1.00	1.19	1.00	.93	1.00	1.20		
Cognition:								
Self	1.38	1.30	1.38	1.06	1.63	1.19	1.42	.29
Other	2.25	1.70	2.38	1.41	1.00	1.07		

These two ego states are at war with each other. The goal of therapy is to empower the Libidinal Ego to be more independent of the Anti-Libidinal Ego.

How then does an object relations perspective shed light on the research data?

First, the data indicate that for the Resolvers alone, there is an increase in the number of client Need statements immediately prior to the resolution of the conflict (T3) and that the Experiencing Chair was the principal contributor of the number of Need statements (M=3.75; Table 4). The shift in the number of libidinal Need statements across the three time periods, suggests that the Libidinal Ego became empowered and made its needs known to the Anti-Libidinal Ego. At the same time, the Anti-Libidinal Ego became more empathic and was responsive to the libidinal needs; there was a change in the mindset of the Anti-Libidinal Ego. In the case of the Non-Resolvers, the number of Need statements for both the Experiencing Chair and the Other Chair remained relatively constant. Although the number of Need statements for the Experiencing Chair was higher at T1 for the Non-Resolvers when compared to the Resolvers, the Other Chair apparently was not responsive to these needs and upheld its controlling and dominating position. The Other Chair, it seems, was responsible for the failure to resolve the conflict. The Libidinal Ego was not empowered.

Second, the pattern of positive and negative affects for the Resolvers is consistent with object relations theory, which states that positive feelings are associated with the satisfaction of libidinal needs and that negative affect is associated with unmet libidinal needs. Therefore at the beginning of the process of resolving the conflict, negative Affect and lack of Need statements dominated whereas at the termination of the conflict resolution process positive Affect and Need statements dominated. The Anti-Libidinal Ego responded to the needs of the Libidinal Ego. In the case of the Non-Resolvers, the number of Need, positive Affect and negative Affect statements remained constant. It appears that the Anti-Libidinal Ego was not responsive to the needs of the Libidinal Ego. Thus, the Libidinal and Anti-Libidinal Ego remained in conflict.

Regarding the pattern of Thought statements (e.g., perception, awareness, interpretation and reasoning), there was a decrease for both the Resolvers and the Non-Resolvers across the three Time segments, but for different reasons. For the Resolvers, as the number of Thought statements decreased, the number of Need and Positive affect statements increased. That is, the Libidinal Ego and the Anti-Libidinal Ego shifted from complaining, reasoning and interpreting to understanding, collaboration and coming to terms with the conflict. The major contributor to this shift, however, was the Libidinal Ego. It appears that there was a reasonable acceptance of the libidinal needs on part of the Anti-Libidinal Ego. Although there is no evidence to support it, one can infer that the Central Ego embedded within the Libidinal and Anti-Libidinal Ego played a signficant role in bringing about a resolution. It is also possible that, with the help of the therapist, the Libidinal Ego was able to become aware of and articulate its needs and the Anti-Libidinal Ego felt safe to listen and respond. In the process, the Libidinal Ego was empowered. With regards to the Non-Resolvers, as the number of Thought statements decreased across the three Time segments, the number of Negative affect and Positive affect statements remained constant and the number of Need statements increased slightly. It appears that the Libidinal Ego and Anti-Libidinal Ego were at a stalemate, with neither being responsive to the other. There was no give-and-take in their interaction. The Anti-Libidinal Ego tried to be reasonable and understanding, as reflected in the decrease in number of Thought statements (Table 4), but this was not sufficient to resolve the conflict. The Central Ego appears not to have been helpful.

The results of this study and their interpretation from an object relations perspective have important implications for research. Greenberg (1983) and Meier, Boivin, and associates' (2001) studies described their results but did not provide an explanation for their findings. For example, Greenberg and associates stated that the client's "depth of experiencing" is related to the resolution of conflicts. In their earlier studies, Meier, Boivin and associates attested that the ability to access, accept and express needs and wants was essential to the resolution of conflicts (Furmanczyk et al., 1981; Boisvenue et al., 1982; Bernatchez et al., 1984; Meier & Boivin, 2001). There was no explanation as to why this might be so. Object relations theory links a client's shift in Need and Want, Positive Affect, Negative Affect and Thought statements to a shift in the psychic structure itself – that is, a shift in the Libidinal, Anti-Libidinal and Central Ego states. But it offers more. It demonstrates how the ego states emerged from the person's childhood experiences, which were transformed into object- and self-representations and then into ego structures through the process of internalization, splitting and projection. It explains how unintegrated ego states (structures) lead to conflicts. Lastly, intrapsychic conflicts become resolved when the needs and wants of the Anti-Libidinal Ego state and the Libidinal Ego state are accessed, accepted and heard.

The findings of this study and their interpretation have, as well, implications for psychotherapy. Understanding the developmental roots of intrapsychic conflicts helps the psychotherapist to be more precise and nuanced in his or her observations, assessments and treatment and to see the specific conflict in a larger perspective. The psychotherapist also has an appreciation of how intrapsychic conflicts can be re-enacted in interpersonal relationships, families and communities. Conversely, the psychotherapist appreciates how often interpersonal conflicts, for example, are reflections of the person's conflicts within himself or herself. According to object relations theory, interpersonal conflicts that seem unresolvable often have their roots in intrapsychic conflicts, and these need to be resolved if there is to be lasting resolution of interpersonal conflicts. It is generally believed that successful psychotherapy is more linked to some unspecific factors such as the relationship than it is to theory and/or technique. The authors of this chapter propose that future psychotherapy research should give some consideration to psychotherapists' ability to conceptualize cases. This is an important skill that has been under-researched.

The model of conflict resolution that emerges from this study could be expressed in terms of a sequence of four phases, namely, Opposition Phase, Empathic Phase, Collaboration Phase and Resolution Phase.

The limitations of this study include the small sample, the use of one therapist for all of the sessions, and the use of already completed psychotherapies (Meier & Boivin, 2001). Future studies could address the following questions.

– To effectively resolve conflicts, is the exploration of client needs as important as the method used (e.g., Two-Chair dialogue, focusing, imagery)?

- Are the findings equally applicable to clients who are either cognitively or affectively oriented?

- Do the resolved conflicts bring about enduring out-of-therapy attitudinal and behavioural changes?

- Are the resolved conflicts part of a more central conflict, such as achieving psychological separation and individuation?

All of these are major questions that must be addressed if we are to have an in-depth and comprehensive understanding of the conflict resolution process (Meier & Boivin, 2001).

References

American Psychiatric Association (1994). *Diagnostic and statistical manual of mental disorders: Fourth Edition.* Washington, DC: American Psychiatric Association.

Auld, F. J. & White, A. M. (1956). Rules for dividing interviews into sentences. *The Journal of Psychology, 42,* 273–281.

Benesh, M. & Weiner, B. (1982). Emotion and Motivation: From the Notebooks of Fritz Heider. *American Psychologist, 37,* 887–895.

Bernatchez, P., Bradley, R., Buis, A., Estabrooks, S. & Fillion, H. (1984). *The Relationship of Client Verbal Response Categories to the Resolution of "Splits": A Further Investigation.* Ottawa: Saint Paul University, unpublished master's research project.

Blanck, G. & Blanck, R. (1979). *Ego Psychology II: Psychoanalytic Developmental Psychology.* New York: Columbia University Press.

Boisvenue, A., Chen, M., Colman, G., Driscoll, E. & MacIver, L. (1982). *The Relationship of Client Verbal Response Categories to the Resolution of Splits.* Ottawa: St. Paul University, unpublished master's research project.

Bowlby, J. (1988). *A secure base: Parent-child attachment and healthy human development.* New York: Basic Books.

Cashdan, S. (1988). *Object relations therapy: Using the relationship.* New York: W. W. Norton & Company.

Cohen, J. (1960). A Coefficient of Agreement for Nominal Scales. *Educational and Psychological Measurement, 20,* 37–46.

Coombs, C. H. (1987). The Structure of Conflict. *American Psychologist, 42*, 355–363.

Fairbairn, W. R. D. (1943/1954). The repression and the return of bad objects. In *An object relations theory of personality* (pp. 59–81). New York: Basic Books.

Fairbairn, W. R. D. (1944/1954). Endopsychic structure considered in terms of object relationships. In *An Object-relations theory of personality* (pp. 82–136). New York Basic Books.

Freud, S. (1901). The Psychopathology of Everyday Life. *Standard Edition, 6*, 1–279.

Freud, S. (1909). Five Lectures on Psychoanalysis. *Standard Edition, 11*, 9–55.

Freud, S. (1923). The ego and the id. *Standard Edition*, Vol. 19.

Freud, S. (1938). An Outline of Psycho-analysis. *Standard Edition, 23*, 144–207.

Furmanczyk, L. & Kenyon, P. (1981). *The Relationship of Therapist and Client Verbal Response Categories to the Resolution of Splits*. Ottawa: Saint Paul University, unpublished master's research project.

Greenberg, L. S. (1979). Resolving Splits: Use of the two chair Technique. *Psychotherapy: Theory, Research and Practice, 16*, 316–324.

Greenberg, L.S. (1983. Toward a task analysis of conflict resolution in Gestalt therapy. *Psychotherapy: Theory, Research and Practice, 20*, 190-201.

Greenberg, L. S. (1984). A Task Analysis of Intrapersonal Conflict Resolution. In L. N. Rice & L. S. Greenberg (eds.), *Patterns of Change: Intensive Analysis of Psychotherapy Process*. New York: The Guilford Press, 67–123.

Greenberg, L. S. (1991). Research on the Process of Change. *Psychotherapy Research, 1*(1): 3–16.

Greenberg, L. & Dompierre, L. (1981). Specific Effects of Gestalt Two-chair dialogue on Intrapsychic Conflict in Counseling. *Journal of Counseling Psychology, 28*, 288–294.

Greenberg, L. & Higgins, H. M. (1980). Effects of Two-chair Dialogue and Focusing on Conflict Resolution. *Journal of Counseling Psychology, 27*,:221–224.

Greenberg, L. Rice, L. (1981). The Specific Effects of a Gestalt Intervention. *Psychotherapy: Research and Practice, 18,* 31–37.

Greenberg, L., Rice, L., & Elliott, R. (1993). *Facilitating emotional change: The moment-by-moment process.* New York: The Guilford Press.

Greenberg, L. & Webster, M. (1982). Resolving Decisional Conflict by Two-chair Dialogue: Relating Process to Outcome. *Journal of Counseling Psychology, 29,* 468–477.

Grotstein, J. (1981). *Splitting and projective identification.* New York: Aronson.

Guntrip, H. (1969). *Schizoid phenomena: Object relations and the self.* New York: International Universities Press.

Guntrip, H. (1973). *Psychoanalytic theory, therapy, and the self.* New York: Basic Books.

Hartmann, H. (1939). *Ego psychology and the problem of adaptation.* New York: International Universities Press.

Hill, C. E.(1978). Development of a Counselor Verbal Response Category System. *Journal of Counseling Psychology, 25,* 461–468.

Hill, C. E. (1986). An Overview of the Hill Counselor and Client Verbal Response Modes Category Systems. In L. S. Greenberg & W. M. Pinsof (eds.), *The Psychotherapeutic Process: A Research Handbook.* New York: The Guilford Press, 131–159.

Hill, C. E., Thames, T. B. & Rardin, D. K.(1979). Comparison of Rogers, Perls, and Ellis on the Hill Counselor Verbal Response Category System. *Journal of Counseling Psychology, 26,* 198–203.

Kaplan, L. J. (1978). *Oneness and separateness. From infant to individual.* New York: Simon & Schuster.

Kernberg, O. (1986). *Severe personality disorders: Psychotherapeutic strategies.* New Haven, CT: Yale University Press.

Klein, M. (1936/1975). Weaning. In *Love, guilt and reparation and other works, 1921–1945.* New York: Delta (pp. 290–305).

Klein, M. (1959/1975). Our adult world and its roots in infancy. In *Envy and gratitude and other works, 1946-1963.* New York: Delta (pp. 247–263).

Kohut, H. (1977). *The restoration of the self.* New York: International Universities Press.

Kohut, H. (1979). *Four basic definitions of self psychology*, paper presented to the Workshop on Self Psychology, Chicago, IL.

Landis, J. R. & Koch, G. G. (1977). The Measurement of Observer Agreement for Categorical Data. *Biometrics, 33,* 159–174.

Lazarus, R. S. (1982). Thoughts on the Relations Between Emotions and Cognition. *American Psychologist, 37,* 1019–1027.

Mahler, M. S., Pine, F. & Bergman, A. (1975). *Psychological birth of the human infant.* New York: Basic Books.

Maslow, A. (1968). *Toward a psychology of being.* New York: Van Nostrand-Reinhold.

Meier, A. (1984). Commentaries on Research in the 1980's. In Whiteley, J. M., Kagan, N., Harman, L. W., Fretz, B. R. & Tanney, F.(eds). *The Coming Decade in Counseling Psychology.* New York, Character Research Press, 194.

Meier, A. & Boivin, M. (1983). Towards a Synthetic Model of Psychotherapy. *Pastoral Sciences, 2,* 137–176.

Meier, A. & Boivin, M. (1984a). *Client Verbal Response Category System: Definitions and Coding Manual.* Ottawa: Saint Paul University, unpublished manuscript.

Meier, A. & Boivin, M. (1984b). *Client Verbal Response Categories and the Resolution of Conflicts.* Paper presented at the Annual Convention of the American Psychological Association, Division of Counseling Psychology, Toronto, Ontario.

Meier, A. & Boivin, M. (1986). Client Verbal Response Category System: Preliminary Data. *Journal of Consulting and Clinical Psychology, 54,* 877–879.

Meier, A. & Boivin, M. (1990). *Client Verbal Response Category System: Development, Definition and Coding Manual.* Ottawa: Saint Paul University, unpublished manuscript, 108 pp.

Meier, A. & Boivin, M. (2001). Conflict resolution: The interplay of affects, cognitions and needs in the resolution of intrapersonal conflicts. *Pastoral Sciences, 20*(1), 93–119.

Meier, A. & Meier, M. (2004). The Formation of Adolescents' Image of God: Predictors and Age and Gender Difference. In R. Dayringer & D. Oler (eds.), The Image of God and the Psychology of Religion (pp. 91-111). New York: Haworth Press.

Mergenthaler, E. & Stinson, C. (1992). Psychotherapy transcription standards. *Psychotherapy Research, 2*, 125–142.

Murray, H. A. (1938). *Explorations in Personality.* New York: Oxford Press.

Perls, F. S. (1969). *Gestalt Therapy Verbatim.* Toronto: Bantam Books.

Polster, E. & Polster, M. (1973). *Gestalt Therapy Integrated.* New York: Brunner/Mazel Publishers.

Reisenzein, R. & Schnpflug, W. (1992). Stumpf's Cognitive-Evaluative Theory of Emotion. *American Psychologist, 47*(1), 34–45.

Tatsuoka, M.M. (1971). *Multivariate analysis: Techniques for educational and psychological research.* Toronto: John Wiley & Sons.

Winnicott, D. W. (1962/1965). Ego integration in child development. In D. Winnicott, *The maturational processes and the facilitating environment* . New York: International Universities Press (pp. 56–63).

Yalom, I. D. (1989). *Love's Executioner and Other Tales of Psychotherapy.* New York: Harper Perennial.

Zajonc, R. B. (1980). Feeling and thinking: Preferences need no inferences. *American Psychologist, 35*, 151–175.

14

Codes of Ethics Resolve Conflict

Peter Barnes

This chapter is written after extensive experience as a chairperson of ethics committees, including those for clinical and professional ethics. My professional ethics experience includes work on both regional and national committees of Canadian Association for Pastoral Practice and Education (CAPPE). The CAPPE Code of Ethics addresses all aspects of the delivery of service, including spiritual care and counselling by chaplains and pastoral counsellors, as well as the delivery of education. This chapter focuses on spiritual care and counselling, to both of which I bring experience, since I am certified in both streams of service.

Professional associations develop and maintain codes of ethics for a variety of reasons. Codes of ethics are generally intended to encourage members to reflect and aspire to a set of values and beliefs that shape professional practice. It is not an easy task to require members to adhere to a set code of conduct or to manage such a code given the individualistic nature of people in North American society.

Consequently, it is to be expected that members will vary in their interpretation of what is acceptable conduct and what constitutes a breach of the code of ethics. This can very well result in conflict within an organization and conflict, or at least difference of opinion, between consumers and the professional members of an association.

A code of ethics includes articles that set desired standards. The membership, as a community, has decided it wants to adhere to these standards and wants them to be consistent with the beliefs the members wish to stand for. This would include standards for things such as confidentiality, advertising and research. This would allow the public to see what an organization's members stand for by their code of ethics.

A code of ethics also consists of standards for professional relationships. When a professional relationship moves towards a personal relationship, there is a point at which there is no return to the professional relationship. This includes instances when there is a power differential in relationships between professionals and clients, families, employees and students. A code of ethics violation in which there is the abuse or misuse of power in a professional relationship is resolved by an ethics complaint procedure, which is intended to insure the professional member does not have the opportunity to further abuse his or her power.

When a code of ethics enquiry does not involve the potential misuse of power in a professional relationship there is the potential to use "peer intervention" to resolve the conflict.

Given this background information, I wish to set the stage for this article, which will seek to be informative regarding approaches to managing codes of ethics and reflective on the experiences of both complainants and member respondents seeking to resolve conflict that has arisen due to a potential breach of the code of ethics.

Relationships

Codes of ethics are first and foremost about relationships – that is, the relationships of clients to members, students to members, other professionals to members, employees to members and members to members. In Chapter 10, entitled "Relationships and Ethics," of Freedman & Combs' book *Narrative Therapy: The Social Construction of Preferred Realities,* mention is made of another relationship – that is, "the interrelationship of ethics and therapeutic relationships, about how each shapes the other" (p. 267). Consequently, in organizations whose members exhibit caring, therapeutic relationships, the code of ethics and its procedures are shaped by the very context or nature of the therapeutic relationships. An organization strives for congruence; therefore, when the organization is centred on the respectful hearing of clients' stories, the code of ethics and its procedures must be consistent or congruent with the empowerment of clients to tell their stories. Professionals are invited "to examine their practices and revise them in terms of the values and relationships that those practices bring forth." (p. 269). Therefore, as society grows in diversity, so too must codes of ethics and related procedures evolve comparatively and consistently. For instance, an organization that promotes good relationships among the professional colleagues and in regard to client's risks standing apart from the cultural norm of Western society "that privileges personal gratification over relatedness" (p. 273). Therefore professionals of an organization that emphasizes relationship must find organizational principles "that have to do with experiences of belonging and being accountable to 'communities that support power-with, collaborative relationships, rather than power-over expert relationships'" (p. 273).

When people perceive that the relationship with a professional member has been inappropriate or inadequate then there may be grounds for an ethics complaint and this may be defined as a conflict between at least two parties: the complainant and the respondent member. More importantly, it must be asked whether the member is being consistent with the principles of the organization.

For instance, when a professional member has abused a trust, a client deserves an opportunity to mend, re-establish or heal his or her ability to trust the member and the organization he or she represents. Sometimes, this may require a detailed explanation of the circumstances, a truthful sharing of what has happened for there to have been, for instance, the disclosure of confidential information – in other words, a restitution to make amends in order to resolve the misunderstanding or conflict.

Eric Erikson's stages of psychosocial development found in his classic book *Childhood and Society* explain a personal violation as generating mistrust that requires healing. One's development is impaired until trust is re-established. This requires healing of emotions, and appropriate measures need to be taken to achieve this healing. One might ask who it is that determines what is an "appropriate measure." In an ideal world, an assessment would determine the "appropriate measure" required to facilitate this re-newed trust. Unfortunately the facilitation of the parties involved to meet and discuss the circumstances is often not easily achieved. Organizations could well learn from First Nations culture and the practice of a healing circle or from some courts of law that practise restorative justice.

Instead, people use whatever means available to seek justice when they feel they have been treated unfairly. This is their way of asking to be heard or listened to by the person(s) involved. An ethics complaint is one way to do this, but one must consider whether it is consistent with the organization's principles. If we accept that in some instances people want and need to be heard, then an acceptable and appropriate response to the initial enquiry is to bring the parties together with a facilitator – that is, in the cases in which there has not been the abuse of power. As noted above, this process may be called "peer intervention."

Healing and Restoration of Relationships

When someone feels violated by a professional or an organiza-tion, he or she wants to be heard. The formal way to do this is to initiate a code of ethics complaint against the individual mem-ber or the organization. When this complaint can be processed quickly the complainant may be made to feel he or she is being taken seriously, regardless of the outcome. The complainant does not want to be dismissed or feel dismissed, which would further jeopardize the relationship with the professional member and the organization.

Consideration must be given to the personal energy required to initiate a complaint against a professional member or a colleague. Doing so sometimes feels onerous, especially when the complain-ant anticipates having to have an ongoing relationship with the professional member.

For instance, a student who feels he or she has been treated unfairly by a teacher or instructor may fear a lower grade or a negative message to potential employers or to a post-graduate pro-gram. This power differential is an important consideration in any potential code of ethics complaint process, and is an obvious factor in the case of a student who lacks power in his or her relationship to the teacher or instructor.

So how does an organization endeavour to level the playing field so as to invite constructive criticism and creative critique without becoming defensive and abusive toward the complainant? It is essential that the person responsible for receiving complaints be accessible, open and a good listener. It is sometimes difficult to maintain objectivity; therefore, the response to the complainant should never be in isolation but rather part of a consultative response that is expedited as quickly as possible. Again, the message to be conveyed is that the complainant has been heard regardless of the nature of the issue or concern.

When the receiver of the complaint deems that there is reasonable substance to it, then every effort must be made to bring the parties involved together with a "peer intervener" who is acceptable to all concerned. This is a restorative act that seeks to resolve any misunderstanding and possibly facilitate reconciliation when there has been an estrangement.

There are instances when "peer intervention" is not acceptable because bringing the complainant together with the respondent member has the potential to compound the original abuse. This is obvious when a respondent member has misused his or her power in relationship with the complainant, especially in a sexually, physically, emotionally or intellectually threatening way. But consideration must also be given to the strength or fragility of character of the complainant. For instance, when a person perceives authority figures as a threat to his or her well-being then the normal exercise of authority may be perceived as a threat to a vulnerable person. In these cases, an alternative to peer intervention must be found to resolve the situation. In fact, the only viable alternative may be an official complaint followed by an investigation, which may be a lengthy process.

Regardless of the severity of the complaint, one of the critical factors has to be the rate at which it is processed. When there is a delay in the processing of the complaint then the potential violation to the complainant and possibly to the respondent member is compounded.

Understanding the Healing or Restitution Process

This process of resolving a code of ethics complaint may be compared to the counselling practice of narrative therapy. The basic process involves the telling and retelling of one's story so as to reframe it and view it with greater objectivity. If this can happen in the context of peer intervention to resolve an ethics concern then there is the potential for resolution and for a win-win result.

In the healing or restitution process, the role of the facilitator is to use "dialogue" rules rather than debating rules. The process follows a specific order.

1. The first step is to have the complainant tell his or her story without interruption by the respondent member.

2. The second step has the facilitator retell the complainant's story without commentary on the content.

3. The third step has the complainant retell his or her story, offering further explanation.

4. The fourth step has the respondent member ask a question for clarification.

5. The fifth step is to have the complainant answer the respondent member's question.

6. The sixth step is for the respondent member to tell his or her story.

7. The seventh step has the facilitator retell the story.

8. The eighth step has the member retell his or her story, presenting any new information for further clarification.

9. The ninth step gives the complainant an opportunity to ask questions for clarification.

10. The tenth step has the respondent member answer the questions.

11. The eleventh step has the facilitator ask the complainant and the respondent member whether there is anything they now see differently after having heard the respective stories.

12. The twelfth step has the facilitator offer the complainant and the respondent member the opportunity to write a note to each other stating their present perspectives on the issue or concern that has been raised.

13. The thirteenth step has the facilitator ask the complainant and the respondent member to state without commentary from the other party, "What do you now think would resolve this conflict to the satisfaction of all concerned?"

14. The fourteenth step has the complainant and then the respondent member answer the question in step thirteen.

15. The fifteenth step has the facilitator ask the complainant and then the respondent member what the answers have in common.

16. The sixteenth step has the complainant and the respondent member ask, "What else needs to be said to resolve this issue or concern?" The complainant and then the respondent member answers this question.

17. The seventeenth step has the facilitator ask the following question: "Does this now resolve the issue or concern or is there anything else that needs to be said?"

18. The eighteenth step consists of the complainant and the respondent member being invited to speak to each other in order to say what needs to be said to resolve the issue or concern to the satisfaction of both.

This process is meant to be a process of reconciliation, to resolve the original issue or concern raised by the complainant in relation to the member. The use of dialogue is similar in function to the Native healing circle, in which only one person speaks at a time and continues speaking without interruption. Sometimes a talking stick is held by the speaker and is only passed on to the other party or parties when the first person has finished speaking.

These processes are truly restorative in nature. Unlike in a debate or argument, the parties involved are required to listen to each other and to see the situation from the other's point of view. This is restorative by its very intent.

Case Reflection

In a case reported recently, an ethical issue was raised with a colleague. The immediate result was that the colleague became defensive and the lines of conflict were drawn. As a result, the relationship became strained and the division became more entrenched.

Consequently, a formal code of ethics complaint was filed and after a lengthy investigation was ruled on by the professional ethics committee, in favour of the complainant. The ruling was subsequently appealed and the professional ethics committee's final judgment was overturned. One has to ask, "What was achieved by this lengthy, divisive process?"

In this case, the respondent member filed a code of ethics complaint against the original complainant and it too was investigated but by a different committee. After another lengthy investigation, a judgment of "unfounded" was given.

One may conclude that these investigations were destructive to all concerned. It is not about who was right and who was wrong, but rather that relationships were broken or estranged as a result of the inadequate and harmful process that was enacted to resolve a code of ethics concern.

In this case, the two investigations together took about 28 months from the first official enquiry to the second judgment. In addition, there was fallout from these complaints as the trust in the organization's ability to resolve these issues was seriously undermined. The result was that at least one health care organization lost faith in the professional association.

An obvious question to be asked is, "Was it worth it?" The obvious answer from every perspective, emotional and intellectual, is "no." Maybe if there had been an attitude of healing or restitution adopted in the original process and if there had been a narrative therapy approach taken then the complainant might have been able to distance himself or herself from the intense negative emotion that was experienced. One may conclude that after a lose-lose experience evident in this case, both parties would undoubtedly wish to go through the code of ethics process differently if faced again with a similar conflict.

What Could Be Different?

Criticism can be constructive, but when it is accusatory then divisions may be drawn, leading to entrenchment and estrangement.

Professional training needs to have the receiving of criticism as an essential component. The acceptance of criticism without defensiveness is a strength of character. Equally, the act of critiquing is an art to be learned. Criticism is an essential component of relationships and therefore it needs to be given creatively and constructively for the benefit of others. And criticism needs to be received objectively rather than taken personally.

What Is the Key to Achieving Win-Win Resolutions?

The key is to dialogue, listen, and practise giving and receiving criticism creatively and constructively to benefit oneself and others, rather than revenge or vengeance and abuse.

Conclusion

Peer intervention processes generally lead to win-win, growth oriented experiences, whereas formal code of ethics complaints generally lead to estrangement or broken relationships. Therefore the following recommendations for training are recommended:

1. That professional organizations' executives be trained to receive ethical enquires without bias and to critique and question complainants constructively so as to help them clarify their thoughts and their feelings.

2. That people be trained as "peer interveners" to offer an opportunity for complainants and respondent members to listen and learn from one another.

3. That professional members be trained in the interpretation of the code of ethics and its procedures, and an ethical culture that truly reflects the beliefs and values of the members in their professional and personal lives subsequently be created.

In brief, the peer intervention process enhances relationships and contributes to the building up of the kingdom of God, or the attainment of enlightenment, or the self-actualization or individuation of the persons involved. However, when an "ethics investigation" is required, the participants should be invited to listen to the other party and respond creatively, and judgment be given with the intention of helping and improving the parties involved.

This may seem like an idealistic objective. In the name of good service and care of others, professional members of organizations that aspire to this ideal must strive towards it in order to model the service they intend to provide.

References

Erikson, E. *Childhood and Society.* (1970). New York: Penguin Books.

Freedman, J. & Combs, G. (1996). *Narrative Therapy: The Social Construction of Preferred Realities.* New York: W. W. Norton.

Epilogue

Getting Beneath the Surface

The brochure for The Canadian Institute for Conflict Resolution contains this caption: "Getting beneath the Surface." Later, it states that the goal of the Conflict Resolution program is "to get at the underlying and deep-rooted conflicts that precede and fuel disputes" and to identify "the underlying causes of conflict" (Saint Paul University, 2006). The implication is that what is seen is not the cause of the conflicts; one needs to look more deeply into the conflict to establish its source and to bring about a resolution.

Reflecting on this caption and reading the chapters of this book raises many questions regarding the origin and nature of conflicts and their resolution. It raises questions regarding the adequacy of current models to understand the "beneath the surface" sources and to appropriately guide the resolution of conflicts. Further, it raises questions regarding the components of these models; the adequacy of working through interpersonal, communal and societal conflicts without addressing the underlying intrapersonal conflict; the phases of the conflict resolution process and the agent for working through conflicts. This epilogue addresses some of these questions and concerns and poses others for consideration and further research.

First, all forms of conflict resolution imply, directly or indirectly, "getting beneath the surface." The contributors to this book propose various "beneath the surface" components of conflicts, such as affect, values, and needs. These components vary according to the purpose of the intervention: namely, to resolve couple conflicts, mediate conflicts brought on by injustices, and work through intrapersonal conflicts.

Regarding the resolution of couple conflicts, Greenberg states that the understanding of adaptive (primary, secondary, instrumental) and maladaptive emotions and motives (e.g., intimacy, identity) resolves conflicts. More specifically, it is by the partners revealing the more vulnerable emotions of fear and shame, and the empowering emotion of anger, that engages the couple in empathic responsiveness and appreciation of each other and ultimately to the resolution of conflicts. According to Rovers, couple conflicts emerge when the partners are not able to harmonize the life forces of individuation and togetherness, with the result that one or both partners seek enmeshment or become emotionally detached or cut off. Their pattern of relating is marked by conflictual cycles of fusion and/or cut-off. The resolution of the conflictual relating pattern entails lowering the couple's anxiety and their emotional reaction to each other, and reducing anger, self-pity, aggressivity, and blaming the other. Marie-Line Morin proposes a couple model of conflict resolution that incorporates religious and spiritual variables such as Fundamental Values, which a person can use to justify, demand, or impose a certain type of behaviour in a relationship. A Fundamental Value is defined as a dominant good – the hypergood – that integrates all other values. A person might expect his or her partner to satisfy his or her needs and aspirations. This model postulates that complete fulfillment can be found only in a relationship with God, not in one's partner. From this it is inferred that conflicts between partners occur when they realize that their soulmate is unable to fulfill their basic needs or that the partner does not correspond to their idealized image of a partner.

Mediation and restorative justice models have a somewhat different focus than the models for resolving couple conflicts. Manley-Tannis argues for a model of conflict resolution (mediation) that encourages persons to open themselves up to each other, to make themselves vulnerable. The opening up entails the expression and balancing of wants and needs within the context of a faith-based community that seeks a peaceful and respectful resolution of conflict. In terms of restorative justice, Morley encourages the emergence of shame, regret, humiliation and remorse in the offender for the harm caused. The emergence of these feelings potentially elicits within the victim an understanding of what it was about the offender's lifestyle, company or habits that led him or her to offend. This approach allows for the offender to apologize and for the victims to express their feelings and to forgive. This approach does not marginalize the offender but maintains the relationship between the offender, victim and community.

With respect to resolving intrapsychic conflicts, Meier and Boivin propose a model that represents a war within one's psyche and the enactment of this war within the context of personal relationships, family, community, society, etc. The war within one's psyche is akin to a conflict between an internalized "child" and "parent": that is, between the two competing forces represented by the "genetic inheritance" and the "cultural inheritance." The root of the conflicts is unmet basic needs, wants and desires. Conflicts are resolved by acknowledging, integrating and harmonizing the needs, wants, and desires of both parties. Unlike the resolution of conflicts between persons and communities, which primarily represent changes in behaviour, the resolution of intrapsychic reflects an inner transformation of the "psychic structure," of negative feelings and judgments into positive feelings, self-acceptance and collaboration. This transformation is reflected in one's relations with others, with the world, and with God.

It is apparent, then, that an effective and credible model of conflict resolution must address unmet needs, wants, desires and longings. It is not enough to address only a person's emotions, be they adaptive or maladaptive. The process of conflict resolution must get "beneath the surface."

Is it possible to develop an overarching model that explains the deeper (e.g., need based) roots of intrapersonal, interpersonal, communal, and restorative justice conflicts and guides the process in resolving these? Meier and Boivin present a model of understanding and resolving intrapersonal conflicts, but is there a similar model available for understanding and resolving interpersonal, communal, societal and other conflicts? Perhaps one can visualize a layered model of conflicts and their resolution akin to Maslow's (1970) hierarchy of needs, with the basic needs at the base of the triangle, the affiliation and self-esteem needs in the middle, and the self-actualization and transcendent needs at the apex. Using this as a metaphor, one could think of a layered model that would place the resolution of intrapersonal conflicts at the base of the triangle; the interpersonal, communal and societal conflicts in the middle; and the transcendent/existential conflicts at the apex. Such a model allows for the perception of conflicts to be primarily intrapersonal, interpersonal and communal, and transcendent/existential in nature. This model would also allow for intrapersonal conflicts to be an essential component of interpersonal and transcendent/existential conflicts. For example, if while working with a couple's conflict it becomes evident that one or both partners are also conflicted within, work might have to be done at the intrapersonal level. It is necessary to exercise caution when assessing for transcendent/existential conflicts. These conflicts, which are often characterized by a quest for the ultimate good and ideal relationship, may indeed represent unfulfilled infant and childhood needs, affirmations and secure attachments. When this is the case, the resolution of conflict also needs to address the intrapersonal conflicts.

It is imperative that those who are interested in the study and treatment of conflict resolution collaborate in developing a clinically relevant model that is applicable to conflicts of varying levels, including intrapersonal, interpersonal, communal, transcendent/existential, and so on. This can best be carried out by building on each other's clinical and research findings. The history of theory building, particularly in psychology, is characterized by fragmentation. One can think of theory building as planting a tree that requires pruning and shaping to maintain its beauty. Theories also require pruning and shaping to maintain their relevance. Theorists, however, tend to dislike what others have done (planted) and do not build on them. Rather they "plant new trees" (e.g., theories), which proliferate and prevent theorists from seeing the forest, or larger picture.

Second, various aspects of the person's internal experience have been proposed as an essential component to be addressed in conflict resolution. Judy Morin, Ford, and Meier and Boivin emphasize the importance of addressing underlying unmet needs, wishes, desires and wants. Greenberg, Rovers, Morley, and Kang,

O'Connor, and Joyce place importance on addressing the person's feelings and using these to achieve a resolution. In coming to terms with brain injuries, Tasker suggests the importance of acknowledgment and acceptance. Marie-Line Morin points to the importance of addressing transcendent/existential variables. Given these aspects of the person's experience, how can one integrate these variables into a coherent description of the origin of conflicts and their resolution? Do some components take precedence over others? If so, with which component does one begin the process of conflict resolution – feelings, values, cognitive processes, needs and wants? Meier and Boivin (1983, 2001) offer a theoretical model that considers needs to be prime directional motivators of behaviours (including conflicts), affects to be responses to either the satisfaction or frustration of needs, and cognitive processes as pertaining to stylistic ways of construing reality, solving problems, managing reality, and evaluating experiences. This model has the potential to integrate transcendent/existential variables within the context of the category: needs.

It is not enough simply to indicate how these aspects of a person's experience are related to each other. It is also necessary to demonstrate how they are connected to underlying organizations or structures. For example, Greenberg relates affects to the functioning of the limbic system. In what way are these experiences related to other intrapersonal, interpersonal, familial and communal structures or organizations? That is, from where do these experiences come? What brings them about? Do they emerge from underlying psychic or system organizations? If so, these need to be articulated and clearly related to the development and treatment of conflicts. An effective and credible model of conflict resolution must address this topic.

Third, when and to what extent does the working through of interpersonal, communal and societal conflicts also require addressing the underlying intrapersonal conflict? To illustrate the intent of this question, one can take the example of anger management programs, which are popular today. By attending such a program, a person might indeed learn how to identify cues that lead to anger, and might also acquire various behavioral strategies to control anger. The changes observed in the person might primarily be at the level of behavioural change. The person might still experience anger within: that is, he or she might still be an angry person. To help this person achieve a sense of inner harmony and peace, it is necessary to address the feelings of anger at the intrapersonal level: at the level of psychic organization (e.g., ego, self), which might be conflicted and disharmonious. The goal is to bring about not only behavioural change, but also an inner transformation, by working at the level of the person's subjective experiences. Using anger management programs as an analogy, might it also be said that to work through interpersonal conflicts, one has to work through them at the intrapersonal level? Might it also be true that to resolve communal conflicts, one has to work them through at the level of the interpersonal, and perhaps also at the intrapersonal, level? Seidl suggests that issues regarding transgender need to be addressed at the levels of intrapersonal, interpersonal and societal so that conflicts can be resolved. What are the indications that conflicts have to be worked through at the different levels? How can this be assessed? A clinically relevant model of conflict resolution needs to address these questions and issues.

Fourth, an integral aspect of conflict resolution is to understand the process that leads to such resolutions. Although all of the chapters touch on this topic, two focus on it directly. In their qualitative analysis of the conflict between a nurse and a chaplain, Kang, O'Connor and Joyce imply different stages that led to the resolution of the conflict. The conflict began with a misunderstanding on the hospital ward, which led to hurtful and angry feelings. In an attempt to resolve the hurtful feelings, the chaplain approached the nurse to discuss what happened. Through mutual explanation and open listening, both gained a greater understanding of what happened and became more respectful towards each other. Negative feelings were transformed into positive feelings and respect, and eventually to apology and forgiveness. Both parties viewed this as a learning experience. In their chapter, Meier and Boivin identified the process of conflict resolution as comprising four phases: opposition, empathic, collaborative and resolution phases. The Opposition Phase is characterized by the expression of negative feelings and negative judgments (e.g., blaming, demanding). The Empathic Phase is marked by one partner becoming more understanding of the other and thereby becoming empathic towards the other. During this phase there is a decrease in the expression of negative feelings and negative judgments and an increase in the expression of positive feelings. In the Collaborative Phase, both agree to work on a resolution of the problem. They identify and express their needs, desires and wishes. The fourth phase represent the final tasks leading the resolution of the conflict. Ford observes that in resolving "incongruences," persons typically identify, express and integrate their basic human needs, wants and expectations. To prevent the emergence of conflicts, Judy Morin advocates that people be aware of their feelings and needs, name them, and then communicate them to those concerned. Fortin and Malette propose a counsellor training model that promotes personal and professional congruency. The positions of Ford, Judy Morin, and Fortin and Malette are consistent with the task of the third phase of Meier and Boivin's model of conflict resolution.

Models of conflict resolution, therefore, must identify and incorporate the process by which they are resolved. The phases proposed by Meier and Boivin in their chapter and by Meier & Boivin (2001; Boisvenue et al., 1982) and by Greenberg (1991) can serve as exemplary models for this task.

Fifth, what roles do mediators, counsellors, chaplains, mentors and other professionals play in the resolution of intrapersonal, interpersonal, familial and communal conflicts? Most conflicts are resolved without the help of a third party. Kang, O'Connor and Joyce point to the fact that people can journey through conflict to resolution without outside intervention. However, in the case of long-standing conflicts, such as within family systems or between communities or nations, the process of conflict resolution is a more complex and lengthy process and requires help from an outside professional. Miles, Cupples, Robinson and Koyle demonstrate that at certain times, such as death, when interpersonal dynamics are complex, anxieties are high, and emotional reactivity is long standing, open conflicts can best be handled with care by an outside professional. Rovers, in discussing therapy with difficult clients, also suggests that calm, directed and focused interventions are needed to resolve deep-seated conflict. Ford indicates that the role of the therapist is to help the client connect with his or her own resources to resolve the conflicts. Greenberg perceives the professional as a coach who guides the couple to move beyond maladaptive, instrumental and secondary emotions, access and express the underlying primary emotions and generally more vulnerable emotions of fear and shame, and thereby become empathically engaged and appreciative of their partner. According to Meier and Boivin, the therapist helps the client to address and work through negative affects and judgments and thereby access the deeper underlying needs for oneness and separateness and for affirmation as a worthy and competent person. Barnes advocates an 18-step "peer intervention" healing process wherein parties come together with a trained facilitator and everyone is given appropriate time and space to share their story until there is a win-win result. All of the models presented above share the need for the coach, counsellor, therapist or "conflict resolver" to guide, not dictate, the conflict resolution process. The clients are helped to draw upon their own resources to resolve their conflicts. This, however, does not address all of the questions, since conflict resolution also takes place within families, communities, institutions and so on. Are there other means that can be used to resolve conflicts when three or more people are involved? When is outside help to resolve conflicts all types warranted, and when are situations best left alone? What degrees of intervention are needed? These questions need to be treated by theoreticians and researchers.

Lastly, very little research has been carried out during the past two decades on conflict resolution. Kang, O'Connor and Joyce demonstrate the use of a Conversational Analysis to conduct qualitative research. For their research, Meier and Boivin used a combined qualitative and quantitative method. Although not presented in this book, Greenberg (1984) used Task Analysis to study the process of conflict resolution. The findings from the three studies are similar in that all acknowledge the importance of addressing unmet needs in resolving conflicts. Studies that address the processes, phases and ingredients of all forms of conflict resolution are needed. These studies need to be guided by an overarching and integrated model of conflict resolution. Although all research by its nature focuses on one aspect of a phenomenon, it is necessary that the results from the conflict studies be explained within the broad context of the etiology and treatment of conflicts. In other words, results need to be contextualized.

Conflict resolution is emerging as a new discipline. The growth of conflict resolution over the last quarter century points to its recognition as a discipline in many circles, including families, organizations, institutions and communities. This book has touched on diverse applications of conflict resolution. More effort is required to develop relevant explanatory and treatment models of conflict resolution.

A person who is at peace within himself or herself will tend to create a home, workplace, community and society that is capable of collaboratively resolving its own conflicts.

The Editors

References

Boisvenue, A., Chen, M., Colman, G., Driscoll, E., & MacIver, L. (1982). *The relationship of client verbal response categories to the resolution of splits.* Ottawa, Ontario: Saint Paul University. Unpublished Master's Research Project.

Greenberg, L.S. (1984). A task analysis of intrapersonal conflict resolution. In L.N. Rice & L.S. Greenberg (Eds.), *Patterns of change: Intensive analysis of psychotherapy process.* New York: Guilford Press, 67–123.

Maslow, A.H. (1970). *Motivation and personality.* New York: Harper & Row.

Meier, A., & Boivin, M. (1983). Towards a synthetic model of psychotherapy. *Pastoral Sciences, 2,* 137–176.

Meier, A., & Boivin, M. (2001). Conflict resolution: The interplay of affects, cognitions and needs in the resolution of intrapersonal conflicts. *Pastoral Sciences, 20*(1), 93–119.

Saint Paul University (2006). *The Canadian Institute for Conflict Resolution.* Ottawa, Ontario. Brochure advertising its programs.

Contributors

Peter Barnes, D.Min., is an assistant professor, Saint Paul University, supervising in Clinical Pastoral Education and teaching in spiritual care and interprofessional learning. He is certified as a specialist in pastoral care and pastoral counselling, a teaching supervisor, and a Certified Canadian Counsellor. He served on professional ethics committees for the Canadian Association for Pastoral Practice and Education for thirteen years, and on clinical ethics committees in St. John's, Newfoundland, and Ottawa.

Micheline Boivin, M.A., is a certified clinical psychologist working with traumatized children and their parents at the Programme Enfance Jeunesse Famille du Centre local des services communautaires de Gatineau, Québec. She is the author of *L'exploitation sexuelle des enfants: Ouvrir les yeux et tendre la main*, published in the book *In Search of Healing*. She has co-authored articles on psychotherapy published in refereed journals, presented workshops on child sexual abuse and the use of puppets in child therapy, and co-presented advanced workshops on the use of mental imagery in psychotherapy.

Maria Cupples, R.N., has been employed as an Emergency Department Nurse by St. Thomas Elgin General Hospital in St. Thomas, Ontario, since completing her nursing training in 1971. She received her diploma in Emergency nursing, as well as BCLS, ACLS, and Advanced Trauma Nursing training. She has co-facilitated a training program in crisis education for hospital staff, and has participated in the filming of the Rogers Cable production "What happens when you come to the Emergency Department." In 1998, following the initial needs assessment, Maria was approached to assist in the development of the Crisis

Support Team. She fulfilled the role of co-facilitator for the team until Spring 2005.

Susan Ford, M.S.W., is a member of the Association of Traumatic Stress Specialists and a Certified Trauma Specialist (CTS). Her practice, Counselling for Change, is located in Ottawa, Ontario. As a Satir Growth Model practitioner, she has earned a solid reputation for helping clients move beyond 'survive' to 'thrive.'

Gilles Fortin, Ph.D., holds a licence in theology from Saint Paul University, an M.A. in psychology from the University of Ottawa, and a Ph.D. in education from the Université du Québec à Montréal (UQAM). An associate professor in pastoral counselling at Saint Paul University in Ottawa, he has served as the dean of the Faculty of Human Sciences since 2005. He is interested in professional ethics, values as they pertain to counselling, experiential learning, and learning styles.

Leslie Greenberg, Ph.D., is a professor of Psychology at York University in Toronto and Director of the York University Psychotherapy Research Clinic. He has authored the major texts on Emotion-focused approaches to treatment; his latest book is *Emotion-Focused Therapy of Depression.* He recently received the SPR Distinguished Research Career award. He conducts a private practice for individuals and couples and offers training in emotion-focused approaches.

Suzanne Joyce, R.N., is Interim Manager Day Surgery and Pre Admission Assessment Units, St. Joseph's Healthcare, Hamilton, Ontario. She graduated in 1971 and began her nursing career in the Emergency Department at St. Joseph's Hospital. She held the Charge Nurse Position for the last ten years in Emergency, before taking the Charge Nurse position in the Day Surgery Unit.

Seung Hee Kang, Ph.D. (Candidate), works as a chaplain in the Spiritual Care Department, St. Joseph's Healthcare, in Hamilton, Ontario. She is an associate member of the Canadian Association of Pastoral Practice Education and a member of Spiritual Directors International and of Ontario.

Michelle Koyle, a case worker for Ontario Works, received a diploma in Business from Westervelt College and a certificate as a Crisis Intervention Counsellor from Fanshawe College. She also completed Crisis Intervention Training from the Ministry of the Attorney General. She is currently completing her B.A. in Psychology and Sociology at University of Western Ontario. Michelle joined the Crisis Support Team in November 2002. In addition to her educational background in crisis work and her experience as a funeral director assistant, Michelle brings a strong people focus to her work as a crisis support volunteer.

Judith Malette, Ph.D., a clinical psychologist, has been assistant professor in pastoral counselling at Saint Paul University since 2001. She received a Ph.D. in experimental-theoretical psychology and did her post-doctoral studies in clinical psychology at the University of Ottawa. Her research interests include images of God, life review, learning styles, and reflective practitioner models.

Richard Manley-Tannis, M.A., attained his B.A. (Honours) in Classical History at Trent University in 1995, and completed his M.A. in Classical History in 1998 at Queen's University. He is a practising Faith Based Mediator and is a candidate in the United Church of Canada, studying Diaconal Ministry through the Centre for Christian Studies in Winnipeg, Manitoba.

Augustine Meier, Ph.D., is a certified clinical psychologist in private practice, a professor in the Faculty of Human Sciences, Saint Paul University, and an Adjunct Research Professor in the Department of Psychology, Carleton University, Ottawa. He provides advanced training in object relations therapy and self psychology. He taught graduate courses in psychotherapy and psychopathology and trained graduate students in individual counselling. He has co-authored articles on psychotherapy and psychopathology in refereed journals. He is the editor of the book *In Search of Healing* and co-editor of *The Challenge of Forgiveness* and *Spirituality and Health: Multidisciplinary Explorations.* Professor Meier is the founder and former president of The Society for Pastoral Counselling Research.

Rev. Adèle Miles, M.Div., is a Pastoral Care Advisor, St. Thomas Elgin General Hospital, in St. Thomas, Ontario. A chaplain and facilitator, she has a solid background in health care, community services, and education, and strengths in crisis intervention, group facilitation, and program development. Over the last 18 years, she has acquired experience in Emergency, Critical Care, Trauma and Palliative Care chaplaincy in both pediatric and adult contexts. Adèle brings a commitment to supporting interdisciplinary teams in the work of end-of-life care. She has lectured, taught and mentored theological and nursing students on communication skills and spiritual issues. In addition to her work as chaplain, she has served as a consultant for health-care staff on handling difficult families.

Judi Morin, M.A., Sister of Saint Ann, is a certified trainer in Nonviolent Communication (NVC). She combines her educational skills (B.Ed. from the University of Victoria) and understanding of theology/spirituality (M.A. in Theology from St. Mary's College of California, Certificate of Theological Studies in the Institute for Spirituality and Worship from J.S.T.B, Berkeley, California) with her skills in NVC in her work as prison chaplain (for 24 years) and in offering courses in the community.

Marie-Line Morin, Ph.D., is a professor in Pastoral Counselling at the Faculté de théologie, d'ethique et de philosophie of the Université de Sherbrooke, Québec. Her research interests relate to the concepts of Fundamental Value and Image of God. Among various applications to pastoral counselling, she has also reflected on the use of these concepts to understand underlying issues in the organization of couple and family systems.

Sherry Morley, B.A. (Honours), graduated from Carleton University in Ottawa in 2004 with a Bachelor's degree in Journalism and Combined Honours in Law. She studied restorative justice in school, completing an in-depth investigation into its theory and practice. After completing her university education, she spent a year and a half in Owen Sound as a journalist and currently works for Rogers News 88.9, an all-news talk and sports radio station in Saint John, New Brunswick.

Thomas St. James O'Connor, Th.D., is Professor, Delton Glebe Chair, in Pastoral Counselling at Waterloo Lutheran Seminary in Waterloo, Ontario. He has written over 30 articles in peer-reviewed journals and two books. His areas of writing include spirituality and health, theological reflection in ministry, qualitative research methodology, narrative therapy and chaplaincy. He is an Approved Supervisor in both the American Association for Marital and Family Therapy (AAMFT) and the Canadian Association for Pastoral Practice and Education (CAPPE).

Rose Robinson is a Physio and Occupational Therapy Aide at St. Thomas Elgin General Hospital in St. Thomas, Ontario. She received her training as a health-care aide from Fanshawe College in 1996, then joined the Crisis Support Team at St. Thomas. There she pursues her passion and enthusiasm for the work of supporting families in crisis. She received the hospital's "Achieving the Best" Award in 2002 for her compassion. Rose has also developed strengths in the areas of professional ethics and problem-solving skills. She is committed to continuous learning, and enjoys sharing her learnings with her colleagues and the community.

Martin Rovers, Ph.D., is an associate professor and AAMFT / CAAPE Supervisor in the faculty of Human Sciences, Saint Paul University, Ottawa. He has published widely in the area of family of origin and spirituality. Martin has brought together family-of-origin and attachment theory in a new paradigm he calls Attachment in Family Therapy (AFT). He is also a psychologist and a marriage and family therapist. His most recent book is *Healing the Wounds in Couple Relationships* (Novalis, 2005).

Helma Seidl, Ph.D. (Candidate), M.S.W., R.N., is a Certified Traumatologist and Post-Traumatic Stress Disorder Counsellor. Her Ph.D. dissertation is entitled *Socially-constructed gender binary: Restricting a healthy transgender self-identity development and self-identity reformation.* Helma is a therapist in private practice, specializing in Transgenderism-Gender Identity Disorder. She is a member of the Harry Benjamin International Gender Dysphoria Association (HBIGDA).

Susan Tasker, Ph.D., recently completed her doctoral studies in Psychology at McMaster University in Hamilton, Canada. Her interests are related to self and interpersonal processes in coping with and supporting the negotiation of meaning-making after major life events such as brain injury. Her practice and research interest in meaning-making extend to parents confronted by the uncertain developmental future of vulnerable babies.